THE COLOUR OF CLASS

How do race and class intersect to shape the identities and experiences of Black middle-class parents and their children? What are Black middle-class parents' strategies for supporting their children through school? What role do the educational histories of Black middle-class parents play in their decision-making about their children's education?

There is now an extensive body of research on the educational strategies of the White middle classes but a silence exists around the emergence of the Black middle classes and their experiences, priorities and actions in relation to education. This book focuses on middle-class families of Black Caribbean heritage.

Drawing on rich qualitative data from nearly 80 in-depth interviews with Black Caribbean middle-class parents, the internationally renowned contributors reveal how these parents attempt to navigate their children successfully through the school system and defend them against low expectations and other manifestations of discrimination. Chapters identify when, how and to what extent parents deploy the financial, cultural and social resources available to them as professional, middle-class individuals in support of their children's academic success and emotional well-being. The book sheds light on the complex, and relatively neglected relations between race, social class and education, and in addition, poses wider questions about the experiences of social mobility and the intersection of race and class in forming the identity of the parents and their children.

The Colour of Class: The educational strategies of the Black middle classes will appeal to undergraduates and postgraduates on education, sociology and social policy courses, as well as academics with an interest in Critical Race Theory and Bourdieu.

Nicola Rollock is Lecturer in Education and Deputy Director of the Centre for Research in Race and Education, U

David Gillborn is Professor of Critical Race Studies and Director of the Centre for Research in Race and Education, University of Birmingham, UK.

Carol Vincent is Professor of Education at the Institute of Education, University of London, UK.

Stephen J. Ball is Karl Mannheim Professor of Sociology of Education at the Institute of Education, University of London, UK.

THE COLOUR OF CLASS

The educational strategies of the Black middle classes

Nicola Rollock, David Gillborn,
Carol Vincent and Stephen J. Ball

Routledge
Taylor & Francis Group

LONDON AND NEW YORK

First published 2015
by Routledge
2 Park Square, Milton Park, Abingdon, Oxon OX14 4RN

and by Routledge
711 Third Avenue, New York, NY 10017

Routledge is an imprint of the Taylor & Francis Group, an informa business.

© 2015 N. Rollock, D. Gillborn, C. Vincent and S. J. Ball

The right of N. Rollock, D. Gillborn, C. Vincent and S. J. Ball to be identified as authors of this work has been asserted by them in accordance with sections 77 and 78 of the Copyright, Designs and Patents Act 1988.

British Library Cataloguing in Publication Data
A catalogue record for this book is available from the British Library.

Library of Congress Cataloging-in-Publication Data
Rollock, Nicola.
The colour of class : the educational strategies of the Black middle classes / Nicola Rollock, David Gillborn, Carol Vincent and Stephen J. Ball.
LC2771.R65 2014
371.829'96073–dc23
2014021201

ISBN: 978-0-415-80981-8 (hbk)
ISBN: 978-0-415-80982-5 (pbk)
ISBN: 978-1-315-74168-0 (ebk)

Typeset in Bembo
by Cenveo Publisher Services

Nicola Rollock would like to dedicate this book to her parents who arrived in the UK from Barbados in the 1960s. Despite the challenges of life in Britain, education remained a firm family priority and for this I am truly grateful.

David Gillborn, Carol Vincent and Stephen J. Ball would like to dedicate the book to all parents (past, present and future).

CONTENTS

ACKNOWLEDGEMENTS

This book is based on an Economic and Social Research Council (ESRC) funded project exploring the 'The Educational Strategies of the Black Middle Classes' (ESRC RES-062-23-1880). It would not have been possible without the contributions of the parents who gave up their time to speak with us. We would like to express our appreciation to them for sharing personal and sometimes painful accounts of their lives and their experiences of schooling their children.

We also extend our warm thanks to our advisory group: Sir Keith Ajegbo, Kwame Kwei-Armah, Professor Ann Phoenix and Dr Debbie Weekes-Barnard for their support and guidance throughout the two-year duration of the project.

Many people have supported us during the initial research project and the subsequent period as we wrote this book. We express our thanks to Anna Clarkson and the entire team at Routledge for their support and guidance throughout. Nicola would like to express deep appreciation to Gregg Beratan, Teresa Dawkins, Joseph Harker, Ann Phoenix and Marcus Ryder for providing encouragement at much needed moments; David is especially grateful to Gregg Beratan, Vincent Carpentier, Neal Carr, Jane Martin, Bevan Powell and Terezia Zoric.

Finally, we are grateful to Margaret Leggett who transcribed many hours of recording for us in a prompt and efficient manner and to Brian Mustoe (Office for National Statistics) for so kindly and patiently guiding us through the data on socio-economic status.

Parts of this book draw on, and expand, analyses that we have presented previously. We are grateful to the editors and publishers of the journals below for permission to use extracts from the following papers:

- Ball, S., Rollock, N., Vincent, C. and Gillborn, D. (2013) 'Social mix, schooling and intersectionality: identity and risk for Black middle class families', *Research Papers in Education*, 28(3), 265–88.

- Gillborn, D., Rollock, N., Vincent, C. and Ball, S. J. (2012) '"You got a pass, so what more do you want?": race, class and gender intersections in the educational experiences of the Black middle class', *Race Ethnicity and Education*, 15 (1): 121–39.
- Rollock, N., Gillborn, D., Vincent, C. and Ball, S. (2011) 'The public identities of the Black middle classes: managing race in public spaces', *Sociology*, 45 (6): 1078–93. First published by Sage.
- Rollock, N., Vincent, C., Gillborn, D. and Ball, S. (2013) '"Middle class by profession": class status and identification amongst the Black middle classes', *Ethnicities*, 13 (3): 253–75. First published by Sage.
- Vincent, C., Ball, S., Rollock, N. and Gillborn, D. (2013) 'Three generations of racism: Black middle class children and schooling', *British Journal of Sociology of Education*, 34 (5–06): 929–46.
- Vincent, C., Rollock, N., Ball, S. and Gillborn, D. (2013) 'Raising middle-class Black children: parenting priorities, actions and strategies', *Sociology*, 47 (3): 427–42.
- Vincent, C., Rollock, N., Ball, S. and Gillborn, D. (2012) 'Being strategic, being watchful, being determined: Black middle-class parents and schooling', *British Journal of Sociology of Education*, 33 (3): 337–54.

ABBREVIATIONS

ADHD	Attention Deficit Hyperactivity Disorder
BESD	Behavioural, Emotional and Social Difficulties
BNP	British National Party
CARD	Campaign Against Racial Discrimination
CRE	Commission for Racial Equality
CRSEA	Critical Race Studies in Education Association
CRT	Critical Race Theory
CSE	Certificate of Secondary Education
DANDA	Developmental Adult Neuro-Diversity Association
DCSF	Department for Children, Schools and Families
DfE	Department for Education
Dis/Crit	Dis/ability Critical Race Theory
EHRC	Equality and Human Rights Commission
EqIA	Equality Impact Assessment
FSM	Free School Meals
GCE	General Certificate of Education
GCSE	General Certificate of Secondary Education
IEP	Individual Education Plan
LD	Learning Disabilities
LSBC	London Schools and the Black Child
LSYPE	Longitudinal Survey of Young People in England
NS-SEC	National Statistics Socio-Economic Classification
ONS	Office for National Statistics
PTA	Parent/Teacher Association
SEC	Socio-Economic Classification
SEN	Special Educational Needs
SENCO	Special Educational Needs Coordinator
YCS	Youth Cohort Study

KEY TO TRANSCRIPTS

Italicised text	Denotes emphasised speech
(…)	Material has been edited out
[square brackets]	Paraphrased for the sake of clarity

PARENT OCCUPATIONS

Below is a list of our interviewees with a note of their occupation and children aged 8–18 years (by gender and age at the time of first interview). All names are pseudonymns. Details of children outside of the selection criteria (i.e. 8–18 years) have been excluded to protect parents' anonymity.

Alice, *Senior Researcher, Voluntary Sector:* daughter 16, daughter 8, plus one younger child [Chapters 1, 2, 3, 5]

Amanda, *Senior Librarian:* daughter 12 [Chapters 2, 6]

Andrea, *Health Manager:* daughter 16, daughter 12

Anita, *Lecturer in Further Education:* son 16, son 14 [Chapters 1, 6, 5]

Anne, *Education Advisor, Local Authority:* son 12, girl 10 [Chapter 5]

Anthea, *Education Manager, Local Authority:* daughter 18, plus two older children [Chapters 2, 5, 6]

Anthony, *Company Director, Voluntary Sector:* son 14, plus four older children [Chapter 8]

Barbara, *Child Health Professional:* son 14 [Chapters 3, 4, 8]

Brenda, *Head of Research, Voluntary Sector:* daughter 16, plus one older child [Chapters 1, 2, 3, 6, 7]

Candice, *Community Development Officer, Voluntary Sector:* twin son and daughter, 10 [Chapters 2, 6]

Cassandra, *Company Director:* daughter 10, daughter 9, plus one older child [Chapters 3, 5, 6, 7]

Catherine, *Senior Management, School:* son 15 [Chapters 1, 5]

Claudette, *Policy Advisor, Central Government:* son 17, son 8, plus two older children [Chapters 2, 5, 8]

Cynthia, *Teacher:* son 10, son 8, plus one younger child [Chapters 1, 3, 5, 6, 8]

David, *Senior Management, School:* daughter 15, daughter 13, son 10 [Chapter 5]

Derick, *Training Manager, Voluntary Sector*: daughter 13, plus one older child [Chapters 6, 8]

Eleanor, *Social Worker*: son 11, plus one older child [Chapters 5, 7]

Elizabeth, *Education Advisor*: son 16 [Chapters 2, 8]

Ella, *Senior Health Professional*: son 11, daughter 9 [Chapters 3, 5, 6]

Elsa, *Senior HR Manager, Public Sector*: son 15, son 13 [Chapters 2, 5, 6]

Esme, *NHS manager*: daughter 17 [Chapter 5]

Felicia, *Senior Solicitor*: son 17 [Chapters 1, 2, 4, 6, 8]

Femi, *Lecturer in Further Education*: daughter 8 [Chapters 1, 2, 3, 5, 6, 8]

Gabriel, *Education Consultant*: son 7, also three other children (two older, one younger) [Chapters 1, 2, 3, 7, 8]

Gloria, *Senior Administrator, Education*: daughter 9, also two older children [Chapters 2, 6, Conclusion]

Grace, *Senior Learning Mentor, Local Authority*: son 17, daughter 12 [Chapters 5, 8]

Isabelle, *Teacher*: daughter 12 [Chapters 2, 5, 8]

Jackie, *Social Worker*: daughter 18, daughter 8, plus one younger child

Janet, *Journalist*: son 9, plus one younger child [Chapters, 1, 8]

Jean, *Further Education Lecturer*: son 9, daughter 10 [Chapters 1, 3, 7, 8, Conclusion]

Joan, *Education Training Manager, Local Authority*: daughter 17 [Chapters 5, 7, 8]

John, *Senior Buyer, Public Sector*: daughter 14

Josephine, *Strategic Development Manager, Public Sector*: daughter 18, also one older child [Chapter 8]

Joyce, *Senior Education Consultant, Local Authority*: son 15, twin sons 13

Juliet, *Communications Manager, Central Government*: daughter 15, plus one younger child [Chapters 1, 5]

June, *Educational Strategist, Local Authority*: daughter 13, also one older child [Chapters 5, 6]

Linda, *Academic in Higher Education*: daughter 17, also one older child [Chapters 2, 4, 5]

Lucy, *HR Director*: son 14 [Chapters 2, 8]

Lorraine, *Researcher, Voluntary Sector*: daughter 15 [Chapters 1, 3, 4, 5, 6, 7, 8]

Malorie, *Education Manager, Local Authority*: daughter 17 [Chapters 3, 5, 6, 8]

Margaret, *Senior Corporate Manager, Private Sector*: son 16, son 11, plus one younger child [Chapters 1, 5]

Mary, *Health Professional*: son 18, daughter 14 [Chapters 1, 2]

Matthew, *Company Director, Private Sector*: son 11, plus 2 older children [Chapters 4, 6]

Maud, *University Administrator*: daughter 16, daughter 14, plus one older child [Chapters 1, 2, 4]

Michael, *Business Owner*: son 16, son 11, plus one younger child [Chapters 3, 5, 6, 8, Conclusion]

Miles, *Senior HR Manager, Private Sector*: son 8 plus three younger children [Chapters 1, 2, 5, 6, 7]

Monica, *Teacher*: daughter 16, plus one older child [Chapters 1, 5, 7]

Ngozi, *Psychologist*: son 17, daughter 15, daughter 14, son 11 [Chapter 2]

Nigel, *Human Resources Manager, Central Government*: daughter 16, son 12 [Chapters 1, 4, Conclusion]

Patricia, *Resources Manager, Local Authority*: son 15, son 13, plus one older child [Chapters 4, 5, 6, 7]

Paulette, *Psychologist*: twin son and daughter 15, plus 1 other child [Chapters 3, 4, 7, 8, Conclusion]

Rachel, *Senior Solicitor, Private Sector*: daughter 12, son 10, plus two younger children [Introduction, Chapters 4, 8]

Ray, *Head of Service, Public Sector*: daughter 13, plus three older children [Chapters 1, 3]

Regina, *Teacher*: daughter 10 [Chapter 1]

Richard, *Director, Voluntary Sector*: son 10, son 9 [Chapters 1, 3, 6, 7, 8]

Robert, *Academic in Higher Education*: son 18, daughter 17, plus 1 older child [Chapters 1, 3, 5, 6, 8, Conclusion]

Ruby, *Community Development Officer for Local Authority*: daughter 16, son 14, daughter 10 [Chapters 2, 8]

Samantha, *Assistant Director, Housing*: son 15 [Chapters 2, 6]

Sandrine, *Senior Programme Manager, Central Government*: daughter 12 [Chapters 2, 6, 7, 8]

Simon, *Teacher*: son 10, son 8, plus one younger child [Chapter 4]

Simone, *Senior Policy Advisor*: son 14 [Chapter 6]

Vanessa, *Community Development Officer*: son 17, son 15, son 13 [Chapters 3, 4, 7, Conclusion]

INTRODUCTION

Background and context

(…) you remember the BNP [British National Party] teacher list that got published? It turns out that my [son's] (…) teacher (…) is a BNP member! (…) I went up [to the school] on the Monday morning and said, 'that woman is not teaching my child I'm telling you now', and basically the headmaster at the time just shooed me out of the office and said, 'Oh we're dealing with it, this is a private matter, this is a staff matter. We'll deal with it. We're investigating it and anyway you mustn't believe everything you read in the press.'

(…) you know when you just have something which leaves a bad taste in your mouth? And (…) obviously all the staff knew [about the colleague in question] but they don't care and the [other] parents didn't care because they were all White parents and they had no issue with it. (Rachel, mother of three)

Rachel lives with her husband and three children in a leafy part of London. She is a Senior Solicitor. Her husband shares a similar high-level professional occupation and together they share a joint income in excess of £160,000 per annum. Rachel is of Black Caribbean heritage. Her comments, above, reveal the complex ways in which certain class capitals operate to advantage her family – for example, all of her children attend independent schools (an indicator of *economic capital*) – yet at the same time such capitals do not always yield guaranteed rewards. Revelation of the teacher's membership of the BNP (a far-right anti-minority party) forces her to consider withdrawing her child from the school for his protection. This highlights not only how race and racism intervene to shape and, in this case, restrict the benefits accrued by her family's class resources – the likelihood of having to seek out a new school, interrupt his education, disrupt the friendships he has built – but also demonstrates how such considerations and dangers are far removed from the realities of White middle-class parents whose children attend the same school. To be White and middle class is not the same as being Black and middle class.

This incident, recounted by Rachel, is just one of many experienced by a relatively invisible demographic of Black middle classes who serve as the subject of this book.

The focus of this book

The low educational attainment of Black pupils has been a feature of policy debates and a concern for Black families for several decades (Coard 1971; Gillborn 2008; Tomlinson 2008). However, there is scant British empirical work that explicitly explores how race and social class *jointly* shape their experiences. Policy debate tends to position Black families as a homogeneous working-class entity and often regards them as deficient, uninterested and uninvolved in their children's education. Yet, the attendance of almost a thousand Black parents, across various social backgrounds, at the regular London Schools and the Black Child conference[1] is just one example which immediately discredits such generic claims. In terms of research on the education of the middle class, studies have tended to focus on the White middle classes and the ways in which they strategise, engage and deploy their cultural capital to their advantage in support of their children's education (Ball 2003a; Byrne 2006; Crozier *et al.* 2008; Vincent and Ball 2007). Similar attention with regard to the Black middle classes and education has, till now, been lacking. In addition, most UK-based research on the educational experiences of Black children has focused on schools and the wider context of education policy (Gillborn and Youdell 2000; Walters 2012). By contrast, our main analytical focus, in this study, is on homes rather than schools; that is to say, we are foregrounding the way in which parents view and interact with schools and how they strategise about education. We should be clear, however, given the long history of deficit understandings of Black families (for elaboration, see Reynolds 2005), that we are not aligning ourselves with research or policy that seeks to blame parents for the underachievement of their children. Rather we are interested in the way in which Black Caribbean middle-class families deploy their social and cultural resources in support of their children's education. We will offer numerous examples in the chapters which follow. Our aim is to explore and analyse the educational perspectives, strategies and experiences of these families, carefully attending to the intersection of race and class in relation to their interactions with schools. Our foremost objective is to identify the complexities of advantage and disadvantage that are played out through these strategies as parents support their children through schooling.

Why examine such questions in relation to the Black *middle* classes? Dedicated examination of this group is important for several reasons. They are a demographic who seldom feature in mainstream public and political debate; they are by and large invisible within mainstream consciousness. And rather than being divisive or creating false boundaries among the Black community (a notion which in itself is worthy of some interrogation) as some have suggested (see Rollock 2013a for discussion), in taking the Black middle classes as our study, we are purposefully and explicitly naming and documenting their experience within a broader historical context of Black people in the UK. Capturing and understanding this provides useful insight into the ways in which ostensible class advantage – that is, being middle class – might be differentially inflected by race and racism. As will become apparent, to be Black and middle class does not mean having transcended racism. This fact alone remains crucial to highlighting the continued subtle pervasiveness and damaging consequences of racism in an era frequently proclaimed as post-racial. Finally, as will become apparent, our findings call for more sophisticated analyses of the ways in which race intersects with class status not just to the *dis*advantage of the Black middle classes, but to the *ad*vantage of their White middle-class peers.

Educational attainment

Respondents are Black Caribbean heritage parents. There are a number of reasons for this. The school experiences and performances of Black Caribbean pupils (especially boys) have, for a number of years, attracted considerable attention and data indicate that this group experiences considerable educational disadvantage. For example, they are over-represented among those identified as having special educational needs and among those who are excluded from school (DfE 2013b; Cassen and Kingdon 2007). The statistics for England show that (with the exception of Travellers and Gypsy/Roma students) Black Caribbean students are least likely to achieve five higher grade GCSEs including English and Mathematics (DfE 2013a: table a).

Furthermore, the risk of low achievement is not limited to those living in economic hardship: 52.8 per cent of Black Caribbean students *not* eligible for free school meals achieve five or more higher grade GCSEs (including Maths and English) compared with an average of 62.6 per cent for all pupils who are not eligible for such meals (DfE 2013: table 2a). However, there are limited data available on the simultaneous impact of social class and ethnic origin and indeed most educational statistics fail to offer an adequate measure of socio-economic status, relying instead on receipt of free school meals (FSM), a crude proxy for family poverty. The most notable exceptions to this are the Youth Cohort Study (YCS) and its successor, the Longitudinal Survey of Young People in England (LSYPE), both government funded projects that collect detailed socio-economic data (DCSF 2008). The most comprehensive cross-tabulation of YCS data for ethnicity and social class, conducted in 2000, indicated that 'African-Caribbean pupils from non-manual homes are the lowest attaining of the middle-class groups. In some cases they are barely matching the attainments of working-class pupils in other ethnic groups' (Gillborn and Mirza 2000: 21). More recent data from the LSYPE suggest a similar picture, in which Black Caribbean pupils 'from middle and high SEC homes' are identified as one of the key groups giving cause for concern after controlling for a range of socio-economic variables (Strand 2008: 3). Thus it would appear that being middle class offers little protection from the lower than average attainment levels experienced by Black students generally while, on the other hand, research on White middle-class families indicates a generally high level of effectiveness in ensuring and sustaining high levels of educational achievement for their children (e.g. Vincent and Ball 2006).

Historical context

The above overview must be put in context. The majority of our 62 respondents are themselves the children of parents who migrated to Britain from the Caribbean in the 1950s and 1960s, responding (like many Caribbeans at the time) to calls for help from the British government in addressing country-wide labour shortages (Ramdin 1987). They came with high expectations not only of opportunities within the labour market but of the potential advantages perceived to be offered by the British education system.

In reality, many Caribbean migrants experienced what might be described as class-downsizing, that is having to accept particularly low-status occupations compared with the positions they had left back home. These were posts that even the British White working class had rejected, characterised as they were as labour intensive with low pay and unsocial hours (Fryer 1984). The prevalence of racial discrimination in employment, housing and policing, as well as other service areas, further reduced the prospect of any 'common consciousness of class' (Sivanandan 1976: 350) between Caribbeans and the White working classes. Sivanandan (1976) points to the government's eager preparedness, on the one hand, to embrace the Caribbean contribution to the labour market and thus benefit the economy while, on the other hand, doing nothing to ameliorate the worsening social relations between Caribbean and White working-class populations.

This was an era without race equality legislation, which was only introduced in 1965; of fraught relations with the police as evidenced, for example, through 'sus' laws; and of an education system that readily treated Caribbean pupils as 'educationally subnormal' (Coard 1971; Tomlinson 1981, 2008). It was the racially minoritised status of Caribbean immigrants and the racism of the wider White society married with their lower occupational status that contributed to Caribbeans becoming a distinct fraction of the working classes (Ramdin 1987). However, many within the Caribbean community fought back, challenging this treatment and advocating to fight racism. A number of community and political organisations such as CARD (Campaign Against Racial Discrimination), the West Indian Standing Conference and the Black Parents Movement were established in order to represent the political, cultural and educational interests of Caribbean communities and to provide a direct means of challenging the endemic racism that they faced (Mullard 1973). The Black supplementary school movement is a prime example of this active resistance. It emerged to counter the shortcomings of the British educational system and to provide a cultural grounding for younger generations through the teaching, for example, of Black history (Gerrard 2013; Mirza and Reay 2000).

Our respondents grew up in families shaped by these histories. We have focused explicitly on those who are now in professional and managerial occupations, a generation that has, in Phillips and Sarre's terms (1995: 54), become 'more credentialised' than their parents. Yet we know that, despite these gains, challenges remain as they continue to experience disadvantage in the workplace (Cabinet Office 2003; Clark and Drinkwater 2007) and wider society.

Black British middle classes

Before describing how we carried out the research which served as the basis for this book, we first provide an overview, from the limited studies available, about the Black British middle classes and, in the section that follows, we offer a summary of key, relevant literature about their African American counterparts.

Class position

We were interested in speaking to Black Caribbean middle-class parents. We took as our measure of class location the Office for National Statistics' (ONS) National Standard Socio-Economic Classification (NS-SEC) which reflects the socio-economic position of persons aged 16 and over, based on occupation title, employment status and whether or not they manage other employees.

Using NS-SEC data from the most recent Census, Table 1 shows the social class composition of the Black Caribbean and White British populations in London and England. In 2011, there were just over 130,000 of Black Caribbeans (26.7 per cent) in professional/managerial posts (i.e. 1.1, 1.2 and 2 NS-SEC). Looking across the Black Caribbean population as a whole, just 6.2 per cent occupy the highest level (NS-SEC 1) whereas over three times as many (around 20 per cent) occupy lower professional/managerial positions (NS-SEC 2). This is depicted most clearly in Figure 1.

Given that over half (56.9 per cent) of Black Caribbeans in England reside in London and, in view of the draw of the capital for employment, it will come as no surprise that most Black Caribbeans in the highest occupation classifications (1.1, 1.2, 2) are to be found in the city (57.6 per cent).

Empirical research

As mentioned previously, there is scant empirical research which examines the experiences of the Black British middle classes. One dated, but useful, exception is a survey-based study carried out by Sharon Daye (1994), which examines, among other factors, the role of race in shaping the objective class position of Black Caribbean heritage men and women in the late 1980s. Daye's research, based on interview and survey data from a London-based sample, reveals the considerable heterogeneity of the Black middle classes both in terms of demographic profile and migration history (though most arrived in the UK between the early 1950s and mid-1960s) and their views about political affiliation and Black representation. In commenting upon the relationship between the *objective class position* of her Black participants (who were in professional and managerial occupations) and their *perceptions of race and class* and how these have been shaped by racism, Daye notes that experiences such as marginalisation and exclusion create dissonance between these two states. In other words, the effects of racism continue to position middle-class Black people as 'outsiders' irrespective of their class position. This, argues Daye,

TABLE 1 Race and social class: White British and Black Caribbeans by socio-economic status (England and London, 2011)

National Standard Socio-Economic Classification (NS-SEC)	ENGLAND				LONDON			
	Black Caribbean		White British		Black Caribbean		White British	
	Number	Percentage	Number	Percentage	Number	Percentage	Number	Percentage
1. Higher managerial, administrative and professional occupations	30,416	6.2%	3,488,992	10.0%	17,439	6.3%	446,128	14.5%
1.1 Large employers and higher managerial and administrative occupations	(7,521)	(1.5%)	(876,755)	(2.5%)	(4,476)	(1.6%)	(95,424)	(3.1%)
1.2 Higher professional occupations	(22,895)	(4.7%)	(2,612,237)	(7.5%)	(12,963)	(4.7%)	(350,704)	(11.4%)
2. Lower managerial, administrative and professional occupations	99,870	20.5%	7,454,246	21.4%	57,544	20.7%	816,209	26.5%
3. Intermediate occupations	68,311	14.0%	4,867,381	14.0%	41,748	15.0%	454,544	14.8%
4. Small employers & own account workers	29,374	6.0%	3,299,973	9.5%	16,995	6.1%	279,297	9.1%
5. Lower supervisory and technical occupations	31,130	6.4%	2,613,458	7.5%	17,303	6.2%	164,757	5.4%
6. Semi-routine occupations	76,555	15.7%	5,125,583	14.7%	41,870	15.1%	319,557	10.4%
7. Routine occupations	57,362	11.8%	4,117,020	11.8%	28,705	10.3%	237,746	7.7%
8. Never worked and long-term unemployed	45,756	9.4%	1,618,073	4.6%	27,572	9.9%	157,250	5.1%
L14.1 Never worked	(27,000)	(5.5%)	(1,118,328)	(3.2%)	(16,320)	(5.9%)	(110,952)	(3.6%)
L14.2 Long-term unemployed	(18,756)	(3.8%)	(499,745)	(1.4%)	(11,252)	(4.0%)	(46,268)	(1.5%)
Not classified	48,959	10.0%	2,284,998	6.6%	28,578	10.3%	200,918	6.5%
L15 Full-time students	(48,959)	(10.0%)	(2,284,998)	(6.6%)	(28,578)	(10.3%)	(200,918)	(6.5%)
L17 Not classifiable for other reasons	(0)	(0.0%)	(0)	(0.0%)	(0)	(0.0%)	(0)	(0.0%)
Total across all NS-SEC categories	487,733	100%	34,869,724	100.1%	277,754	99.9%	3,076,406	100%

Source: Office for National Statistics: Census 2011 <http://www.nomisweb.co.uk/census/2011/dc6206ew>.

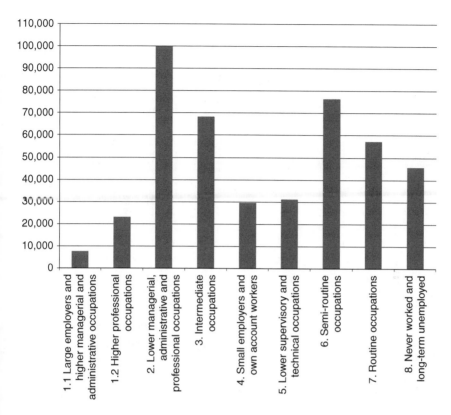

FIGURE 1   Social class distribution of Black Caribbean adults, England, 2011 (NS-SEC categories)

Source: Office for National Statistics: Census 2011.

operates to the advantage of the White majority population by protecting valued, high-status occupations (Daye 1994).

More recently, two relatively small-scale but important studies have sought to capture the experiences of middle-class minority ethnic groups. The first is Louise Archer's (2010) study examining the identities, values and educational practices of several minority ethnic middle-class groups. Participants varied in age and occupation type. Some were students. While the inclusion of such a mix of ethnic groups makes it difficult to draw overarching conclusions, Archer notes that participants felt uneasy aligning with a middle-class identity and, as part of the reasons for this, highlights the challenges (racism, having to work harder than Whites) faced by minoritised groups in the UK. In a separate study of Black professional women, Uvanney Maylor and Katya Williams (2011) report that, despite their occupational status, the women tended to deny that their class status accrued to them – or other Black people within the same class location – any degree of class privilege. The authors contend that this can be understood as 'an emotional need to remain positively connected to the wider Black community' (Maylor and Williams 2011: 353) alongside a desire not to distinguish themselves (albeit it ideologically) from their families.

African American middle classes

While differences in definitions of social class must be noted, there are some potentially useful observations to be made with regard to US research about the African American middle classes. Mary Pattillo-McCoy's (1999) ethnographic study of a Black middle-class community on Chicago's South Side, for example, poses questions similar to those we explore in this book (notably around class identification). Pattillo-McCoy notes the connections among the 'normative' requirements for being middle class (e.g. suburban living, speaking 'standard' English, access to 'good' schools), their necessary economic underpinnings and the history of racism and discrimination in the USA, which have led to racial residential segregation. Pattillo-McCoy's 'middle class' in this context refers to respondents in intermediate (e.g. clerical) and skilled manual positions, which is fundamentally different, as we have seen from the ONS definitions previously described, from the notion of middle class in the UK. However, like Phillips and Sarre (1995), Pattillo-McCoy acknowledges the scarcity of research focusing on the Black middle classes even in the US context, insisting that the 'mainstream' still firmly belongs to those who are White and middle class.

Staying within the USA, Kesha S. Moore's research uses an intersectional approach to identify the ways in which class shapes 'the articulation of a black racial identity' (Moore 2008: 492). Based on a three-year ethnographic study of a Philadelphia neighbourhood, Moore distinguishes between two competing forms of African American middle-class identity: *multi-class* and *middle-class minded*. She demonstrates how, while there are areas of overlap, the former refers to those less securely established in the Black middle classes who have experienced social mobility in their lifetime, thus providing them with a unique 'outsider-within' perspective. These *multi-class* participants commended their capacity to operate comfortably in a range of social contexts and to 'code-switch', depending on the conversational situation. Multi-class individuals worked consciously to maintain 'a symbolic and personal connection' (Moore 2008: 506) to low-income African Americans. *Middle-class minded* individuals, by contrast, were more likely to come from established middle-class families and tended to be more aware or accepting of class differences between themselves and less privileged African Americans. They tended also to situate themselves within environments where most of their contemporaries were also middle class. Again, it is important to take account of study- and country-specific definitions of social class. Moore's respondents were grouped as middle class according to their own determination or based on demographic information (e.g. college education and an annual income exceeding approximately £23,000). While such research may be useful in lending an analytical lens to the British context, it is important to pay heed to these definitional differences as well as to those of socio-historical context. The Black British middle class is considerably newer and smaller than its American counterpart.

The research study

In this section, we describe how we carried out the research and the theoretical framework we used to facilitate our engagement with and analysis of the data. We provide demographic information about the parents involved in the study and also outline ethical considerations about our role and identities as researchers and how this informed the research process.

Method

The research study, 'The Educational Strategies of the Black Middle Classes', was funded by the Economic and Social Research Council (ESRC RES-062-23-1880). We conducted a series of qualitative semi-structured interviews with 62 parents who self-define as Black Caribbean. Aware of the increasing number of Black Caribbeans who have a partner outside their ethnic group, families were included where one or both of the parents self-identified as Black Caribbean. Participants were recruited through a range of sources which included announcements on family and education websites; Black professional networks and social groups (e.g. 100 Black Men of London, Family and Parenting Institute, Black and Asian Study Association); as well as through extensive use of snowballing via existing contacts within the professional Black community. While each participant involved in the study self-defined as Black we noted during the course of our interviews considerable variation in interpretation and engagement with Black identity.

We spoke with parents who had at least one child between eight and 18 years, age groups that encompass key transition points in the child's educational journey. With regard to class categorisation, we sought parents in professional or managerial occupations (i.e. NS-SEC 1 and 2). The category NS-SEC 1.1 includes occupations such as senior government officials, managers in the health service and human resources managers; NS-SEC 1.2 includes lawyers, psychologists and higher education researchers. Finally, NS-SEC 2 refers to occupations such as social workers, teachers and youth or community workers. These occupational groups reflect a particular segment of the middle classes, sometimes called the 'service class' (see Hanlon 1998 for an overview). We also collected information on income, educational qualifications and housing. However, our understanding of class goes beyond these indicators to encompass class as 'an identity and a lifestyle, and a set of perspectives on the social world … class in this sense is … an identity based on modes of being and becoming or escape and forms of distinction that are realized and reproduced in specific social locations' (Ball 2003a: 6). We posit a definition of class that stresses process, 'identifications, perceptions, feelings' (Medhurst 2000: 20; see also Savage 2000; Sayer 2005; Skeggs 2004). This view of class stresses the 'practices of everyday living – practices that are both engaged in, by, and simultaneously encircle men, women and children on a daily basis' (Weis 2004: 4).

As is common in research on parents, most of our respondents are mothers. However, we were especially sensitive to debates about the role of Black men as fathers which often stereotype them as absent or deficient. Consequently, we consciously strove to include men in our sample; 13 of our interviews are with fathers.

Interviews were carried out mostly in London but also elsewhere in England (e.g. the Midlands, Yorkshire, the East of England); we returned, a year later after our initial conversations, to 15 of our respondents in order to conduct follow-up interviews. This second round allowed us to ask additional questions on themes that arose from our analysis of the initial interviews but which were not part of our original research schedule (e.g. we asked whether and in what ways respondents talked with their children about racism), or to revisit original themes in more depth (e.g. the complex relationship between race and class in the formation of identity).

Our principal research questions are as follows:

1. *What role, if any, do the educational histories of Black Caribbean middle-class parents play in their decision-making about their children's education?* We explore how parents' own raced and classed experiences of school may have informed their concerns and choices around their children's education. Are there differences between those who were raised in middle-class homes and those who have achieved middle-class status despite working-class origins?
2. *What are the strategies used by Black Caribbean middle-class parents in their interactions with educational institutions and professionals?* This includes looking at parents' understanding of and involvement in the choice of school, parental involvement with schools and school activities, their monitoring of their children's progress, responses to any problems that may arise in their children's school career, and the use of enrichment activities, private tuition and supplementary schooling.
3. *How do Black Caribbean middle-class parents conceive the relative roles of race and class in shaping their children's experiences (and how do these conceptions influence or inflect their strategies)?* That is, in particular, do they take account of the possibility of experiencing racism in their relations with schools and planning for their children's education?

Analysis

Interviews were recorded digitally and each fully transcribed. Analysis, theorisation and reflection took place throughout the project, enabling us to feed into the ongoing data collection. Adopting this approach meant we were able to progressively focus on identifying new themes and areas for further exploration. Data management and analysis was facilitated by the use of qualitative data analysis software (NVivo). We used a combination of hand-coding and Nvivo to chart regularities in the data in relation to particular themes and to help identify both prevailing tendencies and discrepant cases (Lecompte and Pressle 1993). Some initial theoretical categories were drawn from existing literature, research and theory on race, class and education, and were refined and challenged through engagement with and scrutiny of the data. Given the ways in which Black populations tend to be

'Othered' in empirical research, we were mindful not to merely locate our analysis of their experience through relational comparisons with the White middle classes. While this was useful, on occasion, in highlighting the presence of racism in their lives, we sought to centre respondents' accounts in relation to *their* focal points of understanding and reality.

Profile and demographic background of respondents

Our respondents vary in age, domestic circumstances, education and income. Most (37) were in their forties, with the remainder spread more or less evenly in the thirties and fifties age groups.

We have information on income from 59 of our 62 participants: the majority (21 parents) earn between £36,000 and £50,000; 16 earn between £51,000 and £65,000 per annum and three earn in the highest bracket of £81,000 and above. In terms of education, 49 per cent of the 57 participants for whom we had information hold a master's degree as their highest qualification. As noted earlier, our sample focused on the highest socio-economic categories: 15 are categorised as NS-SEC 1.1; 15 as holding 1.2 occupations and the majority, accounting for 32 respondents, are classified as NS-SEC 2. This is roughly in line with the profile distribution of NS-SEC categorisation described earlier (Table 1).

Individual family circumstance and migration come to bear differently on the financial situation and employment opportunities of each family and respondents vary in terms of the level of detail they are able to provide about the occupations of their parents, particularly prior to migration to the UK. However, some participants describe growing up in relatively poor circumstances, for example their parents leaving school in the Caribbean when aged 12 or 13 years in order to pursue largely manual employment, before later migrating to the UK and taking up what would be considered low-status (within the UK context) working-class posts (usually in the caring or service industries). Some participants speak of how their parents, on arrival in the UK, studied or had to retrain while they worked, in order to increase their job prospects.

Theoretical framework

A theoretical framework helps provide a lens or set of understandings through which research is set up, analysed and interpreted. We employ an *intersectional* analysis to explore the ways in which Black middle-class experiences bring together various configurations of privilege and disadvantage. We are drawn to intersectionality because it emphasises fluidity (Brah and Phoenix 2004: 76) and the importance of different locales, situations, spaces, times, dispositions and subjectivities, for understanding particular interactions and identities (Crenshaw 1995). We are interested in illuminating the ways in which, for different Black middle-class parents at different points in time and in different interactions, race, class and/or gender can come to the fore. This is what Horvat (2003, citing Collins 1991) refers to as the 'both/and nature of race and class'. Specifically, we make use of components of an intersectional analysis that draws on Pierre Bourdieu's work on class and social reproduction and the writings of Critical Race Theorists (CRT) on race, racism and Whiteness, and apply both to our data. Both frameworks allow us to 'see' the world differently.

Bourdieu and social reproduction

Bourdieu's 'method' using the related concepts of habitus, capitals and fields are of direct relevance to our research and we draw on them throughout. Habitus generates the collective dispositions of a particular socio-economic group which are objectively adjusted to the social conditions of particular fields. Habitus is an embodied history; it 'describes dispositions, tendencies to think, feel and behave in particular ways ... expected of "people like us" [although] there are no explicit rules or principles which dictate behaviour' (Reay 1998: 27; Colley *et al.* 2003). Knowledge, values and behaviour are constructed through the habitus but the habitus is always constituted in moments of practice:

> So in the case of the family, the habitus describes not what capital the family owns, but what it decides to do with it; how it chooses to 'play the cards' as Bourdieu describes, the process of investment and accumulation.
>
> *(Brooker 2002: 40)*

We suggest that understanding the workings of family habitus and parental possession and deployment of particular capitals is crucial in understanding how middle-class families seek to and are able to position themselves and their children in relation to education in general and in relation to schooling in particular. The processes by which capitals are deployed require careful contextualising and like most of Pierre Bourdieu's concepts, *capital* has been written about at length (see Kingston 2001; Lash 1993; Reay 2001; Reay 2004; Swartz 1997). Briefly, Bourdieu argues that every individual has a 'portfolio' of capital (Crossley 2008) which can present itself in three main forms: *economic* capital (money and assets), *social* capital (social relationships and networks) and *cultural* capital. The latter can take three forms: *embodied* 'in the form of long lasting dispositions of the mind and body' (Bourdieu 1997: 47), *objectified* (cultural goods, such as books, pictures) and *institutionalised* (qualifications). Again Bourdieu draws attention to the role of the family: 'the scholastic yield from educational action depends on the cultural capital previously invested by the family' (1997: 48). Embodied capital converts 'into an integral part of a person, into a habitus' (ibid.). Clearly not all individuals have access to capitals that are equally valued in particular fields. Moreover, Lareau makes the point that *possession* of capital does not necessarily mean that an individual can realise a social advantage from those resources; the resources have to be activated in social interaction and this requires recognition. Even among individuals who appear to share the same social space, there can be differences in the degree to which resources can be activated (Lareau 1989: 179).

Social capital, in particular, is widely and sometimes rather too broadly invoked. As Horvat *et al.* (2003) remind us, 'education researchers who draw on the social capital concept would do well to specify the nature and social distribution of the resources that are identified by [it]' (2003: 345). Our emphasis on understanding family habitus and the accumulation and deployment of relevant capitals is reflected in the focus on parents' own educational histories and upbringing. The deployment of capitals is a neglected area with regard to Black middle-class families, although Reay (1998), Connolly (1998) and Rollock (2006, 2007a, 2014) have employed and adapted Bourdieu to explore some of the intersecting relationships of social class and ethnicity. With our main analytical focus being on homes and the role of parents rather than schools, we are submitting to empirical enquiry Bourdieu's assertion that:

> Academic capital is in fact the guaranteed product of the combined effects of cultural transmission by the family and cultural transmission by the school (the efficacy of which depends on the amount of cultural capital directly inherited from the family).
>
> *(Bourdieu 1986: 23)*

How Black Caribbean middle-class families deploy their social and cultural resources in support of their children's education is the main focus of this book. We commented earlier that the possession and deployment of social, cultural, economic and emotional capitals by parents on behalf of their children has been well-documented with regard to White middle-class parents (e.g. Ball 2003a, 2003b; Lareau 1989, 2002; Reay 1998; Vincent and Ball 2006; Vincent and Martin 2002). Such research would suggest that Black middle-class parents, in common with middle-class parents from other ethnic groups, possess high levels of appropriate social and cultural capital. However, Lareau and Horvat's (US) research (1999) leads them to argue that although middle-class Black families still benefit from their class position (and interact with schools in different ways than their less privileged counterparts), they still face an institutional setting that inherently privileges White families. A further consideration is that resources may be differently activated by different middle-class groups, and may be open to misrecognition or even denial by institutions. For example, Camille Wilson Cooper cites African American mothers in her research as being seen as 'irrational, threatening and combative' in their interactions with schools (2007: 492). In the UK, Gill Crozier's research (2005) points to the different forms of labour, including emotional labour that Black mothers invest in when supporting their children through school, a process she has referred to as 'countersurveillance' (1998: 129). The intersection of class and ethnicity may mean that the cultural capital of Black middle-class families has relatively less value and therefore effect in the social field of education. This is something we comment upon in the chapters that follow.

Critical Race Theory

We also employ aspects of Critical Race Theory (CRT) to inform our understanding and analyses of the role of race, racism and power relations in the experiences of our sample of Black Caribbean middle-class families. Following the tenets of CRT, we start from the position that race is socially constructed and that which is traditionally defined as 'racial difference' is invented, perpetuated and reinforced by society. In this approach, racism is understood to be subtle and flexible; it manifests differently in different contexts. Indeed, Critical Race Theorists have argued that the majority of racism is hidden beneath a veneer of normality and it is only the more crude and obvious forms of racism which are recognised as problematic by most people:

> Because racism is an ingrained feature of our landscape, it looks ordinary and natural to persons in the culture. Formal equal opportunity – rules and laws that insist on treating blacks and Whites (for example) alike – can thus remedy only the more extreme and shocking forms of injustice, the ones that do stand out. It can do little about the business-as-usual forms of racism that people of color [*sic*] confront every day …
>
> *(Delgado and Stefancic (2000: xvi)*

We also recognise that to be Black is to traditionally occupy a position of relative disadvantage in terms of key areas of social policy and lived experience in the UK. We have already outlined the situation in terms of compulsory education. Data from the Labour Force Survey shows that Black Caribbean men (along with Bangladeshi and Pakistani men) are least likely of all major ethnic groups to occupy professional and managerial positions, although Black Caribbean women fare better (Heath and Yi Cheung 2006). The majority of those occupying the generic category of 'middle class' experience relative privilege in comparison with others from 'working-class' backgrounds. CRT offers a way to uncover mundane and deeply embedded, racialised assumptions and understandings which normalise and centre White individuals, and marginalise the Black population. This underlies our critical engagement with the concept of Whiteness:

> 'Whiteness' is a racial discourse, whereas the category 'white people' represents a socially constructed identity, usually based on skin colour.
>
> *(Leonardo 2009: 169)*

White*ness*, therefore, refers to a set of assumptions, beliefs and practices that place the interests and perspectives of White people at the centre of what is considered normal and everyday. Critical scholarship on Whiteness is not an assault on White people themselves; it is an assault on the socially constructed and constantly reinforced power of White identifications, norms and interests (Ladson-Billings and Tate 1995: 58–60). It is possible for White people to take a genuine, active role in deconstructing Whiteness but such 'race traitors' (Ignatiev 1997: 613) are relatively uncommon. Similarly, it is also possible for minoritised people to play roles and voice perspectives that embrace Whiteness, for example by defending racism and blaming minoritised groups for any inequality they experience (Bell 1992).

Our interviews explore the ways in which Black middle-class parents perceive and respond to this reality, a mainstream norm that has been referred to as 'Whiteworld' (Fanon, 1967: 83; Gillborn, 2008; McKenley, 2005: 16).

Practically, our engagement with CRT, therefore, means that we recognise racism as a reality and remain sensitive to the various complex ways in which this is played out within society and within participants' accounts. We recognise that racism is complex, changing, subtle and a powerful aspect of day-to-day life and, although it saturates society and its structures, it is often not seen or perceived as unremarkable by Whites.

Cautions about intersectionality

'Intersectionality' is a widely used (and sometimes misused) concept in contemporary social science. The term addresses the question of how multiple forms of inequality and identity interrelate in different contexts and over time, e.g. the interconnectedness of race, class, gender, disability and so on. The term originated in the work of US Critical Race Theorist Kimberlé Crenshaw (1995) but has been deployed widely across the social sciences to the point where it is sometimes viewed as a 'buzzword', whose frequent iteration often belies an absence of clarity and specificity (Davis 2008). Richard Delgado, one of the founders of CRT, has warned that intersectionality can be taken to such extreme positions that the constant subdivision of experience into more and more identity categories can eventually shatter any sense of coherence:

> Intersectionality can easily paralyse progressive work and thought because of the realisation that whatever unit you choose to work with, someone may come along and point out that you forgot something.
>
> *(Delgado 2011: 1264)*

We are also aware that there is the problem of how and where the emphasis lies in analysis. Acker (2006), for example, proposes a focus on 'gendered and racialized class practices', with class providing her 'entry point' into 'complex ongoing practices'. However, Acker also acknowledges that gender or race could equally well be an 'entry point' to understanding the operation of intersecting power relations. Preston and Bhopal (2012), by contrast, discuss their commitment to 'foregrounding' race within their analysis:

> Intersectional analysis does not mean that we cannot 'speak' to 'race' alone, and we should address its primacy when necessary.
>
> *(p. 215)*

Similarly Leonardo (2005: xi) contends that CRT writers explore social issues with 'race' (and racism) at 'the point of departure for critique, not the end of it'. Such arguments illustrate the difficulties of our project, of holding *both* class and race together, trying to understand the workings of both, and their points of interdependence for particular social groups and individuals in particular situations at certain moments. We attempt to name and discuss some of these analytical difficulties as we present the data.

The research team

The research team comprised four members: three White professors (two of whom are male) and a Black female doctor. Rollock (2013a) details how this dynamic and the broader considerations of race and racism within the academy informed the research process. However, we note here that we brought different experiences to our approach to the interviews and reading of the data. Rollock shares the same Caribbean cultural heritage and class position as the project respondents and this often presented moments of connection and affiliation to the issues raised during the course of the interviews. For the White team members critical questioning of their ethnic privileges, the power accrued by their Whiteness and the extent of their 'grasp' of the experience of racism was required. This is a fundamentally challenging process and one which is never complete. As Agyeman (2008) notes:

> When researching the Other in the role of an outsider, this also means addressing the role of self in research and engaging in critical questioning of one's own role and scope.
>
> (p. 82)

Solomon and colleagues refer to the everyday embeddedness of White entitlement as 'the din of common sense' (2005: 157), a common sense that places White people at the centre and Black people at the margin. Constant attention to such assumptions was central to our research practice. One of the most explicit ways in which we sought to engage meaningfully with this was by offering interviewees a choice in terms of the ethnicity of researcher with whom they spoke. Respondents were asked, when the interview was being set up, whether they preferred a Black interviewer, a White interviewer or had no preference, and those preferences were met accordingly. Most (37 of the 51 respondents who answered this question) stated that they had no preference and 14 asked specifically to speak with someone Black (Rollock 2013a). While the notion of 'race-matching' or ethnic symmetry between interviewer and interviewee legitimately can be argued to reflect an essentialist engagement with race, we note that the respondents frequently appeared to identify with Nicola, for example, referring to her positioning as one of a small minority of Black academics, or 'switching codes' (e.g. using Patois) at points in the conversation. Of course race, class, gender and individual personalities are all relevant here. It would be a mistake, however, to view the 'outsider' position of the rest of the team as uniformly problematic. For example, respondents often fully explained experiences and interactions, knowing that they would be outside the personal experience and realities of Whites (for a further discussion, see also Edwards 1990;

Hendrix 2002; Mirza 2009a; Ochieng 2010; Rollock 2013a). There are no straight-forward solutions to these dynamics, and we have not solved all the questions, but we endeavour to reflect on the significance of such matters throughout.

Sociopolitical context

Finally, a word about context. Our principal data collection took place between 2009 and 2011, a period which saw a change of government, in 2010, from Labour to a Conservative/Liberal Democrat Coalition. The start of 2009 saw the inauguration of the first Black president of the United States, an event of considerable historic import, particularly to those of African and Caribbean heritage around the world. In the UK, 2009 signalled ten years since the publication of the seminal Stephen Lawrence Inquiry Report by Sir William Macpherson and his panel of advisors (Macpherson 1999; Rollock 2009). As policy-makers and politicians reflected on lessons learnt, they explicitly distanced themselves from the term 'institutional racism', the concept and problem being regarded as irrelevant to today's Britain (Rollock 2013b; Phillips 2009). Policy discourse, under the new government, centred instead on the idea that 'a clear sense of shared national identity' remained the solution to addressing discord expressed by particular minoritised groups (Cameron 2011). In fact, the Coalition's commitment to race equality has been seen as lacking rather than merely weak (Gillborn and Demack 2012). The body responsible for 'creating a fairer Britain' – the Equality and Human Rights Commission (EHRC) – suffered a significant reduction to its annual budget, cut from £70 million to £17 million in 2012 (Holloway 2012; Gentleman 2013), this occurring in the same period when the government also failed to renew the terms of office for the only two EHRC commissioners with discernible expertise on race issues (Muir 2012; Holloway 2012). In addition, procedures that allowed individuals to hold institutions to account for alleged poor or discriminatory behaviour have either been restricted or abandoned altogether; under new employment legislation, employees now must pay a fee should they be forced to take their employer to a tribunal for harassment, discrimination or other unfair practice. Added to this, Equality Impact Assessments (EqIAs), which forced organisations to assess the impact of policies and guidance on marginalised groups, have been dismissed by the Prime Minister as a waste of time and 'bureaucratic nonsense' (Cameron 2012). In short, race equality is no longer on the political agenda and individual action to challenge inequity has been curtailed. It is within this climate that our research on the Black middle classes took place.

Structure of the book

This is a book about social class, race, racism and education.

While we use NS-SEC to identify those positioned as middle class, we are interested in how the Black middle classes feel about the label 'middle class' and how they think it relates to their experience. Such matters are discussed in *Chapter 1*.

Childhood memories and family background play a key role in shaping feelings about class identification; so too do racism and the attitudes and behaviours of the White middle classes. This first chapter is pivotal to introducing the complexities, concerns and ambivalence surrounding not just class location but how race and historical context shape the experiences of our sample of Black middle-class parents. The rest of the book is divided into two key parts. The first, entitled 'The Black Middle Classes and School', centres on parents' experiences of engaging with the education system. At the start of this equation, in *Chapter 2*, are the factors and priorities involved in choosing a school for their child. Often, the emphasis is on the academic reputation of the school; however, this is also sometimes interspersed with queries about the ethnic and class mix of the school's intake. Parents express concern about the type of pupil that their child will mix with yet their apprehensions do not end here. *Chapter 3* reveals discernible tension between parents' aspirations for their children's academic performance compared with the expectations of teachers. In a series of powerful examples, teachers are described as possessing low expectations of Black children's capabilities, especially when compared with other ethnic groups. As we show in *Chapter 4*, such discrepancies in treatment sometimes lead to difficult and painful encounters with the school especially in situations where disability or special educational needs are concerned. In fact, as is apparent in *Chapter 5*, ensuring Black children receive a good standard of education is not something that parents can readily guarantee, leading to many employing a range of engagement techniques and surveillance in a bid to maximise the probability that their child *will* achieve. While it may be easy to trivialise such reports as the complaints of a mere handful of Black parents, it is crucial to remember the wider history of Black educational experience in the UK and that our sample reflects a largely resourceful, agentic demographic. Indeed, Part 2, 'The Black Middle Classes and Society', draws upon precisely this wider frame. The section begins with *Chapter 6* in which we present data revealing how parents work to raise healthy Black children within a wider context in which Black children are often associated with educational failure and disadvantage. There are many factors at play here. Gender plays a significant role; parents express different but equally grave concerns about the challenges of raising Black boys and Black girls. How should sons be protected from the dangers of 'the street' (gangs, stop and search) and how can girls feel proud of their identity and looks in a society which valorises and epitomises White women as beautiful and desirable. These are painful, difficult conversations but perhaps most challenging is establishing the best time to speak with your child about racism. For almost all parents, race remains present irrespective of class status. We witness this most vividly in *Chapter 7* where respondents describe the sophisticated ways in which they deploy a set of complex strategies – 'public identities' (Lacy 2007: 73) – to navigate White mainstream society. In this chapter, we reveal not just how respondents engage with White society – in schools, the workplace, shopping – but also how they come to recognise themselves as occupying a racially minoritised position in society in the first place. We continue with similar themes in *Chapter 8* but expand our analysis to embrace a generational view. We chart the educational perspectives and experiences of respondents' parents, participants themselves and their children. We show how racism is differently inflected, but nonetheless present, across each of these three generations. While we did not speak with the children themselves, their parents describe them as being more firmly located in their class position and as having greater optimism about the state of race relations in the UK. In the final chapter, we reflect on the major findings to emerge from the study.

We begin, in the chapter which follows, by examining how project respondents (who are objectively in the highest socio-economic categories) view and feel about the idea of being 'middle class', and how their understandings are shaped by race and racism.

Note

1 London Schools and the Black Child (LSBC) conference initiative was spearheaded by Diane Abbott, one of the first Black members of the British Parliament. See http://www.blackeducation.info/ (last accessed 12 February 2014).

1

RACE, CLASS STATUS AND IDENTIFICATION

I have multiple identities: I am middle class by profession, working class by birth and attitude and African Caribbean by culture, history and social experience.

Introduction

While we did not set out to explicitly examine Black identity in our interview questions, our data reveal considerable variation in the ways that parents situate themselves in relation to what it means to be Black and their views on wider notions of Blackness. These articulations permeate the interviews irrespective of the theme under discussion. This chapter begins, therefore, by examining how the Black middle classes think about their identity as Black people before turning to focus on how they position themselves in relation to the label 'middle class'.

Black identity among the Black middle classes

For most of the respondents, to be Black is to share a set of cultural understandings, memories and experiences which are transmitted through history, food, music, a belief in a Black community or identity and an experience of racism. These themes and processes function as a form of cultural adhesive, enabling moments of affiliation with other Black people. Felicia's recollection of an encounter while at an exhibition displaying the work of the British Nigerian Turner-prize artist Chris Ofili illustrates this well:

> ... recently a friend and I went to see a Chris Ofili exhibition and I recall that (...) we really enjoyed it. (...) we were sitting down having a conversation about it, laughing because the White people were walking around looking very serious (...) we were laughing saying that we thought they didn't

> understand it and a Black woman was there on her own and she overheard the conversation [we were having] and she joined in because she said she thought the same as well (…) We were just discussing various things; lots of things we were picking out whereas we thought they [White people] were actually passing through quite quickly.

Here we observe how markers of Black identity, symbolised in the cultural imagery deployed in Ofili's paintings, serve as reflections of identity and experience with which the women can relate. This intimate connection with and interpretation of his work serves in their minds to differentiate their experience from that of White exhibition attendees who are positioned as being at the margins of Black knowledge. The exhibition lacks a deep resonance for White people, hence their 'passing through quite quickly'. While we might think of this cultural adhesive as connecting Felicia and her companions, it also introduces an invisible boundary marker between them and White attendees. Interestingly, the exhibition was in fact held at Tate Britain – an establishment, like many national art institutions, steeped in tradition, White privilege and historicity. Yet the acceptance of Ofili's work into this space suggests that his art has successfully navigated some of the very boundaries and cultural norms usually associated with Whiteness. While Felicia and her companions do not comment upon this wider point, the above extract serves to usefully reveal some of the parameters of distinction between Black and White cultural norms.

Robert's articulation of what it means, for him, to be Black calls upon similar signifiers of cultural understanding and connection:

> … although my taste in music is pretty eclectic – it is very heavily dominated by Black music. I like Black humour and so on. I am married to a Black woman; that is very important to me [laughter] (…) in terms of empathy and a common language, shared experience, common frame of reference. Someone who understands what I am talking about instantly. Those things are very important.

We start, therefore, to build a picture of Black identity which extends beyond cultural signifiers. Being married to a Black woman represents, for Robert, a means of immediate commonality and empathetic understanding, concepts that we can begin to think of as fundamental to the notion of what Sivanandan (1993: 66) calls 'a black perspective'.

Femi, who is of mixed heritage and has a White partner, grew up in a mainly White rural area. She explains that the sense of belonging or connection with other Black people, to which both Felicia and Robert refer, is not an automatic given simply because you are also Black. She speaks of being 'devastated' at not having had this bond when she was a young woman, though she is 'aware' or *conscious*[1] now. Contrast Femi with Miles who regards himself as Black in descriptive terms only. In the extract which follows, he has just been asked about the role of race in shaping significant life decisions:

That is not even in the equation. What for me … for nearly everything that I do … is 'have I got the best of x? (…) race is not a big one for me at all other than as I said, I like to think that [I'm] a good example of a person, and I'm also a good positive Black example, and probably in that order, but I don't see any of that as being the mirror of [who I am]. I just think I am who I am and just move on with it. I've been in lots and lots of situations where I haven't even noticed that I'm the only Black person there (…). It's not something that I think [that] 'there's loads of Black people or loads of White people', it's just 'do I like it'? If I go to a football match sometimes I think it's great, sometimes I think there's too many people here, but I don't think about the ethnic mix.

Miles, who is married to a White partner and has three young children, downplays the idea that the colour of his skin has any bearing on his life, reporting that he does not see race either in his personal context or in public spaces. However, there is an uncomfortable paradox to his colour-blindness. In order to assert that he has been in several situations and not 'noticed that I'm the only Black person there' he reveals that he *does* in fact see race but actively goes out of his way to ignore it and to suppress its significance; he denies its relevance to his life. To even see or acknowledge race is problematic. Mary, the mother of two mixed-race children who lives outside of London, conveys a similar sentiment when she is asked about race, stating:

I don't think about people's ethnic backgrounds at all.

And later:

I tend to think more on individual [basis]. It sounds awful because I'm Black, but I don't think of my colour at all, throughout my day I don't actually think about it.

Here Mary offers a hint, a moment of acknowledgement that perhaps she ought to position differently in terms of her raced identity. 'It sounds awful, because I'm Black …' intimates that the way in which she regards herself is somehow different from what she knows to be a more prevalent conceptualisation of Black identity. She recognises that to think in terms of the individual is to be at odds with principles of Blackness. Both Mary's and Miles' interviews stand out for their relative lack of detailed analysis and deconstruction of issues around race and racism. They both tend to stress the idea of individuality: identities are individual and achieving success is an individual act. As we shall see in Chapter 6, this – perhaps unsurprisingly – has implications for the way in which they approach discussing issues of racism with their children. We can draw a stark comparison between their perspectives and the way in which Cynthia, the mother of three Black boys under the age of 15 years, situates herself:

> Whenever I get up, when I go out the door, when I walk down the street, I walk always in my mind you walk as a Black person. You walk as a Black woman, and I feel that I am an example to young Black girls when I see them on the street. I feel that I have to recognise the senior Black people on the street. The way that I allow my children to see me being treated in a shop scenario as a Black person is very important because I think it is always an education for them.

Here we observe the sense not merely of the collective identity that Femi referred to earlier but also the ways in which this is enacted as an intergenerational and gendered form of responsibility. Cynthia's Black identity is conscious, lived, present. It is intricately bound up in seeking to shape and inform positively the experiences of those around her; values of respect and recognition are pivotal. There is a discernible difference to emphasise here with regard to her acts of recognition, which involve seeing and being an example to other Black people, and Miles' commitment to colour-blindness and individualism. We make a distinction therefore between being Black in terms of mere skin pigmentation and being Black as aligned to a political or conscious sense of collective worth and investment (Rollock 2014). Of course, we do not propose that Black identity can be understood merely in these dichotomous terms: being *either* 'conscious' *or* 'incidental' (as we might summarise Miles' and Mary's position), but seek in our analysis to constantly attend to the complexities of being Black within a mainly White society (Touré 2011):

> Its [cultural identity] complexity exceeds [a] binary structure of representation. At different places, times, in relation to different questions, the boundaries are re-sited. They become, not only what they have, at times, certainly been − mutually excluding categories, but also what they sometimes are − differential points along a sliding scale.
>
> *(Hall 1996: 215)*

This framework − thinking of identities as a sliding scale and in a state of constant flux − proves useful when we come to think about how the Black middle classes manage relationships in work and social settings.

Friendship groups and work relationships

One way to conceptualise Black identity within the British context is through the ways in which our respondents talk about friendship groups and relations at work. Our data shows that they engage in delicate, largely invisible acts of artful decision-making and compromise as class (see below) and race considerations collide. An extract from our interview with Alice, a mother of three children each at different stages of education, speaks to these tensions:

> I have friends who work in clerical positions who would only do certain things. It's really weird. If you try and get them to do something else they

don't want to because they feel as though if they were to do it they would be out of place (…) they don't understand why I would want to go to a place that is frequented by White people and they see it as a place that is frequented by White people when it is not (…) if I go to an exhibition or if I go to a gallery for example (…). I am not sure if it is because they think that there are certain things that you can't do as a Black person or that actually I know what it is, I think it is because they think there are certain things that you shouldn't do as a Black person but if you were to do these certain things it makes you very 'unblack' to do them.

This account is interesting for several reasons. First, although Alice's observations are about her Black working-class friends, she initially highlights their class status (clerical positions) and not their race when commenting on their discomfort when attending mainly White spaces. So we are introduced to the idea that (her) middle-class status may enable the development of an identity – forms of Black cultural capital – that allow her to feel more comfortable (or be more accepted) than her friends in predominantly White spaces. And certainly, given their occupations, it is likely that respondents in our study are used to being one of few people of colour in the workplace and to calculating how best to navigate an existence within that context. Our second point of observation is that Alice's criticism is directed at her friends. She suspects that the White spaces she mentions – galleries, exhibitions – epitomise pastimes not traditionally pursued by Blacks and therefore remain unattractive to them.

Versions of an alleged Black authenticity come into play here. It presupposes that there are certain acts with which those who are 'consciously' Black do not engage since to do so is to challenge or interrupt this Blackness. However, we argue that any meaningful critique of Black authenticity must take account of the broader sociopolitical sphere. Questions of Black authenticity, we suggest, only come into play within a wider context of Whiteness. Engaging in White spaces or activities traditionally associated with White people is to risk being subjected to racism or to values and perspectives perceived to be at odds with Blackness (see below). Black authenticity may be understood, therefore, as a consequence of a historic imperative for self-preservation and protection. It is a way of marking oneself off from the dangers of Whiteness, of retaining some (invisible) boundary between *Them* and Us. The parameters of Black authenticity are constantly being remade as racism becomes more covert and complex and as Black people develop increasingly sophisticated tools and resources to navigate mainly White spaces. It is crucial to note that such arguments do not hold with the same resonance for those who might be positioned as 'incidentally' Black since they have less profound investment in a collective Black identity and hence scant, if any, commitment to explicitly addressing the broader issues that affect Black people. Indeed, as we have already noted, those who are positioned in this way tend to deny seeing racial difference at all.

We have already spoken of the ways in which some respondents considered that the boundaries between Black and White people might be understood via the latter's lack of understanding of Black cultural symbols. In the following extract, we look more closely at how these boundaries become reinforced due to stereotypical representations of Black people within wider society:

> Clearly all the friends that I have are not going to be Jamaican [like me]. My Black friends are from Ghana, Nigeria, from wherever, so there are certain sensibilities that have to be negotiated there but the one thing that you don't actually have to explain to someone is being Black. You don't have to talk about it. I mean you might moan about things that happen but you don't have to explain. I have my closest [White] friends whom I have known since I was 11 who would do anything for me but still to this day talk about Black people and their ghetto blasters and I say, 'Well what are you talking about? Do I have a ghetto blaster?' And you know you can constantly be surprised by this.
>
> *(Lorraine)*

Here we see how a certain collective Black identity exists – shaped, partly, in response to the vagaries and turmoil of racism – which can transcend differences of ethnicity. There is no need to account for one's Blackness when with other Black people. Note, in comparison to this, the ways in which race operates when in the company of White people. Despite the longevity of their friendship, race signals an omnipresent discomfort for Lorraine's White friends. Black people are viewed through a narrow, restrictive lens which refuses to make multiple versions of Blackness possible. Being with other Black people therefore represents a certain safety from such limitations (Rollock 2012b), thus serving to reinforce an invisible cohesion among them. Felicia echoes Lorraine's point:

> … I recall talking to one in particular [East Asian] woman about it and she said to me, 'I just don't feel comfortable with them [White colleagues] at all. They don't make me feel comfortable'. Whereas I socialise sometimes but I am aware that when I am socialising it is sort of like I am doing it on the basis that I don't see why I should exclude myself and so I might not enjoy this but you need to learn to interact with me whether you like it or not (…) Someone, one of the most senior of the … runs the whole [organisation] saw me the other day and said hello to me thinking I was another Black woman and when she said the name I said, 'I am not so and so', and she went, 'Ooh I haven't got my glasses on', and I thought no we are both Black and you just assume, even though that person is someone she works very closely with and yet she mistook me for her.
>
> *(Felicia)*

Being in the company of White people means being open to the possibility that race and racism will surface in unexpected, awkward ways. These are moments that are uncomfortable and alienating for people of colour; they are dehumanising. Felicia's account challenges the commonly held view that Black people simply and uncritically exclude themselves from mainly White spaces. To conclude thus is to miss the challenging racial politics that often play themselves out in these arenas. Some White people are not familiar with or at ease around people of colour. Black people retain a hyper-visibility and remain a spectacle in the eyes of the wider White population. They remain as Fanon would say 'overdetermined from without' (Fanon 1967: 87), their bodies stimulating fear and confusion. Still with Felicia, consider this conversation she recounts involving a White colleague who had also been a long-term close friend of the family. The conversation takes place at work:

> [He said] 'Do you mind if I ask you something?' – because in the conversation I had said I was Jamaican – 'Do you mind if I ask you something? Oh maybe I shouldn't?' So I thought right, either it is something totally inappropriate, so now I want to know, so I said, 'Of course just ask away, it is better that you ask.' And he said, 'Do you think that …' (…) the question he asked me was 'Do you think Jamaicans are genetically predisposed to violence?'

The extent to which the question is naive, insulting and does violence to Felicia, who he knows to be of Jamaican heritage herself, cannot be adequately conveyed. That the colleague pauses, hesitates before asking the question hints that there may be some – albeit insufficient – recognition of its inappropriateness. Felicia recalls feeling both amusement and anger at the question yet was somehow able to work beyond this to provide her colleague with a considered response (see Chapter 7). Thus it is not merely talking about the subject of race *per se* with Whites that is saturated with possibilities of danger and insult, as Leonardo and Porter (2010) so powerfully argue, but to be in their presence at all carries risks – the possibility of racial insult:

> The White world, the only honourable one, barred me from all participation. A man was expected to behave like a man. I was expected to behave like a black man – or at least like a nigger. I shouted a greeting to the world and the world slashed away my joy. I was told to stay within the bounds, to go back where I belonged.
>
> *(Fanon 1967: 836)*

These acts of Whiteness (lack of recognition, stereotyping, unwitting insult) serve as perpetual reminders of the chilling permanence of racism in everyday life (Delgado and Stefancic 2000). They remind Black people that they are Black and therefore not equal to White. These are not the explicit, crude one-off forms of racism that grab newspaper headlines. They are small, subtle yet highly damaging everyday incidents which subjugate people of colour and remind them that they are different. These are acts of 'microaggression' (Rollock 2012a; Sue *et al.* 2008).

As we will show in the section that follows, these complex questions around Black identity and the relational role of Whiteness also manifest in discussions with the Black middle classes about class location.

Class status and identity among the Black middle classes

We have detailed information about views on class identification for 59 of our 62 respondents. We have identified five broad groupings that emerge in response to the question 'Do you consider yourself to be middle class?' and to our coding of themes around social class and 'parent class position':

- working-class identifiers;
- working class with qualification;
- interrogators;
- middle-class ambivalent;
- middle-class identifiers.

Participants defined as working-class or middle-class identifiers are the least ambivalent in their identification and are relatively few in number: 4 and 12 respondents, respectively. Middle-class identifiers tend to accept the label 'middle class' by making factual reference to income, the size of their home, occupation or pastimes. This differs considerably to the majority (23 of our 59 participants, almost 40 per cent) whom we define as middle-class ambivalent. Participants in this category tend to regard themselves as middle class but do so with some degree of reservation or hesitation. While existing research on the class identification of the White middle classes also points to their hesitation and ambivalence (Savage *et al.* 2001) we argue, as will become evident below, that the reasons informing these perspectives for our respondents fundamentally differ because of the particular intersection of their histories, identities and experiences as racially minoritised people.

We term a further 12 respondents 'working class with qualification' to encompass those who, while initially ascribing to a label of 'working class', proceed to qualify or expand this to better reflect their personal circumstance. For example, Janet, who is a journalist, describes herself as 'working class but with middle-class values'; another, Richard, draws on his working-class upbringing and the fact that his parents still live in council accommodation to make the argument that his sheer proximity to 'working-classness', despite his objective class status, renders any straightforward identification as 'middle class' problematic.

Finally, we categorise eight respondents as class 'interrogators'. That is, during the course of the interview, they were not able to align themselves with any specific class position. Instead they responded with considerable reflection and thoughtful analysis about the meaning of class, which sometimes included questions about their relationship to it. In certain instances, this is informed by evocative memories of a working-class childhood and upbringing that continues to resonate deeply despite a later transition to a middle-class occupation, a more comfortable home and an affluent lifestyle. In other situations, the very notion of a Black middle class is perceived to be meaningless – a contradiction in terms. Such is the case, for example, for Regina who insists that, while as a group the Black community (again this collective identity) has made some educational progress, they cannot demonstrate the same level of financial and economic mobility or security as their more economically stable and powerful White counterparts. This point is also conveyed by Daye (1994) in terms of the relative economic powerlessness of her Black middle-class respondents, despite their class position.

These five categories provide a useful foundation from which to engage and analyse the data. However, it should be noted that the boundaries between the groups are not fixed or marked by respondents' location. As we will show, these are fluid and porous, reflecting considerable similarity across the groups in reasoning, feelings and thoughts about class. Accordingly, we arrange the analysis that follows thematically rather than subscribing tightly to the groupings outlined above. We reveal moments of tension, ambiguity and sometimes conflicting perspectives held by the same individual, as participants work to make sense of their class position within British society. This reflects social class as a 'relational, emergent, contextual, dynamic, localized' process (Ball 2003: 175). As with those in Daye's (1994) study, for our Black middle-class respondents there are yet further complexities in defining social class that are made awkward by the specific British context: memories, values and connections to a working-class past and ongoing incidences of exclusion from White middle-class spaces.

The British context

For some respondents, questions about whether they consider themselves to be middle class are influenced by distant memories of learning about social class in sociology classes at school or college or by the broader British context against which they attempt to assess their personal situation. Such awareness by no means offers a satisfactory resolution to their analysis as a range of additional factors, such as the interrelated role of specific country context, often comes to bear on these individual memories, perceptions and understandings. For example, Juliet speaks of the ways in which various forms of capital, all of which she argues might be said to relate to social class, are imbued with differing legitimacy according to the norms of the country in question. She describes, for example, her mother as coming from a lower middle-class background and emphasises the importance to the family – and she is referring here to the extended family – of education, with many members having attended university. She also details the forms of historical and political knowledge and networks of 'people like us' readily accessible to her as a child. Yet Juliet remains hesitant to describe herself as middle class precisely because she recognises the different value such capitals have (Bourdieu 1993), when taken alongside the family's financial situation within the British context:

> … as I grew up I felt myself to be culturally Caribbean middle class not English middle class. Caribbean middle class but poor in Britain. (…) there has been a lot more economic mobility [for the Black population in Britain] but that doesn't necessarily equate with class mobility. (…) for example (…) I had a very strong sense of having come from (…) a good family in the

> Caribbean and having a certain social standing so (…) I would see it in terms of like Pierre Bourdieu's stuff around cultural capital; there's a sense [in the Caribbean] of the class cultural capital is greater than the economic …

Country-specific differences in the cost and standard of living and societal values come together in complex ways to shape understanding and feelings about social class. This is a subject echoed by other participants especially, although not exclusively, where individuals had direct or formative experience of having lived abroad. For example, Monica, who is a teacher, self-defines as working class. She speaks of having enjoyed, when younger, a middle-class lifestyle overseas that would not have been available to her family in the UK even if her parents had secured the same occupations. Another respondent, Ray (middle-class ambivalent) outlines the range of variables that feed into reflections about his class position:

> … an article I read recently (…) suggests, based on my income, I am middle class. It placed me in the top 10% of earners in the country. Even though I have argued that class is more than income, all sociological codifications I have seen have placed me in that category despite my discomfort and wriggling. To console myself I rely on the fact that my parents were working class with 'middle class aspirations' which makes me a result of their aspirations. I have multiple identities: I am middle class by profession, working class by birth and attitude and African Caribbean by culture, history and social experience.

Ray's analysis of his class location provides an evocative example of the realities of the ways in which the intersections of place, class and emotion come together to forge an identity that is complex and multi-layered. Formal markers of social class, which attempt to render him straightforwardly middle class, are tempered by the class status of his parents and his Caribbean identity. Values and perceptions about class and race are central. As with many other participants, 'working class' is a childhood identity that is seen to have associations with hard work but also with honesty, integrity and good will, what we might think of as *moral capital*. In turn, these attributes are perceived to be and experienced as at odds with middle-classness, a class location which itself is seen to be deeply infused with Whiteness. We return to this subject later. There is an additional aspect to Ray's subjective class positioning that pertains to his cultural identity and his experiences of racism. Having spent his pre-teens in his place of birth in the Caribbean, he is able to provide a perspective of how he is situated differently in the British context as a Black man, describing in one example the lower expectations that would have existed for him from teachers had he been schooled entirely in the UK. He notes therefore that his 'social identity is significantly affected by racism' so that his reflections of self, what he describes as his 'affiliations', are 'race based rather than class oriented at least when I am in Britain'. Again as with our analysis of Black identity, we are reminded of the continued significance and prevalence of racism within the British context (Delgado and Stefancic 2001), and we can see how, alongside other aspects of his being, racism stimulates in Ray a self-identification whereby any comfortable association with being middle class in the British context carries considerably less resonance.

Respondents also note comparative differences in terms of the economic and financial mobility and success of their African American counterparts (many have friends and family in the US). These observations serve to further obfuscate any coherent conceptualisation of a Black British middle-class identity. Again, race and class work here at multiple levels and in complex ways. For Brenda, for example, the African American middle classes are a more clearly defined group with discernible, 'typical' attributes and who operate within a broader societal context where success is publicly lauded and encouraged. This contrasts with the lack of coherent voice and reservation in celebrating success which she perceives to be evident among their Black British counterparts. Anita also comments on the American situation:

> ... you can live out there in middle class (...) very affluent [areas] like Mount Vernon – it's a very affluent area in New York (...) [also] Atlanta (...) they've lots of Caribbeans there ... For some reasons the Caribbeans that have gone to the States have done great, as opposed to here and Canada. (...) They go there, they work, they achieve because I think that is what America is about. It's about if you can do it ... There aren't those restrictions and here, it is a class country. It's about who you know...

In this sense, respondents are arguing that success in British society is seen to rely on 'class-specific forms of sociability' (Ball 2003a: 80) that is perceived to be less salient and certainly less restrictive in America. Interestingly, Whiteness remains invisible in these analyses about America even though both the African American middle class and the Black British middle class are operating within sites in which social class and race are intimately intertwined and in which they are minoritised.

Black working-class histories

Four respondents describe themselves as unambiguously working class due, among other factors, to a lack of higher-level qualifications and having to struggle financially. For Maud, the term working class was an obvious and simple reflection of the fact that she needed to work for a living, irrespective of the official category into which her occupation placed her. There are also working-class values and lifestyles, developed within the social field of the family, that come to bear on class affiliation:

> I think that the principles and values that my parents taught me and my grandparents taught me stand me quite firmly as being working class (...) Integrity, being a good person, loving your family, loving yourself, loving (...) each other, protecting your family, working hard, providing for your family and (...) education has definitely been a focus in my family.

(Maud)

Again, we witness more evidence of the moral capital seen to be embodied within a formative working-class identity. There is a kind of embodied sacrifice that encompasses certain values around integrity and selflessness, which unproblematically and unquestioningly are seen as exclusive working-class terrain and, we suggest, are deeply infused in the collective Black identity described above. This moral capital has historicity, it is informed by a collective struggle, collective compromises that live and retain legitimacy in the memories of a new Black middle class. Gabriel, who is hesitant about his middle-class location, describes the tensions that this class transition triggers:

> When I see myself as middle class I don't think of the situation of being working class which I understand, I have experienced, I think I have escaped (…) but by escaping it am I closing the door behind me and saying to people that I perceive as not part of the Black middle class or the middle class? Am I communicating to them rejection or indifference or condescension? All those things that I have experienced working when I have been firmly deemed as working class.

The proximity to a working-class past enables empathy with and commitment to the priorities and concerns of the Black working classes (Small 1994) despite the new class location. It speaks to a notion of a particular kind of collective Black identity, the borders of which are delineated by a struggle that has been both racial and economic and which make up the shared 'moral imagination' (Sayer 2005: 960) of many of our Black middle classes. Gabriel is not merely concerned at the idea of leaving this behind but also at the thought of becoming something other, of developing characteristics of a perceived middle class selfish condescension that he remembers experiencing when he was working class. Another aspect of this moral capital is voiced by Cynthia:

> On paper yeah, I'm middle class but I come from working class stock. (…) 'you got to work for everything you need' that was my parents. 'You don't get anything for free; you don't put anything on credit. You save up for it; you buy it cash in hand.' I can just hear my parents now.

Despite her adult class status, the values of her parents retain legitimacy in her life, acting as a form of cohesion across generations. And the past plays a crucial role in shaping feelings about present class location. Nigel recalls memories of a working-class childhood where he had to carry clothes to the launderette and queue to collect fuel for the paraffin heater while his mother balanced four jobs. These histories make up the working-class habitus of many of our respondents. The immediacy of these stories, these memories and advice from a Black working-class past, make, for some, any absolute separation from a definition of working class seem disloyal. It would represent a form of dislocation from a formative previous self that still has presence.

It is also important to note that the relative newness of their middle-class location is accompanied by a degree of uncertainty. Professional achievement does not necessarily guarantee long-term financial security and this explains some participants' reservation about taking up the label of 'middle class'. As Margaret who works in the private sector succinctly put it, most middle-class Black people are only 'one or two pay cheques away from being working class', a fragility that has been researched and commented on by Oliver and Shapiro (2006) with regard to Black middle classes in the States. Again, for our respondents, this lack of security serves as a perpetual reminder of a working-class past.

Defining the boundaries of the Black middle classes

There is a distinction to be made between objective measures of class and those which are affective, that is pertaining to feelings, histories, memories. In this section, we attempt to tease out some of the boundaries that define the Black middle classes even while recognising that these boundaries are newly emerging and forming like 'a flame whose edges are in constant movement, oscillating around a line or surface' (Bourdieu 1987: 13). Even though aspects of this moral capital persist – thus speaking to a desire to retain cohesion and selflessness – patterns of inclusion and exclusion are evident in our respondents' accounts.

We begin with perhaps our most vivid examples. Janet, who self-defines as 'working class but with middle-class values', is one of our 'working class with qualification' respondents. Prompted to describe these values, Janet calls upon certain forms of cultural capital which she regards as more or less acceptable and worthwhile:

> Our son saw a Butlin's Holiday on television and said 'why don't we go there on holiday it looks good?' and (…) my husband said 'I don't wanna go there it'll be covered in people who just wanna drink lager every night and are covered in tattoos [laughs] and watch *EastEnders* and [son] was like, 'what are you talking about?' [laughs] (…) I just said 'well because it's just that we think the kind of people who go to those places don't really think like we do'.

There are judgments and values made in this marking out of class boundaries. Certain acts – 'a couple of foreign holidays a year, reading' – have, for Janet, middle-class status and are assumed to have inherent value and hence legitimacy. She states that her family watch television but only a certain amount (too much television clearly being frowned upon) and not only can 'they not bear soaps' but she does not know 'how people watch that sort of thing'. Janet performs a particular hierarchical class exclusion – what Lacy (2007: 75) terms 'exclusionary boundary work' – to set herself apart from working-class others. She reveals a lifestyle based on arbitrarily perceived categorisations of performing and not performing specific acts of class distinction (Bourdieu 1993). Such distinctions are evident in wider society yet, despite their arbitrariness, they retain (or obtain) value and worth through socially and culturally embedded acts of (middle-) class distinction that seek to define the boundaries of what is and is not intellectual, respectful, tasteful. This class inclusion/exclusion discourse is evident, as we note above, in Janet's remarks about Butlin's holidays, which provide a powerful example of an activity not pursued by 'people like us' and, crucially, acts as a subtle lesson in class politics, taste and 'modes of consumption' to her 9-year-old son (Bourdieu 1993: 37). Janet does not display any of the common discomforts associated with Savage and colleagues' (2001) research that asks (White) participants about class but instead, in order to delineate the reality of her own class position, embraces its arbitrary relationship to status and worth as legitimate, acceptable and unproblematic (Sayer 2002).

Also evident in Janet's accounts about social class is the absence of a discourse of financial struggle, which characterises the comments of some of our other respondents, notably those who self-define as 'working class'. Janet is financially secure enough to be able to make certain choices and to embrace a particular lifestyle. Yet she self-defines as working class because in straightforward economic terms her occupation serves as her only means of income.

This does not, however, complete our understanding of Janet's views about her class location. The reasons why she aligns herself to middle-class values are multi-layered, complex and intersectionally informed by aspects of race and class inequity and worth (Sayer 2002) that exist around her. Later in the interview, for example, she describes the employee demographic of the large, multinational organisation for which she works. Speaking to the intersecting role of race with class she observes that, while most of the employees are White and middle class there are, by contrast, a number of Black people who work in the 'canteen or in the post room and (…) tend to be cleaners'. Only a few Black people – and she includes herself within this – occupy higher-status positions despite possessing relevant qualifications, education and experience. Inequities of race therefore surface irrespective of the cultural capital that she and her Black colleagues possess. Reflecting on the reasons for this, she comments: '[Middle-class White] people tend to choose what they understand and what they know and they don't in a sense relate to you in the same way.'

Therefore, Janet's self-identification as 'working class but with middle-class values' is not only shaped by a distinction against a particular working-class demographic but, significantly, is also informed by the race and class dimensions of her place of work. Even though she enjoys a degree of status in her role (relative, that is, to the majority of Black employees), she remains cognisant of the ways in which power plays out across axes of race and class and how this ultimately benefits a White middle-class majority.

Isolation

Located in the margins of Janet's account is an additional subject to which several participants referred, namely isolation. This manifested in some instances as participants recognised and sometimes resisted that they were (becoming) class distant from friends with whom they had grown up but who remained working class in occupation, tastes and pastimes. To describe oneself as middle class is to not only be disloyal to family and (working-class) friends but is also to enter a terrain where, quite simply, there are fewer Black middle-class people. Catherine, who we have defined as 'middle-class ambivalent', exemplifies this clearly. She regards self-identifying as 'middle class' as 'pretentious', a characteristic with which she does not wish to be associated. In contrast to Janet, she is adamant that she goes on the same holidays, reads the same books and watches the same films as 'everyone else'. Since these leisure activities tend to be highly classed, this reveals something of Catherine's desire, as with Savage and colleagues' (2001) participants, to be 'ordinary'. She does not wish to single herself out as different. Again, we witness this awkward oscillation between class loyalty and formal occupational classification that leads, for Catherine, to the possibility of a classless state. Her resistance and ambivalence about a middle-class categorisation, not easily conveyed here, were reflected during the interview through frequent pauses, as she ruminated upon and struggled with the line of questioning. However, if, as we did with Janet, we probe further about the reasons for her ambivalence, we learn something of the way that context informs her feelings:

> Maybe it's because it's [calling oneself middle class] not with the masses (…) in this country, with a history of being working class (…) it is something to do with poking your head above the parapet and saying [lowers voice, to a whisper] 'I'm middle class' so you know there's not a lot of us there so maybe it's more comfortable to be with the masses.

Not only is Catherine's reluctance to define as middle class located in a loyalty to a Black working class (something we have witnessed already with other respondents) but to actually 'become' Black and middle class is to single yourself out, to become isolated. Her comments speak not simply to the small size and newness of this group but also imply that there is no discernible space or formal membership group in which to be situated. There are few 'people like us'.

The theme of isolation is also conveyed through the careful, detailed evaluations to be made in the management of friendship groups and at social events. Some of our respondents speak of having to manage and 'audit' their social lives along the axes of race and social class (see above). They reflect on the challenges of socialising with long-term friends, perhaps from childhood, who have not made the transition to the middle classes or who might not feel comfortable in mainly (White) middle-class spaces:

> Your friendship group – I mean this is the bit that probably causes the greatest anxiety for me is that the more invested you are in middle-class culture the less likely you are to hang on to your working-class friends, because it's hard to integrate everybody, where you live, where you choose to live (…) when I think about my friendship group, it's hard to maintain friendships with people who don't feel middle class or are suspicious of middle-class things. I have one friend, I've known him for nearly thirty years. He grew up [in care] (…) to all intents and purposes is a wealthy guy but he is so insecure

> about being at dinner parties and places and having those polite conversations
> about bits of literature, art, news, topical stuff.
>
> *(Gabriel)*

We see resonance here with the earlier discussion about friendships. There are the
pastimes, activities and attitudes that are seen to characterise a middle-class way of
life and adoption of these can stimulate in Gabriel's working-class friends feelings
of exclusion. Felicia too speaks of careful decision-making depending on the class
status and tastes of her friends coupled with considerations of the type of event in
question.

White privilege and moral capital

In some ways, the struggle over comfortably owning a 'Black and middle class' identity is tied up in a relational rejection of what it means to be White and middle class.
The latter are perceived to have better financial security and a greater capacity to
truly exercise choice over their own and their children's futures. However, the White
middle classes are also seen to embody privilege and to value individualism, principles to which the Black middle classes have at one time or another been subjected
and with which they adamantly do not wish to be associated:

> I will do dinner parties, and I think yes, I understand that but I didn't grow
> up with dinner parties. I don't think I ate out until I was in my early twenties.
> My parents didn't take us to restaurants to eat and didn't stand in the queue
> saying 'which ice-cream do you want darling?' for five minutes while every-
> body in the back of the queue was waiting. That did not happen. 'Choose an
> ice-cream or there isn't an ice-cream!'
>
> *(Gabriel)*

This anecdote about ice cream is interesting. Gabriel does not explicitly refer to the
race or the class of the parents or child at the front of the queue, yet the example
alludes to the acts of a casual, presumed entitlement and indulgent parenting style
that is oblivious to, and unconcerned about, the needs of others and which, significantly, Gabriel situates firmly outside the norms of his Black Caribbean working-class
family. The White middle classes are not seen to embody behaviours and values
worth emulating. As a result, there is a desire to distance oneself from them:

> I see too many usually White middle-class people who don't seem to live in
> the real world. They just seem to get upset over the most ridiculous things.
> Like I had it yesterday [adopts exaggerated 'upper-class' accent], 'do you
> realise we're only allowed two parking permits where we live!' It's like 'park-
> ing permits'? I can't afford a car! I can't even afford the insurance for a
> car (…) you see them in restaurants letting their kids run absolutely wild.
> At [daughter's] ballet class they sit and they talk through the children's

performances and you look at them and think 'I don't want to be part of your group' …

(Femi)

Clearly there is a level of essentialising here. Privilege and financial security are conflated as a form of Whiteness that remains unseen and taken for granted by the White middle-class actors in Femi's example. Whiteness operates in this instance to maintain a version of reality in which having only two parking permits is uncritically and quite seriously regarded as a problem, while there is, for Femi, another version of reality marked by not even being able to afford a car in the first place.

The ballet incident is relevant to our understanding of Black middle-class identification on several levels. Her daughter is engaging in an activity that is traditionally associated with White middle-class children (Vincent and Ball 2007), although our research reveals that the Black middle classes also share in these pastimes (Vincent *et al.* 2013b). Yet there is tension for middle-class Blacks who enter these spaces traditionally occupied by Whites. Femi is uncomfortable with the forms of parenting, discipline, rudeness and, again, privilege, which she perceives are embedded in a White version of middle-classness and juxtaposed to her form of moral capital. Being Black and middle class she is able to access these White middle-class spaces, but she remains at the edges, made uncomfortable by what she finds there.

Exclusion from White middle-class spaces

Willingness to self-define as 'Black middle class' is, we found, also compounded by the reactions of the White middle classes themselves. It is the moments of exclusion from White middle-class spaces of which respondents spoke most often. Our respondents describe incidents where the White middle classes actively monitor access to these spaces and the ways in which they treat those who may have got in. Jean explains:

> … I've spoken to White middle class people who know my background (…) I've got an education, you know I continue to learn etc. etc. and then there might be still something that they'll say to me that I think 'is it me or is what they've said to me just so not accepting of my experience?' So (…) I'm perceived to be of a certain class by virtue of my race.

(Jean)

Therefore we ought not to think of exclusion in merely physical terms but also in terms of a questioning or rejection of the experiences of the Black middle classes as valid. The cultural capital that Jean possesses in terms of education, while arguably facilitating her access to White middle-class spaces, is not sufficient to ensure that her views and opinions are taken seriously. She seeks to deploy her cultural capital but it is not legitimated or accepted as valid by White others. Again, this sense of being limited by the (White) determinations of one's skin colour (Fanon 1967): Jean perceives that she is expected to be a certain class on account of her race. The notion that she must be working class – that is Black and working class – fuels the assumption that she, therefore, lacks 'legitimate' knowledge – knowledge worth knowing within this White middle-class space. Lorraine has had a similar experience:

> I was talking to one of the clinical psychologists I have been working with and we talked about how I managed [my daughter's] behaviour. So I said, 'Well you know I have tried everything, I have done the carrot and the stick, I have tried star charts, I have done this, I have done that, I have tried motivating her this way' and she went back and she had weekly supervision and she spoke to her supervisor and her supervisor said, 'Well how did she know to try these things?' [Laughs] And [psychologist] said, 'Well she's an intelligent woman, she has researched, she has read.' But clearly because I was a Black woman, single parent, they assumed I knew nothing about parenting.

This example is particularly interesting in the context of debates about educational attainment, Black Caribbean pupils and the need for increased parental involvement. The capitals that Lorraine brings to this situation concerning her daughter (who has learning difficulties), rather than being welcomed as aiding her daughter's advancement, are immediately met with a level of confusion and suspicion by the supervisor. Lorraine's knowledge is not taken as given. Lorraine argues that this reaction must be understood in the context of the stereotypical perceptions that exist about the Black single mother as uneducated, unconcerned and uninvolved in her child's education. It is precisely through these raced and classed restrictions imposed by White gatekeepers that we can better comprehend Lorraine's reluctance to call herself middle class:

> ... I would probably still say I'm working class though that's probably not true, and I think it sounds almost twee to say that you're classless but it almost has to be. I went to [high-status British university]. I speak in a certain way so that if people didn't see me, if they heard me on the phone people would probably think of me as middle class. But, despite having gone to [university], and having had the education that I have and the kind of jobs that I've had I still find it hard to describe myself as middle-class and that's to do with my race.

> *(Lorraine)*

Markers of biography and embodiment, such as university attendance (and in this case a particularly high-status university), accent and occupation serve to position Lorraine as middle class. Yet at the same time there is for Lorraine 'the psychic refusal of becoming middle class' (Reay 1997: 25), that is a certain discomfort and ambiguity in defining herself as 'Black middle class' because of the specific intersection of her 'race' with her class position. This is, in part, as we have already seen, informed by her recognition that her middle-class embodiment and cultural capital is met with confusion and bafflement by White education professionals: 'If I were a middle-class White woman they'd find it easier. I just don't meet their expectations.'

Conclusion

This chapter has explored notions of Black identity and class location among the Black middle classes. There is no single Black identity. Instead, we have noted that it varies along a continuum, one end of which is marked by a denial that to be Black matters and by a focus on individual achievement and rewards. At the other end sits an identity characterised by collective worth, investment and a valuing of history and familial values. We term these 'incidental' Blackness and 'collective' Blackness respectively. Our data suggest that it is impossible to deconstruct a notion of Black identities within the British context without considering the role of racism and without recognition of the wider, sociopolitical discourse about race. We may, at least in part, view both incidental and collective Blackness as strategic responses (not necessarily conscious or explicit) to living within a mainly White, racist society. Similar issues also come to bear on the ways our respondents feel about and respond to the label 'middle class'.

While we have been able to identify five distinct sets of responses (middle-class identifiers, middle-class ambivalent, working class with qualification, working-class identifiers and interrogators), we have been concerned here with the particular reasons cited for affiliating with these five class groupings. Our data reveals considerable complexity in our respondents' class deliberations. They speak of indistinct positioning, of complicated patterns of identification and disidentification, and of inclusion but also liminality. For many there does not seem to be an easy, straightforward way in which to be Black and middle class: histories, cultural identity, the classed British context and racism all intervene to complicate, disrupt and render identities and allegiances uncertain. In an extension to Sayer (2002), we also identify what we term 'moral capital' to encapsulate values of selflessness and collectivity, which they associate with their working-class pasts and to which, despite their new class location, respondents in our study wish to hold on. This presents yet further discomfort since to be middle class is, they argue, to embody undesirable attributes of individualism and privilege, both of which are aligned to Whiteness.

Class, like race, also affects the nature of friendships, with our respondents exercising considerable care and thought over which Black friends might feel comfortable engaging in classed activities such as dinner parties, exhibitions and galleries. Having White friends or work associates increases the likelihood of experiencing racial stereotypes and insults. Whiteness and the actions of White middle-class gatekeepers, therefore, play an important role in our respondents' views and feelings about class position specifically and their sense of belonging and comfort in British society. Many spoke of their awareness that the pervasiveness of racism meant that mainstream White society would always place more significance on their race than their class.

With such factors in mind, the hesitation on the part of the majority of our respondents to self-define as 'middle class' should come as no surprise, and we suggest that Maylor and William's (2011) thesis that the label 'middle class' represents for the Black middle classes an 'irrelevant subject position' may underplay the relevance of the intersectional complexities that we have detailed here and the emotional struggles, challenges and reflections involved in occupying this transitional class state.

Even though our study comes over 20 years after Daye's (1994), we note many similarities in the experiences of the two groups of Black middle-class respondents. Today, there remains a newness to the Black middle classes. As then, they are still relatively small in number and widely dispersed residentially across the UK. Issues of exclusion and marginalisation remain. The Black British middle classes continue to seek a legitimate space with sufficient economic and financial leverage in which they can be 'Black' and 'middle class'. Effectively challenging White resistance to a Black middle-class presence plays an important role in advancing genuine social mobility and race equity. With such considerations in mind, we conclude that it is not yet possible to speak of distinct 'class fractions' within the group in the way that Moore (2008) does. However, within this increasingly post-racial British context it may be possible to think of distinct 'race fractions' (different formations of raced identity) among the Black middle classes, a subject area which Warmington (2014) has begun to examine.

We conclude with a quotation from Lorraine that we feel poignantly summarises the wide-ranging discussion set out in this chapter. Asked whether there was a space, a safe space, in which she might feel accepted and in which micro-management of race and class politics was unnecessary, she states:

> I think it really a very long time since I have felt at absolute peace and totally relaxed with someone else. I think it has to be on my own, in my own space, you know Virginia Woolf and a Room of Her Own, that's what I need, I need to get away into that room to feel relaxed and at peace.

Note

1 Being 'conscious' refers to acknowledging one's cultural heritage and being committed to the positive advancement of those of African/Caribbean heritage. Rollock (2013a: 495) describes this in terms of being 'politically Black'.

PART I
The Black middle classes and school

2

CHOOSING SCHOOLS

Searching for 'the right mix'

I wouldn't have sent her to a school that was all White.

Introduction

In this chapter, we explore the views and experiences of Black middle-class parents as they confront the uncertainties and risks involved in relation to choosing a suitable school for their children. This raises complex questions that go to the heart of parents' understandings and aspirations for their children, not only educationally, but also in terms of their identities as Black people living in a society which most (excluding two parents) understand as marked by inequalities of race.

The chapter begins with a note about the nature of 'mix' as a concept and then explores the general notions of 'good' and 'bad' mixes that emerge in our interviews. Broadly speaking Black middle-class parents seek a degree of *racial* diversity in their children's schools alongside relative exclusivity in *class* terms. Within this general landscape, however, there are competing tensions and contradictions. Although a few parents enjoy 'the right mix' in their children's schools, for most there is no 'perfect' solution. In exploring the parents' views and actions we identify two key approaches: the *academic choosers*, who prioritise educational achievement, and the *social choosers*, who emphasise an array of issues related to their children's social, emotional and even psychological development. Both positions are fraught with uncertainty and risk, especially as the parents weigh the likelihood of encountering White racism and teacher stereotyping.

Mixing and choosing: schools and peers, race and class

There is a large and growing literature on the significance of school choice as a mechanism by which the middle classes seek to secure and hand on their class advantage to their children. Often derided in the popular media as 'pushy parents' (e.g. Hobbs 2013; McDermott 2013; Moore 2011; O'Grady 2009), academic research has sought to explore the details of this situation for middle-class families as they wrestle with the anxiety, uncertainty and risk inherent in making school choices (Ball 2003a, 2003b; Vincent and Ball 2006). Like much previous work on the educational experiences and strategies of the middle classes, however, these studies focused largely on *White* middle-class parents and, by implication, the considerable advantages accrued by their Whiteness. In this chapter, we aim to add to this literature by making more complex the picture in relation to the experiences of the Black middle classes and examining how race and racism shape their decision around school choice.

Social mix (that is a combination of students in class, race and gender terms) emerges in our interviews as a significant concern for Black middle-class parents. It affects their thoughts about the 'right' school to attend, the kinds of peer that will make for 'good' friends and even where best to live. Concerns and preferences about social mix have also been found to be important in research on the school choices of White middle-class parents (e.g. Ball *et al.* 2004), although their concerns trade on the invisibility of their own racial identity.[1] In contrast the concerns of the parents in this study are complexly inflected, in most instances, by a clear recognition of issues of racism and racial identity.

Questions of 'mix' throw into relief the intersection of class, race and gender. As parents discuss their thoughts and fears about school choices, matters of social class, ethnic identity and readings of gendered threat come into focus. Mix involves both seeking others 'like us', in terms of race and class, and avoiding others 'not like us' in similar terms. Choices related to social mix produce a sense of being 'comfortable' for some and being 'outsiders within' for others. Within the processes of school choice the social mix of particular schools can serve, in parents' accounts, as a surrogate indicator for other things – White privilege or school policies that are sensitive to ethnic diversity, anti-racism or the possibility of racism – and perspectives and practices that are conducive or not to minority ethnic achievement.

'Good' and 'bad' mixes when choosing a school

> It's quite a good mixture, although not quite as good as I thought (…) when I went for the open days and stuff, I thought from what I saw it was quite a good mix.
>
> *(Amanda)*

Many parents seek what they call a 'good' social mix when choosing a school for their children. For the Black middle-class parents in this study, a 'good' mix generally has both a racial and a class dimension. In terms of ethnic diversity a 'good mix' means a clear Black presence in the school but with no single dominant ethnic group. Similarly, parents look for signs that the school attracts families who place a high value on education, which is usually related to perceptions of social class background. Respondents feel that the 'right' mix can play a vital role in numerous ways, including helping to minimise the likelihood of experiencing racism in school, creating learning environments that support high achievement among minoritised students, reinforcing a positive ethnic identity and encouraging the skills and dispositions necessary for coping with other ethnic groups. 'Good' mixes are, concomitantly, ways of avoiding or minimising 'bad influences' and negative expectations. However, none of these things are *guaranteed* by a particular mix. In addition, there are sometimes 'trade-offs' made against other factors that are also prized. A good mix, therefore, is one of a number of factors that feed into parents' thinking about key issues like school choice. Ruby, for example, keeps her daughter at a local comprehensive school despite her sense that the school has low expectations of its students; this is because the school's ethnic mix means that her daughter is not isolated as Ruby was in her own schooling:

> And we also thought with my daughter, because she's a bright girl who will do well in life – 'cause she's very much a maths/sciencey person as well, so she's not the most sociable person – we actually also wanted her to be somewhere where she was part of a majority, because it's the only time in her life that's she's going to have that. If she's successful (…) You know, she's gonna be a minority twice (…) she's strong in herself. She doesn't hate being Black, she doesn't hate herself, you know, 'cause that's what I started to feel like. You know, because when you're constantly not seeing yourself, no positive affirmation of yourself in school or within your surroundings …
>
> *(Ruby)*

Ruby, confident in her daughter's academic orientation, therefore puts other factors ahead of the school's academic profile not least its ability to offer 'positive affirmation' of Blackness in the context of a White-dominated society in which Black identity is routinely denied and denigrated (also Chapter 6) regarding the considerations in raising a Black child). Significantly, Ruby's daughter is herself determined to stay at the school and children's preferences, particularly those of older children, sometimes play a key role in school choice. As the following extracts illustrate, parents take a great many factors into account (location, safety, school performance) but the right mix in terms of ethnic diversity is a basic requirement for many of our interviewees:

> So, yeah we chose that school on the basis of the location. The kind of feel of the place as I say, you know, what the tutors were like, and what the other kids seemed like. They had kids guiding us around this school, the kind of look of the place, as in the space and layout, all of these things I took into consideration and yeah, very much a mix (…) some of the other schools were quite heavily Asian and I didn't, you know, I didn't want that but neither did I want it to be heavily White, I wanted it mixed. I wanted my dream [laughs]; a melting pot school.
>
> *(Amanda)*

Now we were both teachers so we understood the education system. We knew that we wanted to get our children into schools where they were going to be emotionally safe and secure, physically safe, and would have an education academic environment that was what we termed middling to higher. And what we were saying was that we felt that we could support our children in any school that provided those three aspects. And the other thing that we talked about was that it needed to be a mixed environment, mixed racially and ethnically. He's mixed as well, had a lot of racism from the kids but not from the staff. And we knew it was a good school academically, but it was mixed, we felt he would be safe in there …

(Gabriel)

It had to be a multicultural school … I wouldn't have sent her to a school that was all White, in an all White area (…) they are a good school: I'm not saying they are *perfect* and my daughters aren't perfect either. And both of them had issues with how those, that particular school dealt with Black students.

(Anthea)

There are compromises involved here, different issues and concerns to be balanced against one another. There is rarely a 'perfect' choice and often parents struggle to reconcile competing demands and concerns. These parents want a school that will offer their children the opportunity to be high achievers, but one in which they will feel 'comfortable', can 'be themselves' and will be safe and secure. They seek to avoid 'bad' mixes, that is schools in which one ethnicity predominates or in which there are too many social class 'others'. For almost all of our interviewees a diverse ethnic mix appears to be a positive social value at school and in social life generally. Many talk of a 'good mix' as a positive quality of schools and a positive learning experience *in its own right*.

With my parents, we had like a safe zone in terms of ethnicity, if you keep to your own group of people, i.e. Black Caribbean, you'll be alright. Now I know that was a mistake because if you cocoon your child with a certain group, there are other groups of individuals that can contribute to your learning … I'm looking for a school that's very mixed … it's a case of learning about every aspect of life.

(Candice)

Racism is an issue that features, to some extent, in every chapter of this book. In terms of choosing an appropriate school, the threat of racism presents difficult and unpredictable problems. As we have already noted, the general social context of racism is different for our interviewees' children in comparison with the parents' own experiences of schooling. Race equality legislation and changing social values have made overt racism less acceptable, although nuanced, subtle and institutional forms of racism continue. The demography of schooling, particularly in London, has also changed. Increasing social diversity, particularly in London, may be changing what it means to live in Whiteworld, but it does not eliminate either the privileges of Whiteness nor the immanence of racism. Nonetheless, this does create a different framework within which decisions about schooling are made:

> He's so lucky, I thought, because he's in a school where half of the children are non-White, which I think is quite good in an area where the ethnic mix is so low.
>
> *(Mary)*

> At his primary school it was very mixed, very diverse, I used to say it was the United Nations of schools. It was lovely.
>
> *(Felicia)*

> I didn't want her going to a predominantly White school because I wanted her to relate to Black people *and* White people (...) I didn't want her going to a predominantly Black school because I think sometimes not all parents are interested in their children's education (...) But it's got a nice mixture here.
>
> *(Sandrine)*

Sandrine's comment that 'not all parents are interested in their children's education' signals the second major – and interrelated – dimension of *mix*, i.e. social class. A small group of parents in the sample explicitly use generalised stereotypes of the Black working class that refer to social characteristics from which they want to distance themselves and their children. (Similar distinctions are also evident in Chapter 1 when parents discuss their feelings about their class location.) For these parents there can be 'too much' mix as regards social class: in the sense of the over-representation of certain class groups, the Black and White *working* class, who are best avoided. Indeed, most of the parents in the sample seek out schools that offer some degree of class exclusivity and ethnic diversity within which they and their children will feel 'comfortable' – a word used often in interviews.

The point we need to convey here is the unstable combination in parents' perspectives and strategies of certainty and ambivalence, as highlighted in Alice's verdict on her daughter's school: 'very good for ethnic mix, brilliant: social mix – all posh'. However, avoiding a 'bad' social mix (in terms of working/under-class peers) can also carry uncertainties and problems where school peers and other parents feel too 'posh':

> You cannot afford to send your child there unless you are middle class (...) it is incredibly middle class, upper class it is to a certain extent. There are very very wealthy children who are there and yes we did feel out of place to a certain extent. Umm, why we felt out of place is um, I don't know [laughs]. It is because we are not terribly wealthy, we are not terribly wealthy and so

we felt out of place for that particular reason, um, but *ethnically* she was fine there and I am glad that she went to a school like that.

(Alice)

Hence the 'poshness' of Alice's daughter's school is both a good thing and a bad thing. On the one hand, many parents want to avoid the risks of 'bad' social mixes, while retaining a sense of positive ethnic identity. These tensions and considerations also speak to the isolation of the Black middle classes as a group (see Chapter 1) – concerned about the possibilities of ethnic and class isolation among the White middle classes while questioning and expressing discomforts with the Black and White working class. We explore these tensions in greater detail below, as we identify three groupings that emerge when our parents talk about the risks and balances they try to manage in choosing the 'right' school for their children: those who find a school that 'ticks all the boxes', those that decide to prioritise academic concerns and those who stress the social mix.

Making mixes: strategy, identity and risk

I was really caught between academics and the social side of things.

(Linda)

Previous research on the White middle class has already documented a considerable amount of strategising and risk-taking (with attendant uncertainty and anxiety) around the issue of *social* mix (Reay *et al*. 2011). However, while some similarities are apparent, our data generated with Black middle-class parents reveals a somewhat more complex situation, as parents try to resolve the contradictions of competing demands within a racialised education system. As our parents share their thoughts about school choice it becomes clear that, for many, there is a fundamental tension between the demands of an academic trajectory and the social sensitivities around racial and social diversity. For a minority of our interviewees the tensions are resolved through the discovery of a school that 'ticks all the boxes':

They've got some really good state schools which have a mix – a wide range of children coming from every single background – but they manage to educate them so that they come out with good results.

(Brenda)

I'm quite lucky that the school he's got ticks all the boxes. I've got a school that's a good moral foundation, good academic achievement, and it's mixed. It's co-ed and it's racially mixed.

(Samantha)

I like the idea it's mixed. It's a true comprehensive ... because you get to engage with different people and that in itself is part of your education

… they do have a good mix of class … there's a large Chinese and African mix as well.

(*Lucy*)

By design, and sometimes by chance, a minority of parents in our sample are in the fortunate position of having local schools, accessible to them, that provide the right balance between social mix and academic performance. For most, however, there is a perceived tension: not all boxes can be ticked by the available schools and moving house is not always possible or desirable (especially in view of some parents' definition of seeking an appropriate racial mix). The majority of our interviewees, therefore, find themselves wrestling with these problems and resolving them in one of two ways. First, there are those who privilege what they view as the 'quality' of education over the possibilities of being subject to racism or being socially isolated – a position we refer to using the shorthand of *academic choosers*; often this leads to using private education. Second, there are *social choosers*, those parents who give a high value to social and ethnic mix as a form of social learning and nurturing.

Academic choosers

I knew before she started school that excellence was my criteria.

(*Isabelle*)

The first group of parents privilege what they see as high-quality education that will give their children future opportunities and advantages. They view this as a price worth paying (financially and in social terms), partly because they view high achievement as a means of avoiding or at least minimising racial disadvantages in the future. For just over 11 per cent of parents in this study, this decision involves using private schooling. Such a choice involves two sorts of risks, depending on location; one risk is sending a child to schools with a majority of White students and/or a majority of middle/upper-middle-class students; the other risk is sending a child to a White majority school with low levels of race-awareness or where they are confronted by forms of overt racism and/or class *and* race humiliations which must be tolerated or challenged. Parents who choose private schools are usually aware of the risks, often because they experienced similar issues during their own schooling. Nonetheless, they weigh up the pros and cons and are willing, at least at the outset, to 'accept' and cope with these risks and attempt to deal with the racisms that may ensue (see below).

The parents themselves are often made to feel out of place by White gatekeepers in these school settings and their attempts at intervention are often rebutted. However, at the forefront of parents' minds is the notion of education as an investment in the future, based on what these parents see as a lack of genuine choice in the state sector. Ideally, these parents want schools that provide high levels of academic achievement (which offers social advantages and kudos – capital – to their children) alongside race awareness and an ethnically mixed intake. For this group of parents the virtues of 'good' social mixes in terms of race and class are subordinated to other priorities, that is the possible *performance* advantages bestowed by private schooling. Race awareness and pride in their Black identity is something that these parents seek to offer their children at home, through their networks and friendship groups. Of course, some private schools may offer 'good' mixes alongside a promise of high academic credentials but many lack any meaningful engagement with race. Some respondents report painful, challenging incidences with their child's school, recalling situations that directly impinge, negatively, on the identity and well-being of the child. In some instances, project interviewees report that issues around race are compounded by being the wrong sort of middle class:

> The social mix of the school does worry me from time to time … it hurts you know when she comes home and says such and such: 'They've been laughing at my shoes'.
>
> *(Alice)*

> I was really caught between academics and the social side of things. Because my son had felt, and I think he still holds it against me, he felt socially very isolated in that school … In a more diverse school, with some Black boys, what might seem to him to be innocent mischief could lead to … I thought leave him where he is and at least I've got more control over what's happening there.
>
> *(Linda)*

> [My son] said, 'I'm the only one who would put my hand up and say I vote Labour.'
>
> *(Felicia)*

Felicia's example is one where some initial 'discomforts' about the ethnic and social mix of her son's private school, located in an overwhelmingly White rural commuter town, proved more than well-founded. Initially, for Felicia an ethnic mix was desirable but not crucial:

> I liked the environment when I had a look at the school. It troubled me that there weren't many Black faces around but that was my experience when I'd gone to school as well, so that didn't put me off. And it very much reminded me of my own school and that had quite a lot to do with it, the look of it, the feel, was like that grammar school thing.

Being in a Black minority at school certainly meant that Felicia's son was socially isolated and the school did little or nothing to engage with issues of racial justice or multiculturalism. As it turned out her son also confronted various forms of racism – overt, subtle, interpersonal and institutional – over a number of years. These had a wearing impact on him, on his commitment to school and on his school performance. When the racist bullying finally came to light Felicia asked her son, 'How did the other Black boys manage, and he said they just ignored it, just pretend you're White'. However, such a response did not sit easily with Felicia or her son: 'He'd always been brought up to be aware of who he is, no apologies.' In one of several exchanges Felicia had with the school about these issues, the head teacher, rather than taking the situation seriously and addressing the ongoing racist bullying, described her son as 'intimidating to his peers', ultimately indicating that he might require an assessment for learning difficulties. (For more detail on the case see Chapter 4.) Felicia's account is a powerful example of the traumatic, painful risks involved in choosing a school that is mainly White and/or has little explicit commitment to supporting race equality. Her son's well being, achievement and identity are all at stake here. On reflection, she says of her son:

> He bounced back from it well, because he did well in his exams and the college he wanted to go to, again this is a selective college, he still got in. But it's held him back, he's not done as well as he would have done if he'd gone to the local state school. I am sure of that …

Felicia's narrative offers a telling example of both the limitations of Black class capitals over and against racism, and the diverse modalities of racism itself. In this case her son's experience of racism is not just denied but also turned back upon him, blaming him as 'the problem'. Felicia's experiences also point to the central importance of resilience on the part of Black families if their children are to achieve in education, over and against the possible damage to their well-being and sense of self.

In contrast to Felicia's experience, however, the school Isabelle found has 'a mix and that's the beauty of the school'. In this case, the school's mixedness is defined in relation to social class and through a range of national identities:

> You have the top end if you like, the children of media people, journalists, well known journalists, people who work in the media, news reporters down to doctors, teachers, and then quite, I guess you know quite humble people – maybe not humble – but people who work in regular jobs. A cross section, it's not top heavy with the well off (…) Visible ethnic minorities are still the minority … there aren't many Caribbean girls in the senior school. There's my daughter and then there's another girl in her year. There's a girl whose parents are Nigerian, that's those three. Then you have a girl who's half Egyptian/half English (…) four or five girls, Indian girls, girls of Asian origin. But there are a lot of ethnic minorities who aren't visible because they are White. A lot of Polish for example, or Italian or Spanish, so the school when you look at their names, you can see by their names that a lot of parents who aren't of English or British descent, but the visible ones are a minority …

(Isabelle)

Despite the mix of nationalities, Isabelle is alert to the possible negative impact of a lack of visible minorities: 'I asked her recently how she felt in terms of her being the only Black girl, she said, "sometimes I think about it but, you know, the attention I get from teachers is because of me not because of me as a Black person". And the attention she gets from teachers is *positive*.'

In contrast, Claudette provides another example of where prioritising academic criteria went wrong. Claudette's daughter went to a 'really good school' but 'it had very few Black kids and the other Black kid was always in trouble, didn't do very well. So she always struggled with having her own identity (…) and the way the other kids treated her she didn't want to go to school.' Subsequently Claudette moved her daughter to a different school, one with a less impressive record of academic performance but a greater ethnic mix.

Mindful of such dangers Ruby, whom we quoted earlier, is critical of some of her Black friends who decided not to send their children to a local comprehensive in favour of private schools where they risk racial and social isolation. Nevertheless, she remains sympathetic to their dilemma:

> They just think, 'you know what, the expectations are always going to be low' [in a state school]. They would rather send their child to the school where they're the minority Black child, but where the school has high standards like a private school or grammar school. Where, OK, they're not gonna get involved in equal opportunities, they're gonna be called the N-word and nothing's gonna be done about it, they kind of accept that with some of the private schools, you know, they kind of accepted that those schools are not gonna be hot on kind of pastoral care and equal opps (…) but at least they'll get through, they'll get the expectations, that they will work hard and they will achieve.
>
> *(Ruby)*

Here the compromise between advantage and identity (a healthy Black identity in a world in which racism is normal, commonplace) is worked out differently. As noted already, Ruby chose to keep her daughter until age 16 in a school that she sees as having generally low expectations for all students because she does not want her to be 'a minority twice' – a Black, female scientist! However, she is mindful of her daughter's own wishes and the choice of sixth form education provider may be very different:

> She's been offered a scholarship [at a private school and] she decided she wanted to go to the private one. I said OK, gotta see what happens. I think she's up for it. I'm surprised; I didn't think she'd want to do it. 'Cause she said 'oh there's not gonna be many Black kids there, I'm gonna be the only one aren't I?' What did she say? 'I'm gonna be like the poor one aren't I?'
>
> *(Ruby)*

Here, race and class concerns intersect dramatically. Alongside being the 'wrong' race, the student may not be the right type of 'middle class', and as we noted above with Felicia, such thoughts about fitting in, about being accepted, are not entirely unwarranted.

Given the risks involved, the qualities and characteristics of the child often play a part in this kind of decision-making. Parents try to judge what they feel that their children can or cannot 'cope with' – as in the cases of Linda and Alice (below) – and this judgment can vary between different children within the *same* family:

> [Daughter 1] is the sort of child who will talk to anybody, so she mixes well. I had no qualms about sending her to a school that was middle class because she can look after herself (…) you have to have a certain strength of character about you.
>
> *(Alice)*

In contrast, at her sister's school (daughter 2) 'they're all from the same ethnic background and I think she might struggle in a school that's as mixed as [daughter 1]'. There can be a variety of social and personal costs involved in choosing for academic advantage, as Alice says, 'we did feel out of place to a certain extent' but 'ethnically she was fine there and I am glad she went to a school like that'. Conversely, Gloria says of her daughter: 'I thought she's clever enough to manage in a state school with my assistance.' There are few certainties.

Of course, we should not automatically expect Black middle-class parents to be any more consistent in their decision-making than their White counterparts. There is a 'mixture of rationalities' (Pahl and Wallace 1985) within school choice and the moral and familial dilemmas of the White middle class are well documented (Ball 2003a; Reay *et al.* 2011). We must be careful not to import an excess of rationality into all of this; utility, aspiration and values do not always fit together easily. Doing what is best for your child is not always obvious and clear-cut. Issues of race and racism heighten the already fraught emotions around choice, and emotions must be a part of our 'moral understanding of human agency' (Morgan 1989). As the data excerpts above demonstrate, these parents are rarely certain that they are doing the right thing and are acutely aware of the sorts of risks they might be exposing their children to if they make a bad choice of school. Linda and Femi represent the different outcomes when social mix (in terms of both race and class) and academic advantage are offset, for different children. Linda feels her daughter can succeed academically despite being in a racially diverse school; in contrast, Femi has decided to move her daughter to a higher-achieving school:

> Because she was very bright I thought she will survive in what you might call a 'bog standard comprehensive school' and she will do well if I push her and make sure she doesn't get into the wrong crowd socially. I want her to have the kind of experience of a wide network of diversity, and she'll manage academically, which I am not sure my son would.
>
> *(Linda)*

> There's [in the new school] many more middle- and upper-class parents, many more White children compared to her current school. It's still London so it still has a good mix but it's different and I am not altogether comfortable with that. But at the same time, her education is the most important thing I can give her and just keeping her where she was, oh well there's other kids like you there. Can I live with that in ten years' time, twenty years' time? I don't know.
>
> *(Femi)*

Femi has moved her daughter away from a school where she was with 'children who are like her' (i.e. Black), to one with a 'different' (greater number of White middle-class children) social mix. She explains: 'I've worked with too many, particularly Black young men who hated school and end up in really bad situations (…) I don't want that happening to her.' Here the wrong mix meant too many Black peers, such that Femi fears that her daughter would be labelled in terms of classist and racist stereotypes reflecting the Black majority intake. Hence she tries to position her daughter differently in the complex matrices of race, class and teacher expectations. Despite all their machinations, planning and deliberate weighing of alternatives, nothing is certain: 'Can I live with that in ten years' time, twenty years' time? I don't know.'

Social choosers

> I wanted him to go to a school that's much more mixed, because society's mixed; we don't work in little pockets you know.
>
> *(Samantha)*

A second group of parents prize 'social learning' in a mixed environment and the ability to function in a diverse social world as a key to their children's social and educational development. These parents judge that there are more important things than academic achievement alone, particularly where the negative impacts of White racism are an ever-present threat. For others, it is a matter of principle and they are willing to accept the risks of comprehensive schooling in order to ensure that their children experience, and draw benefit from, mix and mixing. These parents are willing to find ways of coping with both the possibility that their children will not achieve as highly as they might elsewhere and the temptations of the lifestyles of 'the street' which might be more evident in socially mixed schools. Again, both racial and social-class mixing are taken into account, although not always in equal measure. Indeed, the balance is sometimes judged differently for different siblings, as Gabriel notes at the end of the following quotation:

> Now I'm less concerned about race because I think the whole attitude, culture around racism, is different. Although I think we are moving into a different era now with various things happening on the political landscape, with

the extreme right groups, but I'm more concerned about my children being in a mixed environment with middle-class and working-class kids. I feel that the diversity of race, because we are in London, can be taken as an accepted one for the most part, although we are not talking about my youngest, this is an issue between me and my current wife about which school *she* goes to (…) but to find a school where she would not be the only child [with her particular mix of ethnicity and religion], because we have to throw that [religion] in as well, is a bit of a challenge.

(Gabriel)

Gabriel's primary concern with class mixing is not typical among our interviewees; in most cases it is the racial and ethnic mix that is valued most. Ethnic and 'social' mix are distinguished by many respondents. Indeed, the combined presence of racial and class others which might be perceived as a social benefit in some circumstances can be viewed very differently where the presence of working-class Black peers is seen, as we previously observed, as a possible 'bad influence', especially in relation to our interviewees with sons (see Chapter 6 for further discussion). As Moore (2008) points out: 'Racial and class categories are always understood relative to other groups within the system and are influenced by one's social location and identity.' It is here that contention over what is to count as a Black identity becomes most apparent. The majority of interviewees are very clear about what they see as a positive Black identity (see Chapter 1), which in some instances is inflected by class, although in some cases this is a matter of contention between the parents and their children. This is evident in relation to social mix in several ways and is particularly a concern in relation to boys.

Yes, he has a range, a mix of friends. He has what I can only call his *bad boy* friends, and I keep trying to say to him they are not really friends, they are just kind of fly-by-night people. Then he has his friends from when he was at primary school (…) Because the primary school [they] went to was a little Montessori independent school and that was really nice. But his main contacts are with some boys with all kinds of strange names. I don't even like to think about them really.

(Elsa)

I chose a school that was really a mixture, I don't like this all-Black thing … I'm a bit worried about sending her into the wild.

(Gloria)

I didn't want her going to a predominantly Black school because I think sometimes … well not all parents are interested in their children's education and their behaviour and discipline.

(Sandrine)

The references to 'bad boy friends' and 'the wild' allude to forms of working-class Black street culture with which the parents do not identify. As we noted in the previous chapter, when asked about their class identity a considerable number of the respondents express ambivalence about being middle-class; when viewed from the perspective of social mixing, however, the middle-class identities of the parents look a lot firmer. As we have seen (Chapter 1), the overwhelming majority of our interviewees fall into the category that Moore (2008) calls 'multi-class minded' as opposed to the category she calls 'middle-class'. These are what she refers to as 'two distinct versions of middle-class identity' (p. 502) – a distinction 'based on values and the degree of acceptance of White middle-class ideology' (p. 504). The 'middle class minded' are 'more aware of or accepting of the class differences between them and less privileged Blacks' (p. 505). On the other hand, the 'multi-class', 'intentionally work to maintain a symbolic and personal connection to low-income African Americans' (p. 506). These tensions play out slightly differently in relation to school choice (as indicated by the extracts above) and they also come into stark relief around the issues of where to live and children's friendships. Two examples highlight these tensions and how they are resolved differently. Elizabeth is divorced, has two sons and works as an Education Advisor. Her choice of where to live and where to send her sons to school is in part based on an avoidance of a nearby Black working-class area of the city and the untoward influences she believes might come to bear upon her sons if they went to school there. This is suggestive of a 'middle-class minded' approach. Nonetheless, she is uneasy about her decision and faces criticism from her friends because of it:

> I think probably [pause] my decisions would be more determined by class than race. Actually I have made conscious decisions, which probably sounds really odd, but I have made conscious decisions to like *not* living in Kirkland [Black neighbourhood] with the boys … now I've kind of thought, yeah there's really big houses there and they're really, really cheap, they're like a quarter of the price of this house, but I've been very conscious of I don't want to bring my two Black boys up on their own in Kirkland where there could be influences that I'm not in control of, they're not in control of, and you know, particularly the older one with low self-esteem.
>
> *(Elizabeth)*

She adds, 'I know that sounds awful', which seems to underline her uncertainty. Elizabeth seems to be torn between her *middle classness* on the one hand, and a commitment to her ethnicity, or one version of it, on the other. That is, she is torn between ethnic solidarity and class advantage.[2] She does not have the choice of an area in which to live, and thus choice of school which has, as she sees it, the *right* social mix, that is both Black and middle class. She is hesitant but also tries to be 'honest', and this is perhaps indicative of what Harris (1990) calls a 'multiplicitous self': there is a particular situated intersectionality here. In Harris' terms this is a 'metaphysical dilemma'. Here the intersections of race and class are difficult and painful. They produce social divisions and forms of avoidance and uncertainties about identity and community. These 'intersections of race and class are complicated and personal' (Soto 2008: 12) and again highlight the potent emotions evoked by choice-making:

> I've been accused by Black people of being [pause], you know I should be living here, I should be … I should have been living in Brixton [area of London known for its large Black population] when I lived in London. And I'd kind of thought at the time if I'd had two girls maybe I would have thought differently but I don't know, maybe that's a load of nonsense. (…) I don't know, I kind of told myself it's a race thing but maybe it's a bit of both. [Pause] I kind of like, I kind of like the idea of living with more Black people. [Pause] Maybe there was a class element to it, I don't know, I … But I [pause], I suppose if I'm being honest, because living there would not have been [pause] part of my experience growing up, part of me felt anxious about living somewhere like Kirkland because I suppose I bought into all the stereotypes around it, which, whether they were true or not, but it made me slightly fearful and it wasn't part of my experience and I thought … and then I kind of feared on behalf of the boys and … But you know, I've got friends that, a lot of friends that live in Kirkland and they're, they're fantastic people and I'm really good friends with them and I go there quite a lot …
>
> *(Elizabeth)*

Again we see here the ways that race and class also intersect in particular situations with *gender* (see Chapter 6 for detailed discussion of this issue). Elizabeth's concerns are heightened because she is worried about her sons, as was the case for other parents, and she thinks she may have made different choices if she had had daughters. Ngozi (a psychologist) expresses a similar sense of 'middle-class/multi-class' tensions:

> I want [a predominantly Black, working-class area in South-East London] but I want [that area] with Black people that have high aspirations for their children, for themselves, that are positive about themselves as Black people.

Ngozi speaks emphatically about her children being 'proud to be of African Caribbean descent' and explains that this is one of two things she wants for her children, academic success being the other. Unfortunately, 'in terms of academia, that has been a failure really so far'. These concerns have led Ngozi to consider moving 'outside of London'. She reports her husband as saying 'I actually think we should not have stayed in [area in South-East London] because the negative influences are too powerful.' She explains simply but poignantly: 'We wanted an environment that was Black *and* middle class.'

Ngozi has tried 'really hard to encourage relationships with young people whose families are similar to ours, so the same aspirations academically and socially and personally'. In contrast to Elizabeth, Ngozi sees herself and her family choosing to privilege a raced over a classed identity: 'It's the race that's more important than being middle or working class, but the two do interact.'

Maud has three children, is married and lives in a provincial town, where she works as a university administrator. Maud indicates that she was able to resolve the tensions of class and ethnicity with less difficulty but crucially *within a different geographic space* — she does not live in London. Maud considers her ethnic identity, as Black African, to be her most important consideration but she also wants a high-achieving school and is worried about the problems confronting Black boys, especially in London:

> I think that my decisions of today to even select St Winifred's [school] as an option was because of its population. I wanted my children to grow with people who looked like them. Because I didn't think that removing them from an environment where people who, and putting them in an environment where people who didn't look like them would have a better education. I didn't, I didn't support that. I know that there are some people who say 'oh no, I didn't want them to go to that school; there are too many Black people in that school'. I want my children to go to that school because it is actually high, excuse me, a high-achieving school and more so because it is a Black school (…) and I am letting my children experience that so they would never have this kind of stigma about being Black and being female and being in anyway uneducated. I wanted them to understand fully that they could be all of that and my daughters and, I think *all* of my children have endorsed it, particularly my son because I think for boys it has been difficult in the last decade or so to grow up in the UK — especially in London with the type of stuff that is going on around our Black children and he identified that very early on. Almost got sucked into that kind of negative spiral of violence and crime and, and got out of it just you know, in that, he still had this ambition to do so much more with his life and moved away so that he could concentrate on being who he was. And with the girls I love the way they don't separate themselves from being African as well (…) in every form that we filled in from birth they ask you ethnic origin and we tick African.
>
> *(Maud)*

Maud highlights the complex interplay of factors that Black middle-class parents weigh in making their decisions about school choice. Here social factors (around racial identity) are key but she has also been able to match this with an academic profile: 'I want my children to go to that school because it is (…) a high achieving school and more so because it is a Black school.' But its location outside London is also crucial, especially in view of the perceived threat of gang-related violence in the capital.

It is important to reiterate that although social mix is a significant factor in school choice for these families, it remains one factor among others, important but not necessarily always primary. Indeed, not all interviewees see race and racism as significant in their view of the world. A very small minority (two parents) say they have *no* personal experience of racism:

> ... the consideration was making sure that we lived in an area that was diverse and so therefore the school, *de facto*, would hopefully have been diverse, but that wouldn't have stopped us from sending our children to that school.
>
> *(Miles)*

Nonetheless, for many Black middle-class parents their children's school is chosen to reflect the social diversity of society – particularly those living in London. To reiterate, the diversity that is valued, in most cases, is that of race/ethnicity rather than class. There is an avoidance of schools that have a single predominant ethnic group, but also those that have large proportions of working-class students, Black or White. Those who might in Moore's terms be described as 'middle-class' are few and far between in our study. Nonetheless, there *is* a duality to all of this. For almost all parents the value of diversity is set in relation to a strong sense of identity, as Cynthia explains: 'I feel in order to survive in this society they have to be grounded [in their Black identity] so they can be comfortable in their skin.'

Conclusions

Social mix in school choices is a field of contestation over Black identity and community – what it means to be Black, to be middle class, to be Black *and* middle class. There is a mix of choice and necessity and obviousness and reflexivity evident here which gives rise to some distinct patterns of strategising in relation to school choice where a 'perfect' solution that 'ticks all the boxes' is simply not available to most. On the one hand, among *social choosers* there is the privileging of 'good' mixes and issues of principle, and on the other for *academic choosers* there is the acceptance of an absence of mix in favour of apparently elevated opportunities for achievement and advantage. There are trade-offs and risks on each side. In the former there is a risk of low expectations and low standards; in the latter there is a heightened risk of social isolation and institutional and interpersonal racisms. There are different versions of a 'good education' here, one defined in fairly narrow academic terms and one that involves a more extensive form of social learning, as a preparation for life, for society, for coping with the diversity of the modern social world.

For most of the Black middle-class parents in this study *good* mixes involve ethnic rather than social-class diversity, that is those of other ethnicities but the same social class. Because of demographics, such 'good' mixes are far easier to find in London than elsewhere. 'Good' social mixes at school can serve, as parents see it, to minimise the likelihood of the experience of racism, to create learning environments conducive to academic achievement and to reinforce a positive sense of ethnic identity. There is also the hope that such factors will provide a safeguard against 'bad influences' and the constant threat that children – particularly sons – will become sold on a negative, 'street' version of Blackness that reflects and reinforces White racist stereotypes of criminality and hypermasculinity. An awareness of mix is a means of seeking out 'others like us' and avoiding those 'not like us'. These are difficult questions for parents, especially where some and/or their peers view this seeking out and avoidance as giving up on the wider Black community.

The focus on social mix in this chapter underlines Leslie McCall's point that intersectionality is an effective methodology for 'studying the relationships among multiple dimensions and modalities of social relationships and subject formations' (2005: 1786). Intersections are situated and experienced differently, and race, class and gender come together differently within these families and articulate a variety of subject positions. The way that Black middle-class parents think and talk about social mix is perhaps more reflexive than is the case for White middle-class families. This is a reflexivity based on an alertness to the untoward, to the ever present possibility of racism; this is what Rollock (2012b, after Ladson-Billings and Donnor 2008) terms the 'panoramic dialectic' of racialised minorities who 'occupy a "liminal space of alterity", that is a position at the edges of society from which their identities and experiences are constructed' (pp. 65 and 66). These families are mobile, socially and racially, in the sense of putting distance – when it comes to school choice – between themselves and 'other' sorts of Blackness and between their present lives and their (mostly working-class) origins; they are agentic and resilient, but they are also aware of the many ways in which racism can disrupt their plans and aspirations for their children. We take up this theme in the following chapter, as we examine the barriers and challenges faced by Black middle-class parents in terms of teacher expectations.

Notes

1. Whiteness draws much of its power from 'Othering' the very idea of ethnicity. A central characteristic of Whiteness is a process of 'naturalisation' such that *White* becomes the norm from which other 'races' stand apart and in relation to which they are defined.
2. Moore (2008: 506) gives the example of Marlene who makes the opposite choice and in doing so 'shocks many of her friends and colleagues'.

3

PARENTS' ASPIRATIONS AND TEACHER EXPECTATIONS

My expectations are higher than her teachers.

Introduction

I came from a situation [in the West Indies] where there were no barriers. There were no ceilings placed on my ambition. The Prime Minister of Jamaica was Black. The Governor General of Jamaica was Black and as a child it never occurred to me that I couldn't become Governor General or Prime Minister. However, once I got here, I realised that were I to express similar ambition about the political systems and positions in the UK they would think I was a prime candidate for the loony bin.

(Ray)

… my expectations are higher than her teachers' and I've had many conversations with them about – I think she has difficulties with English, for instance. But they say 'Oh no, no she's fine, it's OK' and that's I think because they're comparing her with girls who don't have English as their first language!

(Lorraine)

In the previous chapter we saw that the greater economic, social and cultural capital at the disposal of Black middle-class parents does not provide a shield from the anxieties and dangers involved in seeking 'the right mix' in terms of school choice and supervising their children's friendship networks in a society where racism remains part of the fabric of day-to-day life. In addition, conscious of the heightened stereotyping of Black men in society, parents are especially worried about the dangers facing Black boys and young men. In this chapter, we turn our attention to parents' experiences of teachers' expectations in terms of academic potential and behaviour within schools. These are especially important issues because teachers act as key gatekeepers to educational opportunity; teachers not only *teach*, they also *assess*, *separate* and decide the academic fate of students who are selected to different teaching groups and forms of curricula from the moment they enter the school system (see Bradbury 2013).

We begin by exploring parents' memories of their own school experiences dating back to the 1960s, 1970s and 1980s. Our interviewees overwhelmingly report encountering teachers who viewed them as having less academic potential than their White peers. Although racist stereotypes play out in more subtle ways in the twenty-first century, most interviewees experience similar problems with their children's teachers. Once again, our interviewees' social-class status appears to offer little protection from White teachers' hyper-surveillance of Black children as potentially disruptive influences. Teachers' greater control and criticism of Black students crosses age and gender boundaries but is most acute in the case of boys and young men. We examine the devastating cumulative effect of these processes through the experiences of Jean and her son Kareem at primary school. The chapter ends with further thoughts on the particular risks facing Black boys and young men in the face of raced and gendered stereotypes that have a centuries old history but continue to influence contemporary education in profound ways.

Experiencing low teacher expectations as a child

> … I am just determined that they are not going to get what I got at school; which was not very much.
>
> *(Richard)*

The majority of our interviewees express a strong concern that teachers overwhelmingly view Black children with relatively low expectations so far as academic potential is concerned. In some cases the parents (mostly schooled in Britain between the 1960s and 1980s) have clear memories of their own experiences at the hands of teachers. For some the racism was crude and obvious: Gabriel, for example, recalls the overt racism he experienced as a child at the hands of White peers *and* teachers. He describes the 'big shock' he experienced when, as a 13-year-old, he moved to a selective (grammar)[1] school in the English Midlands:

> The racism was *ferocious* from the other students in the school and some of the teachers (…) things like calling me names, like 'golliwog' and 'jungle bunny'; putting the blackboard rubber across my brow, marking my face. All day, all day, comments from them. So it was a miserable place …
>
> *(Gabriel)*

Racism saturated Gabriel's experience of grammar school and some teachers made no attempt to hide their view of Black students as intellectually inferior. In one incident he recalls that, after initially being refused membership of the chess club, he went on to beat a rival school's top player only to be rewarded with his teacher's surprised exclamation: 'I didn't think *you people* played chess.'

Our sample is not large enough to draw any definitive conclusions about whether such overt incidents were more likely in academically selective contexts, but several of our interviewees reported especially blatant incidents in selective schools and/or in selective teaching groups within mixed (comprehensive) schools:

> You would get things like, 'Oh I didn't think we had any Black girls in the A set.' Because even though it was a girls' grammar school they had always been used to the Black girls not always being in the top sets and things like that.
>
> *(Brenda)*

> So I went to an all girls' school and I suppose my experience there was overtly racist basically, it was *overtly* racist (...) I was put in the Remedial [special education] Class at school initially and my mum had to fight to get me out into another stream. Because it was just the assumption that you're Black, that's where you belong. So school, I think my school years were a complete waste of time really (...) I wasn't even put in for exams or anything. It was just assumed that we wouldn't, you know, I wouldn't get the results.
>
> *(Barbara)*

Robert (who attended a grammar school in the 1960s) recalls growing conflict between himself and teachers against the backdrop of increasing Black consciousness movements in the wider society:

> ... there was a lot of undermining by people who I think were racist and who clearly had no respect for me as a person; who had no respect for the sort of things that I was positive about ... Black person, Black culture, who my heroes should be and so on. Maybe they couldn't help it because of *their* backgrounds. But I found myself in constant conflict with them. And don't forget that this was a time – 1964 onwards – when, if you like, there was an *awakening* of Black consciousness (...) I would call myself, to annoy them, Robert X, things like that. There was just a *clash* with authority. But obviously it wasn't one-way traffic because it wasn't just *me* railing against them; in a way I was railing against them because I felt that they were very denigrating towards things that I thought were important in asserting who I was ...
>
> *(Robert)*

Conflict with teachers and teachers' low expectations went hand in hand for many of our interviewees when they were school pupils. Indeed, Robert states clearly that anything other than low expectations would have been so out of the ordinary as to arouse his suspicion:

The teachers also obviously played a part in guiding certain people in the Oxbridge direction. So even though I was one of the brightest no one ever suggested that I aspire to that. But you know, towards the end of my time there, I was really so disenchanted that if they suggested something like that, coming from some of them, I would've thought that they were trying to harm me, you know, it was that bad.

(Robert)

Although most interviewees do not report *overt* acts of racism at the hands of their teachers, a clear majority remember feeling that, as children, they faced systematically lower teacher expectations:

For me secondary school was a positive experience socially, the problems came with the expectations of the teachers on me, they didn't expect much (…) school was more of a social place rather than an academic, there was no expectation of me as a child from the teachers, it was just, 'you're here, let's just take you through the system'.

(Cynthia)

Teachers' lower expectations were often difficult to pin down explicitly but became clearer at points of selection, when students were placed in hierarchical teaching groups (streams, bands and sets):[2] the subject options process was particularly memorable for several interviewees. Contemporary secondary schools retain a limited form of the options process at the end of Key Stage 3 when, aged 13/14, students are channelled towards somewhat different academic or vocational curricular routes. Our interviewees attended secondary school prior to the imposition of the National Curriculum and, consequently, the options process represented a major turning point: although presented to pupils and parents as an important chance to 'choose' between alternative subjects, the process has long operated as a form of academic selection that is dominated by the views of teachers (see Ball 1981; Gillborn 1990b; Gillborn and Youdell 2000; Hallam 2002; Measor 1983; Smith and Tomlinson 1989; Sukhnandan and Lee 1998; Tomlinson 1987; Woods 1979):

[One teacher] her expectation of us was nil. I think it was even said to my mum at parents' evening, something about 'don't bother', [she] used those sort of terms (…) we were banded. So certainly by the end of the third year [age 13/14], that's when you chose your options, you were allowed to drop stuff like Physics and Chemistry (…) the Physics teacher said to my mum 'Jean's hopeless at Physics she should drop that as soon as possible'. That's what sticks out. Memory goes 'Jean's hopeless at Physics'.

(Jean)

One of the abiding memories I have about school (…) being told, you know, basically, 'You have to make a choice; we can get you out of Maths and all the rest of it, if you still want to play on the football team and do athletics and the basketball team'. And I knew there was something wrong with that; so I chose not to, and I chose just to go to my lessons and to study.

(Michael)

As we will discuss further in the next chapter, some of our interviewees were barred from all external examinations by their schools. Even when they were allowed to enter examinations, this presented another point at which teachers' low academic expectations led to institutional barriers being placed in children's way, namely the tendency to be entered for the lower-status Certificate of Secondary Education (CSE) rather than the high-status General Certificate of Education (GCE), also known as 'O' levels:

I left school with six grade one CSEs because I wasn't allowed to do O levels. (…) because it was felt that O levels would have been too difficult for me. [laughs] (…) the way the streaming of the school went, there was one set of people who were destined for O Levels and another who – no matter what happened – would be doing CSEs. And I was put in a sort of B stream, so we knew I'd be doing CSEs. And despite the fact that I felt that when I came here I was so far ahead of the children in my set (…) I felt that it was a survival battle to actually get grade one just to prove that I was capable.

(Vanessa)

Several interviewees describe conflict in relation to CSE/GCE decisions but the consequences differed markedly: some (like Vanessa above) made the best of the situation (placated with the chance of gaining the top grade CSE which was officially equivalent to a pass in the GCE) while others managed to negotiate at least some GCE access. Regardless of the eventual outcome, our interviewees remember the process as highly discouraging:

I had to really fight with them to do O levels actually, they automatically wanted to streamline me into doing CSEs because at that time it was CSEs or O levels. I had to fight with them. My parents were really supportive of me and, you know, I can remember having a bit of a stand up with one of the teachers and saying, 'Look, I want to do O levels'. You know, (…) [subsequently took O levels] and I think I got some Bs and I got some As and things, so it was justified.

(Cassandra)

I left school with O levels in four of those subjects that I really enjoyed; English Lit, English, History, Religious Studies, umm but was only entered for CSEs for the remainder of my options – which I just thought was a complete waste of time [laughter] so, you know, even then I could see that I had been put into a certain, certain stream or whatever and I thought well there

> is actually no point to do anything in any of these subjects, so I didn't. Which
> was terribly, terribly counter-productive but that is what I did.
>
> *(Alice)*

Despite the pain and conflict that was often generated by schools' actions over options and 'O' level entry decisions, those flashpoints did at least offer respondents a glimpse of the lower expectations that might otherwise have operated beneath the surface and been less easy to see, let alone challenge. This is one of the key differences between the experiences of our interviewees as children and subsequently as parents, i.e. points of selection within school are much less explicit now than in previous decades. That is not to say that schools are any less selective and exclusionary – far from it. Rather, the points of selection are less visible. For example, the GCE/CSE distinction was apparently overcome when a single exam, the General Certificate of Secondary Education (GCSE), was introduced in 1988. In fact, a strong element of selection remains in most GCSE subjects through the operation of 'tiering', which restricts the grades available to children entered in the lower-tier examinations. There is considerable evidence that Black students are significantly less likely to access the highest tiers, the only exam papers where the top grades can be attained (Gillborn and Youdell 2000; Strand 2012; Tikly *et al.* 2006); however, the existence of tiers is not well known among parents and the decisions are made exclusively by teachers.[3] This makes it even more important that parents maintain a keen interest in the decisions made by, and for, Black students in school. Interviewees report that, although times have changed and racism is rarely as crude and obvious as in their childhood, low expectations among teachers remain a critical concern.

Parental experiences and the expectations of teachers

> You're not gonna walk into the school and someone's gonna call you
> 'nigger'. But the absence of that doesn't mean everything else is [fine]. It's the
> subtlety and I think it is more on an interpersonal level now rather than insti-
> tutional. But of course the people in the institution, so it can become insti-
> tutional because there's so many of them in the one place.
>
> *(Jean)*

British society has changed considerably since the postwar surge in immigration from the British Commonwealth but, as our interviewees point out, it would be a mistake to imagine that the relative absence of *overt* racism signals a sea change in deeper attitudes. Crude and obvious displays of race hatred are now rare; gone are 'the signs in windows: "No Dogs, No Coloureds, No Irish" that were almost iconic in their depiction of London in the 1950s and 1960s' (McKenley 2005: 16). And yet anti-immigrant policy was a central theme in the 2010 General Election and one of the new government's first acts was to announce stricter English language tests for new migrants (BBC News 2010). Notwithstanding a momentary public celebration of ethnic diversity when Black, Asian and Mixed Race Britons secured

Olympic gold medals in 2012, government policy has been robustly, and increasingly, anti-immigrant and anti-multiculturalism (Harris 2013). When it comes to monitoring their children's experiences in school, interviewees are alert for indications of more subtle racism:

> I think the same emotions that drive the racism and the way it manifests itself, the emotions are there, they are the same. The way it manifests itself is possibly more covert now because increased awareness has led to some people wanting to examine what they do and change; and other people wanting to *hide* what they do.
>
> So I think it is more covert, it is more subtle in some ways.
>
> *(Ella)*

Academic selection occurs throughout children's school lives in England and can have a huge impact on their educational opportunities. As we have already noted above, however, the key points of selection, and the processes that lie behind them, are increasingly hidden. For example, students in primary school are assessed and ranked by teachers who then place them in different 'interventions' that can lead to academic routes or more 'remedial' action (Bradbury 2013; Rausch 2012). Later, students are assessed (sometimes using IQ tests) on entry to secondary school and may be placed in hierarchical groups that restrict their curriculum and determine entry to low-status examinations when they are 16 (Gillborn and Youdell 2000). All of these processes have been shown to disadvantage Black students but none of them are open to parental scrutiny (Gillborn 2008, 2010; Tikly *et al.* 2006). As a result, Black middle-class parents have to circumnavigate the veneer of pleasantries that often greet them at parents' evenings (where teachers are keen to run through a brief meeting without detailed feedback on their child's academic performance). Cynthia, who works as a teacher herself, became concerned when she read through her child's work: 'Low expectations; work not being marked; *wrong* being marked *right*; no direction.' She continues:

> we go to parents' evening and they would say to every parent, 'Oh your children are wonderful, well behaved, they're so polite'. Yeah, I got that, that's my job, I don't need to hear that from you. It was nice to hear but I want you to tell me *academically* what's going on, where they're at (...) And I just wasn't getting that, as long as they were nice and polite, it was okay.
>
> *(Cynthia)*

Cynthia's concerns are echoed by many project interviewees, who suspect that White teachers are content with Black students so long as they do not cause trouble and look likely to achieve a basic passing grade (which will add to the school's profile in published performance tables); they see little or no evidence of teachers pushing students to attain the highest possible grades. Vanessa speaks for many when she summarises her son's experiences and the minimal expectations that his teachers had for him:

We had in the final year [aged 16] the expectations from some of his teachers, you picked up that they said 'Well you got a pass, so what more do you want? Where we weren't expecting you to get a pass.' (...) [Eventually] he got a mixture of A stars [the highest possible grade], As, I think his lowest grade was a B for sociology – which upset him because they lost his course-work, his coursework got *mislaid*.

(Vanessa)

When prizes are awarded and extra resources are allocated, Black students are typi-cally notable by their absence. This trend is visible to our interviewees, several of whom detail occasions when their children's achievements were overlooked in one way or another. Robert (below) was angered when his daughter's achievements were absent from the celebrations bestowed on her White peers: 'clearly she wasn't their blue-eyed person'. Similarly, Malorie points to the racially exclusive composi-tion of a newly established programme for 'gifted' children:

... the school was running a gifted and talented programme (...) they selected the young people who they saw as gifted and talented to be a part of this programme and started to do things with them, extended their experiences and opportunities and as I say, found out about it by default. (...) So they chose these young people and do you know what? All of them were White.

(Malorie)

You look at objective things and you make your objective judgments and you see how prizes are being distributed and so on. (...) I remember in one case I actually wrote to the school to point out that [my daughter] wasn't listed in the school magazine as having got a certain award in music, a certain grade in music exams, and they actually wrote to say that it would be cor-rected and they would put something in the magazine next year. So that was something that I did in one case, but the fact is I couldn't quite understand how it was that *her* achievements were omitted; clearly she wasn't their blue-eyed person. Whereas someone else's comparable achievement hadn't been omitted.

(Robert)

Interviews suggest, therefore, that middle-class status is no protection from the low expectations that research has highlighted as an almost constant threat to the school experiences and achievements of Black Caribbean students (Crozier 2005; Gillborn 1990a, 2008; Gillborn and Youdell 2000; Rhamie 2007; Rollock 2007a, 2007b, 2007c). In addition, our data reveal the importance of *cumulative* processes of heightened control and disciplinary punishment alongside the lower academic expectations. This issue is explored in the following section via detailed consideration of the experiences of one interviewee and her eight-year-old-son.

'It's like you're trying to break his spirit': cumulative processes of criticism and control

Drawing on her research with 22 Black British families,[4] Gill Crozier reached the following conclusion:

> According to the parents' accounts the young black people in this study have had a pattern of cumulative negative experiences that have often contributed to their demotivation; in a number of cases their permanent exclusion from school, and in most cases leaving school at 16 with fewer qualifications than their parents had expected.
>
> *(Crozier 2005: 595)*

Similar patterns of heightened teacher surveillance emerge in our data, suggesting that middle-class status, enhanced cultural and social capital and even a high-profile role as a parent representative in school are no protection from these processes, which appear to run deep in English schools. Rather than present a succession of brief quotations on this matter, a more detailed description of a single case will more accurately convey the sense of frustration and despair generated by the *cumulative* damage suffered at the hands of repeated unfairness. The case concerns Jean (a lecturer in a further education college) and her nine-year-old-son Kareem.

Jean reports that her son's personality has drawn attention throughout his schooling. Teachers have commented on his 'charisma and charm' but these have been viewed as a problem and Kareem has been portrayed as a bad influence on his peers:

> ... he's been labelled as being charismatic but in a *negative* way. Yeah, so from reception [the very start of formal schooling aged four], 'Oh he's got this charisma and charm that he manages to lead the other children astray'.
>
> So what is it? This is the sort of label that he's been getting. I mean I would have thought that charisma and charm was something quite *positive*.

Jean feels that over time a pattern of almost continual criticism developed as an over-reaction to the minor nature of the problems and cast her son as a repeat offender:

> ... this has been going on for a while. Little silly things. I'd come in to school [to collect] him and now [the teacher is telling me] 'He's done this today' and 'He's done that'. And hand on heart, he's never physically hurt someone. He's never been aggressively rude and abusive or offensive to adult or child. It's maybe attention-seeking, silly boyish eight-year-old behaviour that I think you should be able to manage if you're a professional.

A notable flashpoint occurred when Kareem was selected to attend a class especially designed for Black children seen as at risk of failing. Although this intervention might sound positive and well-intentioned, Jean feels that a lack of proper planning and resources resulted from the simple – and erroneous – assumption that a course for Black boys would not require the same level of skill and professional preparation taken for granted in other parts of the curriculum. She explains:

> The danger is sometimes, with some of these initiatives for young Black boys, is the only qualification for [leading] an intervention is that you're a Black male. Erm, [pauses]. *It's not enough.* You know, I've met many a Black male who actually [she addresses an imaginary 'mentor'] *keep away from kids at all costs.* Yeah, so this guy (…) You recognise your target group is maybe children who are having some problems focusing, concentration, so actually you [should] come equipped with some strategies to get them on board. And in this one-hour session, apparently Kareem disrupted it so bad that [the adult] couldn't continue.
>
> What's Kareem doing?
>
> He's rocking on his chair, and he might be going [drums fingers on the desk] and making the other boys laugh.
>
> Now I wouldn't mind if he got up and kicked you and punched you … well I *would*, but [I could understand the reaction] if it was something *extreme*, but it was *low level*.

In addition to her frustration at what appeared to be an overreaction from the staff member concerned, Jean also detected that a no-win situation was developing where her son was *always* deemed to be at fault. On this occasion Kareem was disciplined for distracting his peers, but in previous meetings to discuss his behaviour the issue had been reversed, with the accusation being that Kareem was too easily distracted by others:

> I've had this conversation with this man where, you know, one of Kareem's things [targets] is to not be distracted by others.
>
> Oh. *So* when *he's* doing the distracting and others are being distracted, surely *they* should be spoken to, not to be distracted by him?
>
> Now it sounds like I'm being really picky here but – so he gets in trouble if he's a *distractor* and also if he's *distracted*.

The situation came to a head over an apparently tiny matter which highlights the devastating cumulative nature of the problems that can face Black children and their parents, regardless of social class. Once again, the context might appear superficially to be a positive multicultural situation (a project concerning the election of the USA's first-ever Black president). As Jean explains, her son was highly motivated and engaged by the topic; he produced exceptional work and, cooperating with peers, he won an exciting reward which was summarily taken from him as an additional punishment for a completely unrelated and minor infraction of playground rules.

> … the icing on the cake was when he did this activity in a class, in his class, and erm, it was all around the Barack Obama stuff, which I thought was really

positive. They did their own election campaign in groups and his leadership skills came to the fore, [he] came out with some stuff for his campaign and his group *won*. So their reward was to run the class for the afternoon the following week. And he was so inspired by this Barack Obama. He'd done some writing on him, cut some pictures out, and made a scrapbook thing at home. He'd done this in class as well and was really really looking forward to it and had ideas of what he was gonna do, and then he was excluded from that.

Yeah he was excluded from that.

His teacher wouldn't allow him to do it because at lunch time when the bell rang, he wasn't lining up. He was put in the office. He was put in the office and then his teacher saw him in there and decided not only was he gonna miss his – he missed his play time [recess]. I would have thought that was the sanction for not lining up. Missed his play time but also he wasn't going to take part in the after lunch campaign. (...)

It's like you're trying to break his spirit to a certain extent. Erm, and he's not a crier, my boy's not a crier, but he was crying now that he didn't want to go to school and this had been going on for weeks now.

Jean is a professional educator and was active in her son's school as chair of the governing body (officially the most high-profile role available to a parent). These roles might be expected to generate a certain amount of respect from fellow educators in her son's school but this was not the case:

I'm chair of governors and they've just no respect. If there's no respect for me, it translates into this for your kids. And I'm not missing out – I mean obviously I've really *summarised* it – I'm not, he's not done anything that I've missed out. Like he's kicked someone or sworn, he's not done *anything* like that. And I agree some of the behaviour was really *irritating* at worst, but actually I don't think it warranted that repeated kind of ... [her voice trails off]

Jean moved Kareem to a new school where his relationship with teachers has been much improved. Her case captures, in painful detail, the cumulative damage wrought by a process that showed her son no understanding and her no respect. At no time was Kareem accused of any major rule-breaking but the sense of continual – often unfair – criticism drove mother and son to a point where neither could continue with the school. Fortunately, Jean's personal networks and understanding of the system (her middle-class cultural capital) helped her to secure an alternative school for her son, but the damage was done and continues to be done to other Black children in the same situation.

It's different for boys?

I think as a Black *guy* and not a *small* Black guy, you know, the instant perception is of, in the street, is of someone who might be dangerous, might be a little bit violent, might be a little bit angry. I am not the first person people come up to and ask the time.

(Richard)

There are very few African American men who haven't had the experience of walking across the street and hearing the locks click on the doors of cars. That happens to me – at least before I was a senator. There are very few African Americans who haven't had the experience of getting on an elevator and a woman clutching her purse nervously and holding her breath until she had a chance to get off. That happens often.

(President Barack Obama)[5]

The intersection between racialised and gendered inequalities is complex and prone to oversimplification. In terms of academic achievement, Black Caribbean students of *both* sexes are less likely to succeed in school than their White counterparts. However, the average achievements of Black boys are lower than those of their female peers and the gap between Black and White boys is bigger than the gap for Black and White girls.[6] Clearly, both gender and race are significant factors. This complexity tends to be overlooked in much popular discussion about race and achievement. As we noted earlier (see Introduction) the educational landscape in contemporary England is dominated by the erroneous assumptions that White 'working-class' children are the lowest attaining group and that race inequality is no longer an important issue. When race inequality *is* mentioned in the media, it is frequently assumed that the 'problem' relates only to Black *boys* and the blame is laid at the door of the children, their families and communities:

> African-Caribbean boys are still at the bottom of the league table (…) They have failed their GCSEs because they did not do the homework, did not pay attention and were disrespectful to their teachers.
>
> *(Sewell 2010: 33)*

> Black boys aren't being failed; many are failing themselves. Those who went to school in London have their stories about the unteachable black boys who viewed the whole idea of education as effeminate.
>
> *(West 2010)*

These kinds of perspective trade on the stereotypical view of the Black male as hyper-masculine, prone to acts of aggression and unsuited to academic study (stereotypes that have a long history in education in the US and UK: see Brown and Donnor 2011; Gillborn 2008; Ladson-Billings 2011). Black female sexuality has also been fetishised (Gilman 1992; Pajaczkowska and Young 1992) and Black young women and their mothers face a range of negative stereotypes inside schools (Mirza and Joseph 2010; Youdell 2006: 119–24). This complex interplay between race and gender is present in the experiences and concerns of the Black middle-class parents in our study (for further discussion see Chapter 6). In particular, a strong theme throughout the interviews is the greater threat of stereotyping and exclusion perceived to operate against Black boys and young men – a gendered stereotype documented in numerous school ethnographies (Connolly 1998; Gillborn 2008; Rollock 2007c; Wright 1986). As Kareem's case above highlights, even very young Black boys can find themselves singled out for unwanted negative teacher attention. Similarly, Paulette identifies a clear pattern to teacher/student interactions in her son's primary school where Black boys appear to be cast in an especially negative role:

> There were all these issues about him at primary school, 'yes his work is excellent but he can't sit still, he is out of the room, he is out of his seat' all that nonsense – 'he is answering back' (…) so I felt given the way that the school was responding to him, the primary school, erm given the way that the primary school responded to Black boys: Black boys were always in trouble, Black boys were always outside the head teacher's office, there was that kind of … Black boys had a particular *part* at that school. I just felt that he was going to hit secondary and I can see it going pear shaped.
>
> *(Paulette)*

Paulette's words are particularly significant because, despite his teachers' judging his work to be 'excellent', her son was increasingly experiencing a pattern of cumulative criticism (similar to Kareem's case discussed above) in line with the role into which the school cast Black boys as a group. Several of our parents discuss the difficulties they face in balancing a desire to support their sons against such labelling while also being conscious of the danger of dispiriting them by seeming to suggest that the odds are entirely stacked against them. No matter how carefully they try to strike this balance, however, their sons' perceptions are often painfully clear:

> My son said to me this morning … (…) 'if you are a White kid, you can just be a kid, you can just be a child. But if you're Black, you're a *Black* child.' You know, you can just *be*, it's much easier if you're White but if … Black comes first. And he's 14 and he was saying that, as an example, that his friends, his White friends just have a different experience, a completely different experience, a freedom that [my son and his Black friends] don't have, that he feels he doesn't have as a Black child.
>
> *(Barbara)*

Barbara's teenage son poignantly captures the ever-present threat of racialised labelling and racism in a world where his White peers 'can just be a child. But if you're Black, you're a *Black* child.'

Interviewees, therefore, are especially concerned that Black boys and young men face a persistent and significant threat of racist stereotyping. It would be a mistake, however, to fall into the trap of forgetting that stereotyping (although most pronounced for boys) is by no means absent from the lives of Black students of all ages and both genders. As Femi's six-year-old daughter discovered, stereotypes of Black threat and physicality appear to know almost no limits:

> My six-year-old daughter who is yay high [indicates height of a small child] had 'threatened and intimidated' the teaching assistant. Now, first of all, my daughter doesn't do that at home, so I'm wary; and second, I'm thinking you're a teaching assistant, how can you be intimidated by a six-year-old-girl who hasn't spat on you, hasn't kicked you, hasn't thumped you – what exactly did she do that is so threatening because I struggle to understand a situation where you would be threatened?
>
> *(Femi)*

Conclusions

Almost all interviewees complain that their children's teachers expect too little of them academically. The significance of these findings is powerfully conveyed by the fact that individual parents involved in our study (with children of different ages) consistently report similar challenges when faced by teachers and by the sobering realisation that previous generations of Black families have had similar experiences.

The Black middle-class parents in this study often draw upon their personal experiences when describing how racism in education has changed over the decades. Some (like Gabriel, Barbara and Robert) vividly remember the actions of racist White teachers and peers; others remember the racism as being less overt but standing out at points of selection, such as the subject options process or decisions that blocked their entry to high-status 'O' level examinations. A common thread in the interviews is the parents' belief that racism in schools is now less overt and much more subtle than before. Nevertheless, they remain vigilant for signs of racism, particularly in the low expectations of teachers who seem content to accept mediocrity from Black children so long as they achieve a basic passing grade (good for league table performance) and do not 'cause trouble'. Unfortunately, low academic expectations appear to go hand in hand with heightened sensitivity to any possible sign of disorder or indiscipline, even when dealing with very young children.

White teachers' heightened sense of danger from Black children, especially boys, is a common theme in previous research on both sides of the Atlantic. Of special significance in our interviewees' accounts is the way that a series of relatively minor issues and distractions can quickly build into a cumulative process that can destroy children's confidence. We described in this chapter the case of Jean and her son Kareem; theirs is by no means the only example, but by examining the case in detail it is possible to gauge the enormous hurt and frustration caused by an incremental process of repeated unfairness and exclusion at the hands of White teachers. Jean is at pains to emphasise that she is not presenting a sanitised account of her son's behaviour and her despair and anger at the school's treatment of her son is tangible.

In this and the previous chapter we have seen that factors concerning race, class and gender are all in play as Black middle-class parents try to guide their children through the education system. We noted in the previous chapter that for many middle-class Black parents their greater social and economic capital does not present any easy answers to the problems of finding a satisfactory balance, 'the right mix', when faced with the pressures of racism in the education system and the dangers of the street and a racist society more generally. Similarly, we see here that middle-class status also does not guarantee protection from low teacher expectations and hyper-surveillance in disciplinary terms. These are issues facing the parents regardless of their children's age and gender but are, in the parents' eyes, especially pronounced for Black boys and young men. A similar pattern emerges in the next chapter as we add a further dimension to our analysis of parents' experiences of the education system, by examining how race, class and gender intersect with notions of disability.

Notes

1 Grammar schools restrict entry to students who have passed some form of academic selection.

2 Streams, bands and sets are forms of academically selected and ordered teaching groups: *streaming* usually refers to a system where children are taught in the same selective grouping for all subjects; *bands* are considered to be broader than streams, sometimes comprised of several groups thought to be relatively equal in 'ability'; and *sets* are selective groupings designed specifically for one or more subject areas. See Hallam (2002).

3 The introduction of the 'English Baccalaureate' (EBacc) as a new measure of overall achievement makes teachers' decisions about access to high-status courses even more important (Gillborn and Demack 2012).

4 Crozier's interviewees covered a wide range of social class backgrounds 'from professional to unskilled and unemployed' (2005: 587).

5 Transcript from President Obama's press conference reflecting on the 'not guilty' verdict in the case of the fatal shooting of Trayvon Martin, an African American youth killed by a neighbourhood watch member. Video available on the White House YouTube channel at: http://www.youtube.com/watch?v=MHBdZWbncXI (last accessed 22 July 2013).

6 In 2012, 63.7 per cent of White British girls achieved five higher-grade passes, including English and Maths, compared with 56.3 per cent of Black Caribbean girls (a gap of 7.4 percentage points); 54.2 per cent of White British boys achieved this level, compared with 43 per cent of Black Caribbean boys (a gap of 11.2 percentage points) (DfE 2013: table 2a).

4

RACE, CLASS, DISABILITY AND 'SPECIAL EDUCATIONAL NEEDS'

You're Black, that's where you belong ...

Introduction

> I took [my son] to get him educationally assessed and they said that he had
> dyslexia (...) I took him up to Great Ormond Street [Hospital] to get his
> hearing tested and they said he can't hear half of what's going on. So when
> the teachers are always saying 'he's distracted and not paying attention', he
> can't hear. (...) they were just very happily saying [he] doesn't pay attention,
> [he] doesn't do this, [he] doesn't do that, but, you know, *he can't hear ...*'
>
> *(Rachel)*

'Educational subnormality' is no longer a part of the contemporary educational
lexicon. But the phrase has important connotations for the Black British community, many of whom remember how the term was applied with disproportionate
frequency in relation to Black children whose subsequent removal from mainstream
schools had a damaging effect on their educational prospects (Coard 1971;
Richardson 2007). Terminology has changed but Black children continue to have a
particularly difficult relationship with 'special education' and understandings of disability in society (MIND 2009). In this chapter, we look at how disability and 'special educational needs' (SEN) feature in the experiences of our interviewees and
their children. Fifteen of our interviewees (around a quarter) mentioned disability
or related issues during their interviews and some important patterns became clear.
In the sections that follow, we consider the problems that interviewees experienced
in getting schools to take their concerns seriously and examine the continuing battles they face despite being armed with formal assessments and despite the

considerable social, cultural and economic capitals at their disposal. We begin by detailing the key terms and debates in this field, including an outline of race inequities highlighted by previous research. By applying a race/class intersectional perspective, we offer a new and sometimes disturbing account of how racism continues to work through the constitution of 'disability' and 'special needs' in education.

Race, class and disability: theory and practice

Before we consider interviewees' experiences in detail, it is necessary to set the scene by outlining some of the key issues that have been examined in previous work in this area. First, we clarify key points in relation to terminology and debates about issues such as ability, disability and 'special educational need'. We then outline the broad patterns of inequality that have been mapped by previous research.

A word about words

'Race' and 'disability' are ideas that share several important characteristics. Both are commonly assumed to be relatively obvious and fixed but in fact they are socially constructed categories that are constantly contested and redefined. As with 'racial' categories, so too the definition of disability varies between different societies and over time within the same society. Received wisdom tends to view both race and disability as individual matters of identity and selfhood but a critical perspective views both as categories that actively re/make social oppression and inequality: as Roger Slee (2011: 36) points out, this relates to C. Wright Mills' famous entreaty to understand issues in their social, historical and structural context, that is as *public issues* not mere *personal troubles* (Mills 1959: 14–15). The struggle to challenge 'common-sense' assumptions necessarily extends to the words that are used to frame debate and construct critiques:

> Although readers new to this literature may be bewildered by these exchanges [about which terms to use or avoid], what is at issue is far more than a choice of words; the debate is about the best way to understand and contest disability and the multiple oppressions that are associated with it.
>
> *(Barnes et al. 1999: 7)*

Colin Barnes and his colleagues choose to adopt 'the terminology of the British disabled people's movement' by using the term *impairment* to refer to 'a medically classified condition' whereas *disability* denotes 'the social disadvantage experienced by people with an accredited impairment' (Barnes *et al.* 1999: 6–7). Hence impairment only becomes disabling when confronted by socially constructed problems and assumptions, e.g. 'not being able to walk or hear being made problematic by socially created factors such as the built environment ... and the use of spoken language rather than sign language' (Beratan 2012: 45; see also Oliver 1996). However, the term impairment has itself been criticised as inherently derogatory and, for example, in the field of developmental issues (such as dyslexia and autism) the term 'neuro-diversity' is sometimes preferred (see Developmental Adult Neuro-Diversity Association n.d.).

The overall picture: racism and ableism

In the UK the majority of contemporary research on social justice and SEN focuses on the difficulties encountered by parents as they try to negotiate the system and secure equitable treatment for their children (e.g. Nind 2008; Riddell 2009; Todd 2003). This work takes social class as its main preoccupation and has, almost by default, been concerned with the position of White working-class parents. Relatively little research has focused on the intersection of oppressions based simultaneously on the explicit analysis of race, class and disability; there is, however, a track record of work on racism and ableism. In the UK, for example, two of the most important works in the then fledgling field of multicultural education examined the over-representation of Black children among those designated as 'educationally subnormal'. These children usually found themselves facing chronically low teacher expectations and were often taught in segregated facilities (Coard 1971; Tomlinson 1981). As the field of multicultural and antiracist education developed, however, research concerned with race inequality rarely included an explicit concern with disability and vice versa (Barnes *et al.* 1999: 89–91). Nevertheless some writers (especially in the US) have continued to focus on how race and disability combine in complex, sometimes contradictory ways.

> An interesting paradox in the racialization of disabilities is that civil rights responses for one group of individuals (i.e., learners with disabilities) has become a potential source of inequities for another group (i.e., racial minority students) despite their shared histories of struggle for equity.
>
> *(Artiles 2011: 431)*

Alfredo Artiles has been one of the most prominent academics to pursue research in this field and his work points to the fact that African American students are typically over-represented in certain types of SEN provision. The history of antiracist struggle in the US and UK has documented very clearly, and over many years, that *certain* disability labels are disproportionately mobilised in relation to Black students (Artiles and Trent 1994; Artiles *et al.* 2004; Oliver 1996; Tomlinson 1981). As Beth Harry and Janette Klingner note, in relation to the US, Black (African American) students face much higher 'risk rates' in categories 'that depend on clinical judgment rather than on verifiable biological data' (2006: 2). These patterns have a long history and they continue today: the most recent comprehensive study of SEN demographics in the UK (Lindsay *et al.* 2006) revealed that rates of Black overrepresentation are especially pronounced in the category defined as 'Behavioural, Emotional and Social Difficulties', where Black students are more than twice as likely to be labelled as their White peers.[1]

Theorising the intersections of race, class and disability

Work in the US has gone beyond focusing on the general over-representation of Black students in SEN and has begun to raise fundamental questions about the nature of the categorisations that are deployed in relation to certain groups of students and the quality of education they receive as a result. In a landmark paper entitled 'Why is there Learning Disabilities?' Christine Sleeter argued that the notion of Learning Disabilities (LD) emerged specifically to protect the privileged position of children from White *elite* backgrounds:

> Rather than being a product of progress, the category [Learning Disabilities] was essentially conservative in that it helped schools continue to serve best those whom schools have always served best: the white middle and upper-middle class. This political purpose, however, has been cloaked in the ideology of individual differences and biological determinism, thus making it appear scientifically sound.
>
> *(Sleeter 1987: 212)*

More than 20 years after Sleeter's original article, Wanda Blanchett revisited the issues and, drawing on a range of recent US research, concluded that there are important race inequalities in the quality and nature of provision that students experience despite having the same official designation of 'learning disabilities':

> Middle- and upper-class white students with LD receive accommodations and modifications within the general education classroom setting while students of color with the same labels are educated in self-contained [i.e. segregated] settings.
>
> *(Blanchett 2010: 4)*

For Black students the correlations between race and SEN placement appear to be relatively stable on both sides of the Atlantic, with minoritised students being over-represented in particular categories that often lead to segregated provision and lower attainment. Research is less useful, however, when the issue of social class is added to the mix. Although Sleeter's original argument addressed race, disability and class simultaneously, later work has tended to deal with disability and *either* race *or* class. Blanchett, for example, describes work that looks at socio-economic factors and work that looks at race, but none of the studies (quantitative nor qualitative) deals simultaneously with race, class and disability to explore whether class modifies the experiences of Black students in relation to notions of disability. There is, however, a growing demand for research that deals systematically and simultaneously with multiple dimensions of inequality in relation to the construction and application of disability categories. Artiles (2011) has called for an 'interdisciplinary' approach that explicitly addresses the intersection of race and disability and 'documents the very *production* of inequity' (p. 443, original emphasis). Zeus Leonardo and

Alicia Broderick (2011) argue for a radical reconceptualisation of scholarship in Whiteness and Disability Studies to explore the oppressive work these categories and processes achieve in mutual, symbiotic relation:

> Whites and smart people are only real insofar as social institutions like education, and formidable processes like common sense, recognize certain bodies as White and certain people as smart. Historically and materially, these ideologies have operated not in isolation from one another, but as inextricably intertwined systems of oppression and exclusion.
>
> *(Leonardo and Broderick 2011: 10)*

In a similar vein Subini Annamma *et al.* (2013) propose a new conceptual framework, Dis/ability Critical Race Theory (DisCrit), as a means of unifying a fundamental concern to deal seriously with the jointly constituted nature of racism and ablism. This is where our present study can potentially make a significant contribution. In looking at where notions of SEN and disability appear in our data, we are able to explore the intersectional nature of race, class and disability in a new way; examining through the parents' eyes how race, class and disability are mutually constituted and negotiated in the everyday routine of schooling. Our key concerns in this chapter, therefore, do not relate to questions of over- and under-representation, as if there were some objective *real* notion of disability into which Black middle-class students should gain rightful admittance or avoid wrongful categorisation. Rather, we are interested in how understandings of disability are made, asserted and contested in schools. In particular, we seek to understand the experiences of Black middle-class parents and their children as they encounter labels being used against them or alternatively how they attempt to use labels to access additional resources.

Assessing 'special needs': parent vs. school perspectives

> I didn't necessarily want her to be labelled as *special educational needs*. I just wanted her to get the support that she required to get through secondary education.
>
> *(Maud)*

The troubled history of race and SEN is well known within the Black community and, as we have seen in previous chapters, middle-class Black parents are only too aware of the potential dangers of being negatively labelled in school. The decision to pursue a formal SEN assessment, therefore, is not one that parents take lightly. Indeed, sometimes parents view the label as too great a burden or risk; in Maud's case, above, she studiously avoided her daughter being formally labelled in this way and preferred to work closely with teachers, including the school's head teacher, to build knowledge of her daughter's condition and encourage greater sensitivity and understanding:

I was very much involved with anything (whether it was things going smoothly or things weren't going so well) and I was *always* involved (…) My approach wasn't so defensive with the school. I became more engaging. So rather than saying 'you shouldn't be doing it this way', I said 'let's work together and see how we can make [my daughter's] education more productive'. (…) There is always some event or other that I am involved in; they ask me to do things and I am happy to oblige. And that's helped, that's helped me get recognised in the school as a parent who supports the school and in turn has given my children extra support. Now it shouldn't be the case that because your mum's in the school, and quite vocal, that your child gets extra support but for me it was any means necessary.

(Maud)

We discuss parents' strategies for engaging with their children's schools in greater detail in the next chapter. Although many adopt such conscious and strategic approaches, few enjoy the level of success that Maud describes. Although she comments that such tactical manoeuvres 'shouldn't be the case' Maud successfully negotiates the situation. For the majority of respondents who feel that their children need additional support, however, a more formal assessment of their needs is often seen as a vital step in the process.

The government's advice for parents of children with disabilities (DCSF 2009) sets out a process whereby the young person's needs can be identified and suitable action taken to support them successfully through the education system. The guide sets out a series of stages that should typify the process:

- The parents and/or school identify that the child is having problems.
- An assessment is arranged through the school or the local authority.
- The nature of the child's needs is identified and adjustments are recommended.
- The school then acts on these recommendations and the student is better able to fulfil their potential.

The guide includes advice on appeals procedures but tends to assume a shared understanding of 'SEN' and envisages a constructive and trusting relationship between parents and teachers:

If you think your child may have a special educational need that has not been identified by the school or early education setting, you should talk to your child's class teacher, to the SENCO (this is the person in the school or preschool who has a particular responsibility for co-ordinating help for children with special educational needs) or to the head teacher straightaway … Working together with your child's teachers will often help to sort out worries and problems. The closer you work with your child's teachers, the more successful any help for your child can be.

(DCSF 2009: 9)

In our data there is only *one* case that comes close to this model of mutually supportive and proactive parent/school interaction in relation to such issues. Matthew is extremely positive about the help and support that his son's primary school has supplied, confirming his own worries about his child's development and helping to identify professional support:

> Before [he] was diagnosed, this is in junior school, there were issues with his behaviour which nobody could quite understand (…) inability to grasp, very early on, very basic concepts and remember things and also his behaviour, his lack of attention, mood swings. But it was the school that picked up on it actually, they realised that he wasn't developing very fast (…) the school brought in a speech development person to look at [him] and then they noticed that he was way behind age-wise and so we went along, they said maybe he's got ADHD [Attention Deficit Hyperactivity Disorder] so we started that process of going to psychologists all instigated by the school …
>
> *(Matthew)*

As is characteristic of many parents in this research, Matthew and his partner mobilise their considerable class capitals (personal networks and research skills) to find out as much as possible about the issues and their best ways of proceeding, in this case pushing for a formal 'statement of special educational needs' as a means of securing a binding commitment to the resources and support that their son should receive from school:

> The moment that was mentioned, ADHD, we ourselves went and got educated. We read everything, we bought the books, we spoke to certain people who were experienced and we started to understand what was going on. And then at that point, we knew we had to fight for statementing, again with the help of the school. And I felt the school gave us that help.
>
> *(Matthew)*

Even in this single positive case, therefore, the parents' own research, contacts and commitments play an important role. Although Matthew views the school's involvement as supportive, he reports the need to resist an initial push toward a drug-based response from the school and other professionals:

> The very first thing you know as part of that agenda is they're always offering you drugs at every step (…) so there was a huge pressure but we refused the whole time, 'No. We're not putting him on drugs, we'll deal with it' (…) when you read about the personality changes in children who have these drugs – because it suppresses them – just imagine for a second: [he's] a bit of a handful but imagine him quiet, sitting in a corner because of drugs. No, we have to find a way, and there's a big school of thought also, which is well written, that you need to change the environment around the child, so you

don't change the child and plonk them into, you know, you help the environment to change, you educate yourself …

(Matthew)

To reiterate, despite their differing views on the utility of medication, Matthew's experience with his son's primary school stands out from our data as the *only* case where a positive experience comes anywhere close to the kind of process envisaged in the official SEN guidance. Contrary to the official expectation of a school/parent *partnership*, interviewees tend to report a negative experience (in line with the research described earlier); they encounter schools whose reactions range from a lack of interest through to outright disbelief and hostility.

The reaction of teachers (including senior leaders) emerges in our data as a considerable barrier to parents' attempts to access the help and support they need. In almost every case it is the parent (rather than the school) who takes the initiative in seeking to explore whether the child has an impairment that might be assessed and positively addressed.[2] This involves parents deploying a range of class-related resources, for example utilising their *economic capital* (to finance expensive specialist assessments) and also their *cultural and social capital* (often using friendships and professional networks to help them negotiate a complex and unpredictable system). For example, because of her own specialist professional education, Paulette is aware that a sharp discrepancy in a child's performance on a range of different types of task can be a sign of a learning disability (DANDA 2011). Yet when she drew this to the school's attention, she was simply informed that her daughter's *true* level of attainment was the lower level and that her concerns were misplaced and unwelcome:

> A discrepancy was emerging, in that she would get a B for a piece of work that she had spent time doing [at home] and then she would get a D or an E even [for timed work in class]. So I then contacted the school and said, 'look there's a problem here'. And they just said 'well, she needs to work harder.' So they were actually not at all helpful and I ended up having a row with the Head of Sixth Form because she accused me of being 'a fussy parent'. And what she said was that my daughter was working to her level, which was the timed essay level, she was working to a D.

(Paulette)

Paulette is annoyed and frustrated that her professional knowledge is dismissed so readily by the school. In a further manifestation of the low expectations that characterise so much of our parents' experiences of the system (and as we discussed in Chapter 3) she discovered that the school views her daughter's *higher* levels of achievement as at best anomalous, at worst suspicious:

> I felt really frustrated and actually very angry that they wouldn't listen. Because I could see that, yes, OK in a class of thirty you could overlook that,

but if someone's actually pointing out to you the difference [between timed classwork and homework] and you are still saying, 'well actually, you know, we don't see that', and 'is someone actually helping her with her homework?' Which is what I was asked, because she is getting better grades when she is producing work from home, so it got really unpleasant.

(Paulette)

Paulette paid for a private assessment, which diagnosed a form of dyslexia, and eventually moved her daughter to a private institution that followed through on the recommended adjustments. Paulette reports that her daughter's performance in Advanced level examinations (aged 18) improved dramatically: from two grade Es and an ungraded (failing) result before the adjustments and change of school to three passes at grade B.[3]

The low academic expectations that Black parents and students encounter almost routinely within schools (despite their middle-class status) take numerous forms. For example, in many ways Vanessa's son was well liked by his teachers but their lack of academic ambition for him meant that they were unconcerned by his passivity in class. She feels that years have been wasted:

Each time I went to school, or if I passed the window, [he] would be sitting looking out the window and I was convinced that he was somewhere on the autistic spectrum (…) but because [he] could sit for an entire lesson silent and not be disruptive, all they ever said was [in a patronising tone] 'he's so handsome' and 'he's so quiet' and I said 'Yes, but that's not normal is it?' (…) So when he actually saw the psychologist he was just about to leave junior school – so he was about 11. So all the support that he could have had, the learning plan, *nothing* was done at all. So we wasted a lot of time that he could have been supported.

(Vanessa)

We noted earlier that Matthew's experiences stand out from our data as the only positive case that followed the relative pattern of mutual support between parent and school envisaged by official SEN guidance. In our data there are two further occasions where the impetus for an SEN assessment came from the school rather than the parent, but these cases are much less positive. In both cases the Black student is a boy who has been racially harassed by White peers; in both cases the schools' actions served to divert attention from accusations of racism and refocus attention onto a supposed individual deficit within the Black child.

Simon describes how his son was excluded for reacting violently to racist harassment. In a situation that echoes previous research on the over-representation of Black students in exclusions (Blair 2001; Communities Empowerment Network 2005; Wright *et al.* 2000) it seems that the school refused to take account of the provocation and violence that the young man had experienced at the hands of racist peers and, instead, chose to view his actions in isolation:

... someone called him a 'black monkey' and he responded by beating him up (...) I just don't think the school really understood the impact, or how isolated pupils can feel when they stand out physically, and that's just something that I don't think they get.

(Simon)

The process culminated in Simon's son being labelled as having 'behaviour and anger management' problems. In a strikingly similar case, Felicia discovered that her son was experiencing racist bullying. Initially she was encouraged by the school's reaction:

I started being concerned about his performance and then the little things, like he'd be coming home and his shirts were ripped and he'd say he'd been playing rugby, but his shirt was completely torn in two (...) eventually he said about the comments and what had been going on and how they'd been behaving towards him and essentially the racism he had been tolerating. So I contacted the school and arranged to see the Head of his year. (...) the Head of Year was quite shocked and quite encouraging in terms of our conversation; calling and saying, you know, 'Really sorry. We've let you down; we've let [your son] down; we didn't know this was happening'.

(Felicia)

Unfortunately the school's reassuring words did not translate into action and, when Felicia sought further information, the situation deteriorated (see also Chapter 6):

Nothing happened. I'd asked them about what policies they have for bullying and racism, they said they have got a policy and I said I'd like to see it. This is a school with loads of money, [but they said that] all the computers were down during our meeting. [She laughs signalling disbelief] The place has got hundreds of computers. So [they said] they couldn't print it off for me to take with me that morning but they would send it to me. And I waited for two days and didn't get it; third day, I sent an email saying 'I was promised this.' 'Oh it's coming.' When it finally came, it said *draft* on it. So I wrote back to them saying, the fact that it says draft suggests that (a) it's not in place and more importantly the parents don't know about it (...) My son's class teacher had said to my son that I'm asking *too much* but not to tell me.

(Felicia)

The situation became even worse when Felicia unexpectedly received a phone call on a Sunday afternoon:

I got this telephone call out of the blue one Sunday afternoon, from his class teacher, suggesting that he have some *test* – I can't remember exactly how this conversation went because it was such a shock; it was five o'clock on

Sunday afternoon – that there might be some reason for his under-perform-ing: not the racism at the school that I told them about, but there might be some reason, that he might have some *learning difficulties*.

(Felicia)

Both Simon and Felicia sought to resist the school's actions and to insist that the racism experienced by their children be addressed. Neither was successful. Instead they met with an escalating insistence that their child was in the wrong:

I wrote and explained [to the Head Teacher] I'm concerned that nothing has really been done and, having been told that it was accepted that he'd been let down, that nothing was being done and that perhaps he ought to, you know, [the Head Teacher] needs to talk to the boys [responsible] and their parents. And I had a stinker of a letter back from him essentially suggesting that my son was some sort of latent gangster (…) that he talked to some of his peers, who said they found him *an intimidating presence*, all sorts of things! If you'd looked at his school reports for those four years, there's never been any sug-gestion of bad behaviour, in fact most of the teachers say he's a nice boy. That his peers found him an intimidating presence, that something about the *rap culture*, he talked about specifically about *bling* (…) basically telling me off about this monster I've produced.

(Felicia)[4]

Our data, therefore, reveal that the first stage in SEN procedures is fraught with problems and risks for Black parents, even when they can call on considerable middle-class capitals. In almost every case where parents believe that their children might have a learning disability that could usefully be addressed, it is the parents themselves – not the school – who take the initiative in seeking advice and arrang-ing a formal assessment, often in the face of suspicion or explicit resistance from the school. In our sample there are only three exceptions to this pattern and in two cases the school initiated SEN assessments following incidents of racist bullying against Black children. The schools failed to support the children by taking action against their aggressors and instead invoked SEN proceedings, actions that the stu-dents and their parents experience as a sign of the schools' lack of understanding and their reluctance to address White racism.

'I don't think they want to know': schools' reactions to SEN assessments

I don't think they want to know. And as long as they think academically she's doing OK, that's where they're concerned. I'm concerned with her performing to the best of her ability, which I don't think she does, and I think they're con-cerned with her reaching their target grades, which is I think a different thing.

(Lorraine)

Having negotiated the first stage in the SEN process (usually by paying for a private assessment in the face of official inaction) parents face the task of presenting the assessment to the school. In principle, the assessment should indicate action that can be taken by the school and/or local authority to better support the child. In some cases the assessments suggest fairly basic adjustments; for example, where children are identified as having specific learning difficulties such as dyslexia, recommendations might include use of a laptop computer in class or the provision of additional time to complete examinations. In some cases the assessments point to more profound issues that require far-reaching changes. Regardless of the nature of the issues that are identified, however, in almost every case our interviewees report that schools' reactions are at best slow and uncertain, at worst actively hostile and obstructive. Nigel was advised that his son should use a laptop in class; ready to buy the machine himself, Nigel was stunned when the school refused permission:

> So we have gone up, we thought it would be a *fait accompli*, we thought we would get the laptop. We were going to buy the laptop, the school wouldn't have to *buy* it, you know, we would do all of that, and they said no. So we had a long conversation with the head, who we were very friendly with, and they said that it would set a precedent.
>
> *(Nigel)*

The schools' rejection of Nigel's approach was unusually clear and direct. Much more common is an initial reaction which seems positive and constructive; only later, after months (and sometimes years) of inaction does the schools' actual lack of concern become apparent despite their supportive rhetoric. In some cases such lack of concern comes across as deliberate obstruction. Lorraine's experiences illustrate this pattern: as a trained researcher Lorraine is able to use her professional contacts to access information and wider support networks in order to explore possible ways of understanding, and helping, her daughter. Unfortunately, the school's positive early reactions and promises remained unfulfilled:

> I have a daughter who now has been diagnosed with autism, I actually do want to get much more involved in the school and how they deal with her. But I think for the school it's easier if they don't get involved with me. So, for instance, going in and having meetings; her Head of Year says 'oh, you know, I understand now, we'll do this, we'll do that' and then that just doesn't happen.
>
> *(Lorraine)*

Attempts to follow up promises by telephone or email frequently prove fruitless. Government advice, noted earlier, informs parents that 'Working together with your child's teachers will often help to sort out worries and problems' (DCSF 2009: 9), yet in reality it can take up to a month to simply *meet* the relevant member of school staff:

> ... it's almost impossible to talk to the Head of Year on the phone because she's always teaching or 'somewhere else'. It may well be *a week* before she gets back to me. And then it may be another 2–3 weeks before a meeting is scheduled. So the lack of communication, I find quite difficult.
>
> *(Lorraine)*

Repeated visits, and even enrolling highly trained support, do not guarantee success:

> I – together with other professionals – had been in to school to talk to the SENCO [Special Educational Needs Coordinator], to talk to the Head of Year, and *they had done absolutely nothing.* So there were *constant* visits to try to get them to take some kind of action to help (…) You know, at first I thought it was me not being forceful enough, but as I said, I was accompanied by a Clinical Psychologist who tried to get them to help as well and *they* failed.
>
> *(Lorraine)*

Although the school maintained a pleasant façade, and talked about making relevant changes, looking back Lorraine is frustrated by their continued inaction. Even when a SEN specialist offered free dedicated training for staff members, the suggestion was met with silence:

> I went in with the Clinical Psychologist who has experience of autism; what we were saying to the school was that [my daughter] needs this particular kind of intervention and we felt very strongly that *all* her teachers should know about this. The Head of Year's response was, 'None of us know anything about autism.' So the Psychologist wrote to them, she wrote *three times* offering to come in and do a day with staff about autism and they never responded to that at all.
>
> *(Lorraine)*

Even when parents succeed in accessing an assessment *and* having a formal Individual Education Plan (IEP)[5] agreed as a record of what the school would do, they typically encounter patchy or non-existent follow-up. This pattern emerges regardless of whether the assistance is sought within the state system or in a private school. Rachel describes her constant vigilance at her daughter's private school:

> I went to parents' evening recently. I went round to see all of the teachers individually. And I said, 'Have you seen her IEP? Have you read it?' Not all of them had. Some of them didn't even have it. 'And what have you done differently to accommodate that plan?' You know, 'How are you catering for my daughter?' I'm paying for her education, so I just said to them, you know, 'What are you doing to make life easier for her?' You know, some of them had thought about it and some hadn't. (…) I went immediately and complained to the headmistress – who was there – because I thought why – don't

advertise and promote yourself as a school that is good at pastoral care and being supportive if, when you have a child who has learning needs and you have an IEP, and the staff can't be bothered to read it. It's not good enough. She said, 'Oh, which teachers were you talking to?' and 'I'm going to get on to it and I'll get back to you.' And I haven't heard from her since.

(Rachel)

The failure to circulate accurate information among staff (about students' needs and how their impairments might present in class) can have very serious consequences, not only leading to conflict and distress but, in one case, meaning that a child was denied access to an examination:

[There are] two or three teachers who have got very annoyed with [my daughter] because she has done things which they don't like, but which I think are because of her autism. And so they have thrown her out of lessons, made her stand in the corridor. So this particular teacher threw her out of a class in which everyone else was informed of when they had to submit their work. So [she] didn't know and when she *did* submit it, it was too late and she wasn't allowed to submit her coursework. Absolutely unbelievable. (...) I said to her when she got her results, 'How did you manage to get a U [ungraded result]?' Because I had seen some of the work she had done (...) and then she explained to me that she wasn't allowed to submit the work.

(Lorraine)

'This is your first lesson on what it means to be a black boy in Britain': SEN, segregation and psychiatric racism

Psychiatry is never very far away when there is talk of positive representation ... for the solution is always to be found in altering individuals and not institutional practice ... [In schools] psychiatric racism is effected by means of psychology, as a major sub-discipline of education science; and the whole issue of educational subnormality and black children's behaviour is the zone in which psychology blurs into psychiatry because of the obvious pathological implications of educational backwardness and behavioural disorder.

(Francis 1993: 186 and 203)

To this point in our analysis, we have explored the ongoing battles that Black middle-class parents face in attempting to ensure that their children's needs are recognised and taken seriously. We have seen that, in the experience of our respondents, SEN labels appear to be resisted by schools where they would act as a catalyst for additional resources and other opportunities being made available to Black students, for example in the case of specific learning disabilities such as autism and dyslexia. In contrast, labels relating to 'emotional' and 'behavioural' difficulties appear in our data where children have been subject to racist violence from White peers but their schools' response shifts the focus from problems in the school onto the Black child themselves, exactly the kind of 'psychiatric racism' that Errol Francis described twenty years ago.

In a qualitative interview-based study such as ours it is difficult to draw wider conclusions with any certainty; nevertheless, it is significant that this pattern of experience connects directly with the wider patterns of race discrimination and SEN found in previous research. For several interviewees this is not the first time they have encountered racialised understandings of disability. Patricia, for example, recalls how Black students were over-represented in the bottom of five selectively ranked 'bands' in her state secondary school in the north of England. In the fifth 'band' students were denied access to public examinations and teachers used openly derogatory and disablist language:

> ... quite a lot of Black people were what they called, in [my secondary school], *below the line*. And 'below the line' was a term [used] not by the kids, but by the teachers. The teachers called it 'Man and Mongo.' Like *Mongolians*. Mongo. Remember they used to call erm ...
>
> *NR*: Down's syndrome?
>
> Down's syndrome, that's it. (...) [Band] four was the cut off point at which they'd *allow* you to take Maths, English and a science if you wanted to go to an exam. 'Below the line' you weren't taking any exams. You could go to school; you could cut out of the catalogues; they'd do a lot of sticking and gluing. They might get the sex talk (...) it was like 'Man in the Environment'. It was to teach them how to live, basically. That's all they were doing. Those people, they weren't gonna take any exams. (...) A lot of the Black kids were doing 'Man and Mongo'.
>
> *(Patricia)*

Although such overtly degrading terminology is less common in contemporary schools, Black students continue to be over-represented in low-status teaching groups and in categories such as 'Behavioural, Emotional and Social Difficulties' (Gillborn 2008; Hallam 2002; Lindsay *et al.* 2006). Barbara (who we discuss in Chapter 3) knows from her own experience, as a child, how quickly pseudo-scientific labels can be applied on the basis of racist stereotypes:

> We were the only Black family in the county, much less the village. So I went to an all girls' school and I suppose my experience there was overtly racist basically, it was *overtly* racist. (...) I was put in the 'Remedial Class' [special education] at school initially and my mum had to fight to get me out into another stream. Because it was just the assumption that you're Black, that's where you belong ...
>
> *(Barbara)*

Her experiences as a child, plus her professional training in child health, mean that Barbara is acutely aware of the dangers facing her son. She and her partner remain constantly vigilant and actively challenge any labelling at the very first indication of trouble. She recalls, for example, a point in her son's very first encounter with school when it was necessary to challenge the language being used about him because a single incident could have been recorded as indicating a more generalised psychological problem:

> he was in nursery, not even in Reception, and there was something on his report about 'inappropriate response to social conflict', you know, with *categories*. (…) when we went to parents' evening my partner said, he said 'Oh you know, the report was very good, it was very positive. There's just one thing we don't understand, can you clarify? What do you mean by this. "an inappropriate response to social conflict"?' So she said, 'Oh well, there was this incident (…) it's fine now.' And [my partner] said 'well we are a bit concerned about him having that on his record' and she changed it. She was really apologetic and she said 'There's not a problem with [your son]' she said, 'The only problem [he] has; he's a very bright boy.' And I thought that's a sad indictment …
>
> (Barbara)

As we noted earlier, the over-representation of Black students in SEN provision is well documented in both the US and the UK, although the statistics are rarely, if ever, broken down by race and social class simultaneously. Our data clearly reveal the ways in which racism and racial stereotypes intersect with notions of dis/ability with damaging consequences for respondents and their children. Further, while class status enables interviewees to proactively solicit (sometimes independent) advice, guidance and information to support their children, attempts to make good of these capitals are thwarted and resisted by the school. However, if necessary they can, and do, seek alternative provision (e.g. private schooling) for their children. In another example, Linda was shocked to receive a note from her son's school saying that he had been placed in segregated SEN provision. When she challenged the school to justify the decision, she discovered that the required procedures had not been followed. Worse still, the school had no plan for how to support her son to enable him to progress:

> All I got was a letter saying 'We've decided he needs to be in the special needs group, he's in it.' (…) I asked what was the special needs procedure? They hadn't gone through it basically. But they insisted that he stay in this class and it was a nightmare (…) I said 'I don't understand why he's in this class; he doesn't understand why he's in this class; I'm asking you where are the areas that he's failing on? Or not doing well on? And what does he have to do to get out of this class?' The teacher just looked at me. (…) I said, 'I'm in education. If I've a student who's failing, I need to identify *where* they're failing, *what* they need to work on, what input they need to help them with it and what I want to see as evidence of improvement.' (…) They hadn't got

a learning contract for him or anything like that, learning plan, whatever they call it, and so they wrote one in a week. 'Cause they didn't have anything written down and it was really terrible …

(Linda)

Unfortunately, the majority of Black students do not have parents with a professional training who can research procedures and mobilise considerable cultural and economic resources in order to increase the chances that schools follow the formal procedures and actually conceive of a way forward. A measure of the continuing danger faced by Black students, especially boys,[6] can be gleaned not only from respondents' attempts to protect their own children, but also from their experiences witnessing the operation of the contemporary education system where there remains clear evidence of an assumption that disability represents a stable, unyielding, life sentence of educational underachievement. Paulette's experiences are especially important and highlight the continuity between current practices and the racist segregation and labelling exposed by the pioneering work of Coard (1971) and Tomlinson (1981).

Paulette works as a Psychologist and sometimes her role requires her to visit schools: she has been profoundly disturbed by what she describes as the 'brutalisation' of Black boys in segregated provision in a state secondary school. She describes a class of boys physically separated from the mainstream school – 'they weren't in the main school building':

> The class was predominantly Black, not many students but they were really unruly, and I was really shocked at how unruly they were. (…) the SENCO said to me, she said, 'Well, that's what you get.'
>
> *(Paulette)*

Upon further investigation Paulette discovered that the class had come about as a result of the school's decision to selectively group students in hierarchically ranked teaching 'sets' – an approach that is especially common in secondary schools (Hallam 2002). This form of grouping has been known to generate problems for particular groups of students who are consistently placed in the bottom groups, denied a full curriculum and often taught by less experienced teachers; Black students, and their White peers from poorer backgrounds, are often over-represented in bottom sets (Araujo 2007; Ball 1981; CRE 1992; Gillborn 2008; Gillies and Robinson 2012; Hallam 2002; Hallam and Toutounji 1996; Sukhnandan and Lee 1998; Tikly *et al.* 2006; Wiliam and Bartholomew 2004):

> What they do is, because the boys are in sets from the time they come in and those boys are in the bottom sets. And the bottom set has been written off as boys who are just not going to get anywhere. And literally they kind of turn into animals, they really had, because of the way that they had been treated and because of the expectations. (…) And I just felt that there was something that that school – you know it sounds crazy – but something that that school

did, actually *did*, to particular Black boys. I'm not saying that Black boys go there and they don't achieve because many do, but there is *a particular group of boys* perhaps underachieving, you know the type that I'm describing – who perhaps have an unidentified need – not doing so well at school. The school *does* something to them because they don't, literally the Deputy Head said to me when I made the complaint [about what she had seen in the class], 'Well you know, what do you expect, they are in bottom sets?' (…) And I just think, I just thought that what it is, is that maybe the school just brutalises those children, *unintentionally*. Am I making sense?

(Paulette)

Paulette goes on to describe the fate of a Black student whom she has known for some time. She explains that in primary school, despite having been diagnosed as dyslexic, his attainment was 'good' to 'average'. But the secondary school has interpreted the SEN label as automatically signalling a generic and untreatable deficit:

Because he had dyslexia they had put him in bottom sets for everything, even though he was an able student. So from year seven [aged 11], what do you do? He just became completely de-motivated, completely disaffected. He had completely given up. And that was such a shock to me, it was such a shock.

(Paulette)

This boy's fate is particularly significant. Many young people achieve highly despite dyslexia; indeed, it is exactly the kind of learning disability that – as we explained earlier – Sleeter (1987) views as an explicit part of attempts to protect the educational privilege of *White* middle-class America. Under the right circumstances (with sensible adjustments to pedagogy and through the use of simple assistive technologies) the student could have had a very different experience. But in this school the combination of SEN and race seemed to automatically condemn the student to the very lowest teaching groups where his confidence and performance collapsed.

Despite the statistical evidence on the over-representation of Black students in SEN (noted earlier) it is beyond the scope of this research to judge definitively whether the kinds of processes witnessed by Paulette are significantly more likely for Black students – where racist and disablist processes combine and are amplified – than their White peers. However, our data certainly contain incidents that support this analysis and the overwhelming picture from our findings is that racism intervenes to further complicate the use of SEN as a weapon against Black children.

Earlier in this section, we described Linda's experiences when her son was placed in a SEN group with no consultation and no obvious plan to support his progress. The experiences that they endured during this period (when he was aged 12) prompted Linda to have an explicit discussion with him about the wider significance of racism in society and, in particular, his own positioning as a Black male (an issue we look at in further detail in Chapter 6):

He'd come home from school; he'd be upset because he'd been at class with kids who couldn't read and write (...) it was draining and he was *insulted* – he didn't want to go to school. (...) and this was the first time I had to have this conversation with [him] about being a Black child in Britain.

And I said to him, 'This is your first lesson on what it means to be a Black boy in Britain.' And I said 'You've got a number of choices; you *either* accept what they're telling you about yourself, that you're not very good and you can't do stuff – even though you know that you can be, you know, and you shouldn't be in that class. You've got a choice, you either feel bad about it, accept what they say and just feel like crap. Or you remember who you are and what you're able to do and you work hard and prove them wrong, or you just get angry, act out, and fulfil another stereotype of Black boys. That's the choice you've got and this is ... you're going to get more of it later on in life, so you might as well learn *now*, that you've got to fight that, you know.'

And it was horrible to have to say, *he was twelve*, but I needed to kind of give him a framework for understanding what was happening to him. For me, it was about he was being perceived as a Black boy, which was that he was troublesome, you know. He was either talking too much or he was too quiet. You know, so he buckled down and I had to really really work on his self-esteem while he was in that class, you know, and after a term they took him out [of the class], it was ridiculous ...

(Linda)

Conclusion: whose needs are being prioritized?

Oppression is a bundled set of relations that reinforce one another, so there is little to suggest that advantages in terms of one relation necessarily contradict the enforcement of another relation.

(Leonardo and Broderick 2011: 9)

'Race' and 'disability' are socially constructed categories of difference and exclusion that have a long history of complex intersectional relations. Some of the most important early work on the racist operation of the English educational system exposed how particular notions of disability (concerning 'educational subnormality') operated to segregate Black British students from mainstream classrooms with damaging consequences to their educational achievements. Understandings of disability have changed over the years but the racialisation of these issues continues. On both sides of the Atlantic there is a long-standing pattern of Black over-representation in categories that rely heavily on the judgment of White teachers who perceive an 'emotional' or 'behavioural' aberration in the actions of Black students. Recently, however, there have been growing calls for studies that deal with race/disability intersections in more detail and this is precisely the opportunity afforded by our in-depth work with Black middle-class parents. In addition, and perhaps most significantly, the socio-economic profile of our respondents allows us to look at how social class issues operate in this mix.

Despite the relatively advantaged socio-economic profile of our sample, our findings suggest that 'disability' continues to operate as a racialised barrier to equity in English schools. Indeed, an intersectional analysis reveals new dimensions that illuminate the simultaneously raced and classed nature of particular understandings of disability in education.

Only one of the 62 respondents report an overwhelmingly positive experience, where the systems operate as they are envisaged in official guidance, and there is a mutually respectful and supportive relationship between home and school. In all other cases there is a degree of tension and mistrust, often leading to conflict and a breakdown of home/school relations. When respondents believe that there might be an issue worth investigating through a formal assessment, in most cases they report that their concerns were dismissed. Even when they draw on specialist knowledge to support their argument, interviewees report that schools continue to resist such moves and prefer, instead, to assume that the child is simply not working hard enough or that their low achievement is simply an accurate measure of their limited talents. The exceptions to this rule are two cases where the school initiated SEN procedures after being informed that White peers had been racially harassing the student. Rather than seeking to meet the needs of the child, therefore, their actions serve to shift attention away from institutional failings onto a supposed deficit in the individual Black child.

We noted earlier that our approach does not make judgments about the onto-logical status of any disability labels or truth-claims; our aim is not to pronounce on the supposed 'accuracy', or not, of labelling processes, but rather to understand how notions of disability are constituted and the significance of race/class intersections in those processes. For example, Christine Sleeter's analysis proposed that 'learning disabilities' emerged as a category 'created by white middle-class parents in an effort to differentiate their children from low-achieving low income and minority chil-dren' (1987: 210); our data suggest that learning disabilities (including issues such as dyslexia and autism) are policed by schools in ways that position Black parents as illegitimate *regardless* of their class status. In all but one case, in the face of school resistance our respondents had to seek private assessments outside the state system. Then, armed with the requisite assessments (and even when accompanied by spe-cialists), they continued to face resistance to having their children's needs acknowl-edged and acted upon. So far as disability labels and processes are concerned, therefore, our parents' enhanced socio-economic standing does not seem to alter schools' approaches to the issues: negative understandings of SEN act to deflect accusations of White racism and serve to segregate some Black students from the mainstream; meanwhile, attempts to access additional resources for Black children are resisted at virtually every stage.

We have focused, in this chapter, upon the different strategies that Black middle-class parents seek to deploy in order to protect and advocate on behalf of their children on matters of disability and special educational needs. We follow this, in Chapter 5, by examining more closely parents' various modes of engagement and involvement with school.

Notes

1 The most recent major study of these issues found that, relative to White British students, Black Caribbean students are 2.28 times more likely and 'Mixed White and Caribbean' 2.03 times more likely to be categorised as BESD (Lindsay *et al.* 2006: table 5a).
2 The two exceptions, where the school was the first to raise the question of a SEN assessment, are highly significant and we discuss them later in this chapter.
3 Moving to a private institution is by no means a guarantee of success, as Rachel's experiences (below) demonstrate.
4 Felicia's experiences strongly echo the processes described by Adrienne Dixson in her account of how raced, classed and gendered stereotypes intersect in the exclusion of an African American boy accused of making threats (Dixson 2006).
5 According to official guidance an Individual Education Plan should include details of: 'what special help is being given; how often your child will receive the help; who will provide the help; what the targets for your child are; how and when your child's progress will be checked; and what help you can give your child at home' (DCSF 2009: 12).
6 Heightened concern for the dangers faced by Black boys and young men is a recurrent theme in our interviews; see, for example, Chapters 2, 3 and 6.

5

PARENTS' ENGAGEMENT AND INVOLVEMENT IN SCHOOLS

You find it helpful sometimes to use your status.

Introduction

Patricia Hill-Collins recalls a day when, as a 16-year-old, she attended a movie and witnessed a young White usher violently remove two Black children. When she went to complain she found several Black adults already informing the manager of the incident:

> Ignoring them, the manager turned to his teenaged employee and asked him what had happened. Red-faced and stammering, the usher denied hurting the boys and, if that were not enough, claimed that he had seen the boys sneak into the theatre. After hearing his employee's testimony, the manager turned back to the adults. 'You must have been mistaken,' he flatly stated. He turned his back on all of us and simply walked away. (...) On that day I learned that, in some situations, gender, age, social class, and education do not matter if you are Black. The usher and the movie theatre manager could see only race and their perceptions of race clouded their judgment.
>
> *(2006: 2)*

In this extract Hill-Collins vividly illustrates that there are times when social class and other resources that are held by Black people can be negated by racism; on occasion, the complexity and fluidity of contemporary life can be stripped away in the face of a simple, crude colour-line. The event she describes took place in the early 1970s in the US. In a different time (the present) and location (England), our research project explores the intersection of class and race (and to a lesser extent gender) and how these social dimensions shape Black middle-class parents' strategies for and interventions around their children's education. None of the strategies are guaranteed success – the racism that Hill-Collins describes can still intervene – but our interviews with Black middle-class parents reveal a wide variety of dispositions, strategies and interventions all aimed at supporting their children as they negotiate the demands of schooling.

We begin this chapter by considering the general context within which the parents operate, a context defined by a long history of racialised and classed exclusion where many Black children soon learn that they must 'work twice as hard' as their White peers. As we have already noted, in contemporary England there is still a widespread assumption that Black people are, virtually by definition, working class. We explore how the Black middle-class parents in the study work against this *misrecognition* by drawing upon a range of social class capitals, including economic, social and cultural resources. Some parents talk explicitly about particular 'strategies' that they and their friends deploy. All of the parents in this study are deeply committed to protecting and supporting their children as they move through the education system but some interesting differences emerge when considering the style of intervention that parents pursue. In particular, we identify a continuum of involvement that reflects differences in priorities, aspirations and forms of engagement with teachers and schools.

We conclude by emphasising that although many of the parents' strategies are proving successful in guiding their children through the education system, they demand considerable labour as they draw on all available resources. This labour can be thought of as intersectional work, that is working on and at the intersections of race and class.

Being Black *and* middle class: strategies for recognition

Comparing, for a moment, our respondents' experiences with those of White middle-class parents documented in previous research, it is clear that the basis for the engagement of Black middle-class parents with the school system, their orientation towards it, lies on radically different ground to that of White middle-class parents. There is, however, some commonality in terms of *strategy* (see also Lareau 2003; Archer 2010) as both White and Black middle-class parents perceive schooling to be a risk – a risk, that is, that their children's academic potential may not be fully realised. Middle-class parents do not generally maintain an unquestioning trust in the education system (especially the state education system), rather displaying a restricted or 'managed trust' (Vincent and Martin 2002: 116). The perception of 'risk' for Black middle-class parents is heightened by their awareness of, and often their own experiences of, racism and low teacher expectations when they were children (see Chapter 3 for further details). The parents in this study, therefore, share an urgent need to manage the risks faced by their children and, as we illustrate below, they draw on their particular resources of social, cultural and economic capital in order to do so.

The parents marshal their resources against the 'symbolic violence' (Bourdieu and Passeron 1977) of the education system, which deems, for example, Black children's cultural knowledge inferior. Indeed, it can be argued that the potential 'violence' to the life chances of the children, to their educational and labour market opportunities, and to their well-being and self-esteem are real and solid and not merely symbolic. Data on exclusion rates, achievement levels and access to high-status universities (see Equality Challenge Unit 2012; Gillborn 2008; Shiner and Modood 2002; Strand 2007; Tomlinson 2005; Wright 2012) are all well documented indicators of the challenges facing these families. Several parents speak of high levels of educational achievement as offering their children choices in later life, and the space and agency with which to define themselves. White parents may express similar priorities, but Black parents have a more urgent rationale; strong educational credentials are understood as offering their children the best chance of success in a UK higher education sector where Black students are markedly under-represented at prestigious universities (Vasagar 2010) and a labour market in which race discrimination remains a significant factor (EHRC 2010a). The importance of working hard and gaining qualifications are common themes, well established among Black parents coupled with the recognition that the automatic rewards and privileges incurred by Whites are not equally attributed to Blacks:

> [My mum's] favourite saying was you've got to work twice as hard as the White person next to you. And I know lots of – I thought it was just my mum that used to say that until my friend said, 'Yeah, my mum says that as well' [laughs].
>
> *(Monica)*

> A perception that Black people need to work harder to actually get where they want in life, and that's something that nearly every member of my family has said.
>
> *(Miles)*

> A common thing they [his parents] used to say was that 'your White counterparts are going to get where they're going. You need to work twice as hard to get to where they are'.
>
> *(David)*

> It was always a perception, always the feeling I got that because you're Black you need to work twice as hard.
>
> *(Grace)*

> [My daughter] has to realise that, you know, in education, in the workplace, they have preconceived ideas about her and she has to work, I dare to say it, *twice* as hard.
>
> *(Esme)*

Strategies to minimise risk encompass investments both out of school (such as encouraging achievements in extra-curricular areas: Chapter 6) and within school. The latter involve defending themselves and their children against *misrecognition* and by deploying resources to position themselves as assertive but reasonable advocates for their children and their children as good and responsible learners. This is the area on which we concentrate here, highlighting, in particular, parents' different approaches to teachers and their awareness of the risks inherent in naming racism.

Defending against *misrecognition*

> Symbolic violence can do what political and police violence can do, it only does it more efficiently (Bourdieu and Wacquant, 1992, p. 166). This is because symbolic violence is an act of cognition and misrecognition that 'lies beyond – or beneath – the controls of consciousness and will' (Bourdieu, in Eagleton, 1992, p. 113).
>
> *(Everett 2002: 66)*

As we have documented in previous chapters, Black middle-class parents report that in most cases they and their children face not crude and overt racism (although that has by no means disappeared) but subtle yet pervasive 'mundane' racism, that is degrees of misrepresentation and *misrecognition* of both parent and child that can be highly insidious in their effects.

In Chapter 3 we explored the low aspirations that teachers seem to hold of Black students, despite their social-class background. Cynthia, for example, describes how her interactions with teachers at a state primary school convinced her that for the White teachers 'there was only a certain level of achievement that my boy as a Black child could achieve'. She feels that she cannot trust the system to educate her children to 'their true and fullest capacity' and as a result suspended her own teaching career to home-school her three young children. This strategy illustrates the interplay of race and class in the parents' lives; it is driven by Cynthia's determination to avoid her sons being positioned at a particular nexus of race and gender, as deficit and dangerous, despite their class background (we discuss Cynthia's approach to raising her sons in more detail in Chapter 6). Additionally, giving up her paid work leads to financial sacrifices, and is ultimately made possible by her husband's professional salary. She describes the importance of giving her children a 'grounding' in Black history and cultures to ensure their confidence, and a strong, proud self-image, something which the school is seen as incapable of providing, 'only I can speak that [grounding] into their lives (...) I just make no apology for it.'

Misrecognition is also an issue in relation to teachers' assumptions concerning parents themselves. Among our interviewees, for example, Black women often feel that they face being caricatured through racist assumptions that they lack knowledge, sophistication and an appropriate demeanour:

Sometimes people categorise you, they expect you to be whatever stereo-typical kind of screeching, not able to articulate, Black female.

(Cassandra)

Class – and supposed *working-class* – deficiencies are also visible here. Several mothers speak of the assumption that they are lone mothers and fathers speak of being perceived as a potential physical threat, subject positions at particular structural intersections of race, class and gender; Lareau (2003) notes the same assumptions impacting on Black fathers and Rollock (2007c) describes how these same stereotypes impact Black students in a London school. Similarly, in the USA, Cooper cites African American mothers in her research as being seen as 'irrational, threatening and combative' in their interactions with schools (2007: 492). Parents in our study respond to these stereotypes by deploying class-based resources, especially forms of social and cultural capital, to seek to escape particularly negative intersectional positioning:

And you find it helpful sometimes to use your status, what job you do. And people treat you differently. I don't necessarily want to say I do x, y and z, but I found that if you don't sometimes say that, they treat you in a way, my own experience as a Black woman – oh, you're a single parent – there is a category they read off as to who you are without really knowing anything about you.

(Eleanor)

Here we see two forms of misrecognition. The first is in the Bourdieuian sense that many teachers fall into the trap of assuming a kind of given, almost *natural*, link between Blackness and a working-class, disrupted family background. Second, there is misrecognition in a more everyday sense, that teachers fail to recognise the middle-classness of Black middle-class parents because their raced identity takes priority. As Lorriane notes, there is a sense in which the very identity of being Black *and* middle-class is 'difficult' for teachers to comprehend:

I think I'm seen because I'm the kind of parent that does go into school … knowing what my rights are and having read up on subjects, I think that the staff in the school find me difficult. And that is to do with class and its expectations … Along with being uncomfortable about this is a middle-class Black woman. They are not used to dealing with that [laughs] and if I were a middle-class White woman they'd find it easier. I just don't meet their expectations.

(Lorraine)

While professional status and particular forms of cultural capital (knowledge about the education system for example) are helpful, they can serve, as Lorraine notes, to increase the amount of labour (or concerted work) that Black parents have to do, as they attempt to counter and navigate around the discomfort of White school staff. As Valentine notes (2007), 'when individual identities are "done" differently in particular temporal moments, they rub up against and so expose the dominant spatial ordering that defines who is in place/out of place, who belongs and who does not' (2007: 19). In this sense, our interviewees are often treated as being 'out of place', unusual, an anomaly since being Black, in the UK, is commonly read as being working class. This is a theme to which we return in Chapter 7. In dealing with these and other pressures, Black middle-class parents adopt a range of strategies both in relation to their engagement with the education system and within society more broadly. We focus in this chapter on their engagement with the education system.

Strategies, dispositions and cultural capitals

> That's one of the strategies that I've actually advised other parents to do.
>
> *(Anne)*

All of the 62 parents in this research place great value on education and academic achievement. The parents commonly monitor their children's academic progress and speak with them about their experiences at school and their aspirations for the future. They draw upon a range of strategies intended to enhance their children's educational experiences, and are all ready to intervene at school if they judge it necessary. At the time of the interviews almost a third (20 out of 62) are, or had been, involved with a governing body or active in Parent/Teacher Associations (PTAs). Detailed analysis of the parents' orientations towards schooling, however, reveals some important variations in practice, which can be thought of as differences of strategy, priorities, actions and intensity of involvement. We can best illustrate these differences by considering the cases of Margaret and Michael, and Claudette.

Margaret and Michael are a couple; she is a senior corporate manager while he runs his own business. They moved their children from private to state school, citing the latter as more ethnically diverse and better value for money. They display a strong focus on academic achievement:

> Before he started at the [state] school I wrote to the headmaster and ... to the deputy head ... 'My child is coming to your school, he's always gone to private school, but I love your school. But be warned I have very high expectations of my child, so my message is do not mess up!'
>
> *(Michael)*

> We couldn't really fault [the state school] and I tried very hard to fault it because I ... didn't want to fall into this notion that because the school is local and it's not fee paying we would send him there.
>
> *(Margaret)*

I not only want [my child] to do really well in his GCSEs, I want him to do very well. *Very* well.

(*Margaret*)

Despite the couple's choice of strongly academically oriented secondary schools, all their children have extra tutoring because, Michael says, 'it makes you go that extra step'. Michael and Margaret also believe in giving their children a strong steer in terms of their future direction, and in this way they differ from many parents in the study who spoke of not wishing to or indeed being prevented from (by the young people themselves) directing their children in particular ways:

I would like [my son] to study at one of the best universities in the world (...) I think we fail our children in leaving them to make their own decisions. (...) This year we've organised for [our eldest] to shadow one of the chief executives at a ... global PR company.

(*Michael*)

All of this is informed by an awareness of the continued existence of racism and discrimination against Black young people, and a history of low academic attainment in state schools, particularly for boys.

Claudette is a policy advisor. She self-identifies as mixed race and Black British; her son is educated at state school. Claudette's view differs from that of Michael and Margaret in a number of ways. Like them she is proactive in relation to her children's education but, in stark contrast to Michael's view that 'we fail our children in leaving them to make their own decisions', Claudette emphasises the degree of space that she has allowed her son to make his own choices over his education, 'I never, for any of my children, told them to go to college, and when [my son] was dithering, I just said "don't go if you don't want to".'

[He] has been allowed to have his own way of thinking to a certain extent at home (...) it's allowed him to make up his own mind about certain things, to find his own level of motivation. It's also kids having an opinion and being able to express that opinion [that's important].

[My sister] raises her kids [as we were raised] in the sense of complete control over what they do and looking at their homework ... She would make the kids redo and redo their homework.

To use Bourdieu's terms, we see here two key areas of subtle difference between Claudette, and Margaret and Michael. The first is in terms of the relative priority given to schooling and academic achievement. This, we suggest, is a difference in dispositions, in terms of what feels 'right' and 'natural' to parents in relation to their parenting and their priorities for their children – what could be called a family habitus. The second set of differences lies in the possession and activation of capitals. There are differences in the possession of economic resources between these two families, the cultural goods they possess and the kinds of social networks to which they belong. Indeed, Claudette appears less firmly established in the middle-class than Margaret and Michael. For example, while Margaret has no difficulty identifying herself as middle-class, Claudette is ambivalent, and says 'Nobody has ever considered me to be middle class, never.' Margaret, Michael and Claudette represent opposite ends of a continuum of involvement that can be discerned when Black middle-class parents in the study explain their approach to dealing with schools and teachers; in the next section we consider the continuum and different clusters of parent positioning that emerge from the data.

A continuum of involvement

In order to better understand the strategies, actions and priorities of the parents with regard to their children's education, we examined a range of factors including differences between them in social positioning, dispositions towards education, and also the differing degrees to which they possess (and activate) economic, social and cultural capitals (see Introduction). The Black middle-class parents in this study fall into four main groupings or clusters along a continuum. At one end there are those who are *determined to get the best* (such as Margaret and Michael above) while in the middle are those who are *being watchful and circumspect* and those with *a fighting chance*. At the other end of the continuum are parents (such as Claudette above) who prioritise other factors and might be described as *hoping for the best*.[1] There are few consistent differences in parental priorities and strategies according to respondent's income, occupation or educational attainment, although there are tendencies, which we detail later in this chapter, according to the gender of the children or the child's grandparents' class position/attitude towards education.

Determined to get the best

Excellence was my criteria.

(Isabelle)

Parents at this end of the continuum display the following characteristics. They are clear about their long-term planning, tutoring or moving house to get their children into particular identified schools, or perhaps moving into an area with lots of 'good' schools when children are young in anticipation of their later needs. Isabelle provides an example of this long-term strategising. When her daughter, then aged five, was not accepted for entry to an independent school, she and her husband arranged tutoring for the child, who sat the exam twice more before gaining a place: 'I never really considered her not getting through [the exam] … It wasn't an option her not getting in.'

Some, but by no means all, of this cluster use private schools. However, all share an intense focus on academic achievement: 'We wanted them to be in a school where the general ethos was unambiguously achievement – academic achievement oriented' (Robert). Their trust in the school system, especially the state system, is very limited (often because of their own experiences – see Chapters 3 and 7), and several talk about their perception that state schools are too ready to accept 'mediocrity' in levels of attainment, a settlement which they refused for their own children (see Cynthia above). Isabelle has similar concerns: 'Excellence was my criteria (…) No teacher was going to do that to [my daughter], decide how far she could go.' Here, on the issue of seemingly entrenched low expectations of Black children, race and class come together in a family habitus that insists both on the child achieving highly, and the teacher having high expectations of the child.

For these parents the possession and activation of cultural, social and economic capital makes possible the extra tutoring and activities that abound. The home becomes a site of pedagogy and also 'exposure' to high-status cultural activities.

> [My daughter is] an all rounder, she's done a lot of things. I've made sure she's experienced lots of things that I have never had a chance to experience. She's travelled a lot (…) she plays the clarinet, she plays the guitar, she does horse riding. She recently returned from the USA, she was one of a group of 12 young people that was sponsored …
>
> *(Malorie)*

As noted above, this cluster also maintains high levels of surveillance of the school and are ready to argue in defence of their children's interests. Joan, for example, eventually persuaded her daughter's primary school to move her up a year group for literacy and numeracy: 'That [experience] taught me a lesson, that I had to fight for my child's education. Otherwise she will become mediocre. The system will allow her to become mediocre because that is all they want to deal with.'

There is a tendency for this cluster to have high levels of educational qualifications and incomes towards the mid–high end of the scale (upwards of £60,000 p.a.), and to self-identify, sometimes reluctantly, as middle class (see Chapter 1).

Being watchful and circumspect

> I make sure that they are not under the radar.
>
> *(Alice)*

In the middle of the continuum of parental involvement there are two clusters that show a mixture of occupations, incomes, educational qualifications and attitudes towards a middle-class raced identity. The main identifying attribute of one cluster is *watchfulness*. Although achievement is important, these respondents do not display the intense focus of the *Determined* cluster, and tend not to indulge in long-term planning to ensure achievement above all else. Watchfulness is not, however, a passive state. These parents actively monitor, they ask questions and they act on their observations. In general, however, this cluster does not see the need for and/or have not had experiences that result in radical action (such as moving schools).

Their involvement, like Anne's (below), comprises taking the initiative – and thus challenging stereotypes of Black parents as uninterested – but they generally remain within the limited boundaries of what schools judge to be 'appropriate' parental involvement (see Vincent 1996). That is, they email questions and ask for meetings, they draw teachers' attention to (and the phrase is a considered one) their concerns, suggesting, in effect, that they adopt a more proactive role as partner with the school. Their relationships with school are largely positive (which is not to say that they have unlimited amounts of trust in the professionals). Being proactive is a feature of all the parents' accounts, although the *Hoping* cluster (below) are less proactive than others. For this *Watchful* cluster, proactivity consists largely of monitoring the child, monitoring the school and making sure the teachers are aware of the particular 'needs' of their child.

> He's just started secondary school and I'm seeing some traits of the same children that I'm working with, who are underachieving and who are at risk of being excluded, in my son and I'm thinking to myself, I need to devise a strategy to ensure that this boy achieves. One of the things I'm seeing, I'm identifying that there's this lethargy about homework, peer pressure, I'm seeing a lack of interest in the curriculum, I'm seeing in a sense some stereotyping from perhaps some of the teachers, maybe one or two, and since I've identified that, I've probably been down to the school twice now, just to check on him, make sure how he's doing, make sure his work is up to date. And I discovered a few things that I need to work on, like not handing in homework.
>
> *(Anne)*

> At every single stage of my child's education, I make sure that they are not under the radar. This is ridiculous how much I bother their teachers to make sure that they know that there is a child here.
>
> *(Alice)*

Anne consciously describes her visits to school as a 'strategy' – one she shares with other parents – and views it as raising the profile of her child while challenging the stereotypical misrecognition of Black parents as uniformly uninterested:

> I'm very much in contact with the school because that's one of the strategies that I've actually advised other parents to do when they suspect that their children are underachieving or know that their children are underachieving (…) The teachers have been very, very supportive, but also very surprised that I've wanted to see them before parents' evening or before they asked me to.
>
> *(Anne)*

As they have fairly frequent monitoring interactions with the schools, it is in this cluster that we can clearly see the ways in which the parents 'do conversation' (dialogue, engaging with the institution: Vincent and Martin 2002). This requires a careful balance so as to be interested and engaged without being condemned as 'pushy'. As Eleanor notes:

> You've got to sort of play a game in a way (…) you don't want to come across as a know-it-all because people will perceive you in a different way, so sometimes you have got to sort of, what I call 'humble', play it down a bit. But at the same time you have got to be able to show people that you know what you are talking about and when it comes to your child you will stand up for them.
>
> *(Eleanor)*

Similarly Cassandra speaks of deploying her class resources to alter or pre-empt racist stereotyping:

> Class is about having a professional standing, having a certain level of aware-ness and understanding of your place in the world and how you can impact on things around you. And so I think that class and being a Black middle-class woman has occasionally allowed me to (…), transcend being a Black woman.
>
> *(Cassandra)*

The dangers of naming racism

Cassandra suggests that her reasoning, non-threatening style avoiding explicit men-tion of race and racism, backed up by her and her husband's professional status, improves the chances of her voice being heard (we examine this further in Chapter 7). For example, she describes 'gently' prompting her daughter's head teacher to introduce more multi-ethnic books in school.

> They changed all the books. It was awesome really. This is perhaps another example where class and race can merge. I did not go in there as, you know, 'we are Black people and you should not have this and that and the other.' [Rather] 'it is a little bit dated and it would be really good … if the children could have resources that would reflect their experiences.' Well [coming from] Black parents who work in business and medicine, whatever, [the head teacher] took it on board.
>
> *(Cassandra)*

This is a successful strategy and in the school's purchase of the new books, she achieves the result she is looking for. However, to describe her demeanour as *simply* a strategy, a ploy, a form of performance, would be to downplay the embodied dispositions and capitals that form her identity, her investment in particular classed forms of respectability and 'appropriate' behaviour (Skeggs 2004).

Ella, with a child at a private school, echoes Cassandra's view of the need to engage schools using a particular style of demeanour and language:

> [Teachers at the school] have a lot of pressure from the parents and my feeling is, you know, you watch what they are doing, because education is too important to leave to the teachers alone, but they do have expertise and you have got to respect that. So you keep a sort of watchful eye on what's going on, but you've got to work with them (...) You have to be careful of your language and be very circumspect in how you challenge people in authority. I don't think they like to have things rammed down their throats or shoved in their faces, and so I tend to be very circumspect in how you deal with them, but it got the same result.
>
> *(Ella)*

Ella describes a particular example of how this strategy can play out and is especially careful ('circumspect') in relation to the issue of *addressing* racism without *naming* it as such; after several incidents, she began to question the validity of the reprimands issued to her son:

> So I had to work with the head of the middle school to alert her to the fact that this was going on and she was very sensible. I found she was very sensible in her approach. I didn't have to spell out too obviously what my concerns were. I think she was very able to read between the lines. (...) Some of the playground assistants ... it was a training issue and yeah they've got a difficult job to do, trying to watch so many children, and I think sometimes they went for the easy option of not always finding out what actually happened. If you're not careful some children could receive a label or a tag which they would have to struggle to shake off. We just kept a very close eye on it and made sure the appropriate people were aware ...
>
> *(Ella)*

By positioning the adults' behaviour towards her son as due to a lack of training, Ella goes to some lengths to avoid explicitly naming racism. In her second interview we explored this in more detail and she makes it clear that this is a conscious strategy:

> I have never actually been in a situation where I have gone out and said 'you are racist' or 'I think this is an act of racism'. It is something I am very reluctant to do because you get *shut down* [claps her hands emphatically] (...) once you mention to people you think they have been racist, they clam up. But what you *can* say is that 'this behaviour is a problem ... how can we tackle it and turn it round?'
>
> *(Ella)*

Careful strategic consideration of the appropriate conversational tactics allows some parents to maintain a channel for dialogue with their children's school, in order for them to monitor as closely as possible both child *and* school. While monitoring and surveillance is common among White middle-class parents (e.g. James *et al.* 2010) Black middle-class parents have to work against a range of racist stereotypes (of both themselves and their children) which, by definition, do not pose a problem for their White peers. As a form of resistance and refusal of such stereotypes, Black middle-class parents in the *watchful* cluster use their dress, speech and demeanour to position themselves as knowledgeable, interested, enthusiastic and proactive in their dealings with schools. Femi, for example, describes investing in a particularly visible form of 'good' mothering to combat racial stereotypes. This is working at the intersections of class, race and gender – intersectional identity work, in other words.

> I won't let my daughter go to school unless everything is ironed, her shoes are polished (…) There's no way she's looking scruffy because I will not let people make that judgment about her …
>
> NR: What judgment about her?
>
> That if you're Black, you're working class, you're scruffy, you don't care and that's all you ever can be (…) we've always made sure her lunch box and everything in it, you know, there is a real pressure there to make sure that everything in it is healthy and just right and seen to be just right; it's not just that it's got to be right and appropriate, it's got be *seen* to be appropriate. We make sure that when we fill in letters for the school, we don't keep them at home for two or three days, they go back immediately the next day.
>
> *(Femi)*

A fighting chance

> I know how the systems work and how to escalate things.
>
> *(Juliet)*

This cluster contains those who step outside the boundaries of what most schools judge to be appropriate behaviour by challenging the school directly, sometimes in connection with their own child, but also on wider issues to do with inequality and injustice. Here race and racism are often named explicitly in parents' interactions with schools. Parents in all the clusters speak of assumptions and expectations which ignore, disadvantage and discriminate against Black children: what Linda describes as 'cultural racism'. It is in this third cluster, however, that parents translate their individual experiences of low expectations and/or stereotyping into collective concerns, on which they take action:

> So when OFSTED came I gave them every single email that I sent, every single response that I've had back and [the school] came out 'unsatisfactory' on community engagement.
>
> *(Patricia)*

> There was one particular teacher who used to pick on [my daughter] all the time and I wrote some very stroppy letters to the school, because I do like a good stroppy letter. And I said [my daughter] has told me things and other parents have told me things, I don't know whether this has been fed back to you, but I am getting the impression that there are a particular set of girls who all seem to be girls of colour who are not treated the same way as others. And I asked the headmistress to look into it, and that teacher left shortly after. But I will yeah, if [daughter] does something wrong she knows that I will come down on her like a ton of bricks, but if she's in the right and people haven't bothered to ask her the actual story, I will also defend her all the way and I don't care how far I go (…) I know how the systems work and how to escalate things.
>
> *(Juliet)*

Whereas parents in the *watchful* cluster try to work within the school's notion of 'appropriate' language and behaviour, parents in the *fighting chance* cluster are prepared to step outside these boundaries, often in quite deliberate ways. We suggest that some of the parents we identify as 'watchful' may well take up a 'fighting chance' position if compelled to do so by particular circumstances within the school. This is clearly an area which warrants further examination in future research. We turn to Juliet, who we categorise as located in the 'fighting chance' group. Dissatisfied with what she perceived to be unfair and unprofessional behaviour by a senior teacher, she challenged her directly:

> I said to [my daughter] 'OK look here you are going to have to leave the room now and I need to talk to your teacher and this is something you don't need to see.' I said 'I don't know who you think you are talking to but this is my child she needs a decent education and it is your job to give it to her.' (…) I'm sorry but sometimes people just need to be told things about themselves. I don't like having to do it (…) this teacher has been very off with me ever since, but she's done what I asked.
>
> *(Juliet)*

Respondents across the sample are aware that, even if they themselves do not feel marginalised in a school system dominated by what Jean calls 'the language of Whiteness', other Black parents might. In response, many, especially in this cluster, feel compelled – driven by a connection to a wider notion of Black identity and struggle – to support other Black parents or to raise awareness through, for example, offering resources for Black History Month. As Jean notes: 'Sometimes you don't want to be championing everything because you're Black but actually if you don't then who will?' Her comment speaks poignantly to the way issues of race and cultural diversity still remain marginalised within the school context. It is in this cluster, therefore, that we see a shift away from the individualism normally understood to characterise (White) middle-class families (e.g. Ball 2003a; Jordan *et al.*

1994), as Black middle-class parents speak out against discrimination and prejudice inherent in a White-dominated education system.

Hoping for the best

> Education is important but (…) my children's happiness is far more important.
>
> *(Elsa)*

At the other end of the continuum from the *determined* cluster are those parents, like Claudette (whom we described earlier in this chapter in contrast to Michael and Margaret), who might be thought of as *hoping for the best*. Here we use the word 'hope' not as a vague, wishful fantasy, but in the sense of a critically informed hope born from a recognition of the complex and dangerous situation facing Black children in the English school system.[2] One of the defining features of this cluster is that academic achievement is viewed as important but not at almost any cost; the family habitus is one that allows more space for the child's *own* voice. These parents are proactive with regard to education and their children's achievement and well-being, but less focused on school and schooling. Elsa comments: 'Education is important but at the end of the day my children's happiness is far more important.' Similarly:

> I want him to get his grades, I want him to pass, but, I just don't think, I don't want him to be all, it's got to be all As. You know, just get some decent grades and then move to the next, the next step.
>
> *(Anita)*

Anita deliberately avoids putting pressure on her son, whom she describes as 'not academic in any shape or form'. Nevertheless, now aged 14, she feels that he has learnt important lessons and is doing 'really, really well':

> He found for himself that [other children in bottom sets] behaved really badly and he couldn't learn. He found he realised that what we were saying is true. I think that's not having pressure, giving him time to kind of grow up (…) He's doing really well at school. Really, really well. He's not in the top set but I think he's in B set for most things. And then a couple of C sets.
>
> *(Anita)*

Anita's description of her son as 'doing really well' and yet not being placed in the top teaching sets would be an oxymoron for parents in the *determined* cluster, but here parents are prioritising a different view of their children's best interests and reflecting a different understanding of the world, a different family habitus.

Another defining feature of this cluster is that a local (though not necessarily the nearest) school is understood as important, and for some, state school is a political priority:

> We believe state education is really important. We've got friends who send
> their children to private school (…) we couldn't do that.
>
> *(June)*

In some cases parents are restrained from too much contact with school or too
much monitoring by the resistance of their teenagers. 'Oh my children didn't want
me to go anywhere. "No please don't do anything. Leave it" (…) she said "Oh no
mum, please don't go to school." OK, that's fine with me' (Anthea). Catherine is
less sanguine. About her son, whom she considers to be underperforming, she says:

> He is strong minded and when I say [he] resists parenting; as a parent there
> will be things that I want to do or certain responsibilities I feel I have which
> [he] resists. Whereas he is resisting on the grounds that I'm coming at them
> from an academic, with my academic hat on, or my educationalist hat on, not
> my parenting hat on. So there will be other parents that are *allowed* to get
> more involved in their child's education and in their homework and every-
> thing else, but I'm held at bay.
>
> *(Catherine)*

This induces considerable frustration, as she considers her son to be 'below the
radar' at school. Illustrating the school's low expectations (Chapter 3), she notes:
'Because he's [seen by his teachers as] a nice boy and not kicking off, he's almost
being allowed to underperform.' However, Catherine persists in the arena that she
can more fully control – her son's out-of-school time, insisting on a range of activities, including music lessons.

Having outlined the key characteristics of each cluster, we must reiterate that the
differences between clusters are fairly subtle and are differences in attitude and priorities. There may be some similarity in practices, for example many of the *hopeful*
cluster use tutors on occasion, and likewise most of their children have been
involved in doing extra-curricular activities. Interestingly, there is a tendency for
the parents in the *hopeful* cluster to be education 'insiders'. Most have education to
degree level themselves and have incomes towards the mid–low end of the scale
(£40,000 and under), and express reluctance about or refusal to see themselves as
middle class.

Conclusions

In this chapter we have explored the numerous strategies that our interviewees use
as they negotiate the education system, whether in state-funded or private schools.
There are no guarantees of success and the variety of approaches demonstrates the
complexity and uncertainty of the situation (see Rollock 2012a, 2012b). For parents like Robert the *determination* to achieve the highest levels of academic achievement is the dominant driving force. At the other end of a continuum of differing
styles of interaction with school are parents like Elsa, Anita and June who explicitly

prioritise a wider range of factors, including their children's health and happiness, their wider political solidarities, or the importance of taking seriously their children's own wishes and desires. These parents prioritise a wider range of concerns and are *hopeful* of protecting and supporting their children as they grow and find their way in society. Between these contrasting positions are groups of parents who can be seen to adopt two broad types of approach. The first is those like Alice and Anne who frequently visit the school and ensure that their children do not fall 'under the radar'. These parents are extremely *watchful* and concerned but also take care to strike a balance in their interactions with schools – as Eleanor puts it, trying to avoid being seen as 'a know-it-all' but simultaneously demonstrating that 'you know what you are talking about' and need to be taken seriously. More outspoken are the parents, such as Jean, who sometimes consciously decide to step outside the limits of polite/non-threatening codes that she describes as 'the language of Whiteness'. These parents are often involved in *fighting* for justice alongside other parents and, when the situation is judged to require it, they are prepared, in Juliet's carefully chosen words, to 'escalate things'.

In order to help navigate and chart the differing parental approaches we have used heuristic labels to describe these broad clusters that emerge in our interviews: those who are determined to get the best; those who are watchful and circumspect; parents who strive for a fighting chance; and those hoping for the best amid a myriad of sometimes conflicting priorities. But, as we have tried to stress, none of these positions are simple or static. And none of them are passive; each cluster represents an active engagement with schools and teachers; the variety reflects not only differences in family dispositions and habitus, but also the sheer uncertainty of striving for health and success as a Black parent in a system where misrecognition and stereotyping are a constant threat. In the next part of the book, we look at how these same motivations play out in relation to the wider issues raised by the relationship between the Black middle-class and society.

Notes

1 It should be noted, of course, that our interviews present a snapshot of a particular point in time and that parents' level and focus of involvement do not necessarily remain static over their children's school careers. Thus parents might cluster at different points on the continuum at different moments in their parenting histories, although we believe that movement from one end of the continuum to the other is unlikely.

2 For a discussion of different understandings of the notion of hope within a critical perspective see Bozalek *et al.* (forthcoming).

PART II

The Black middle classes and society

6

'MAKING UP' THE HEALTHY BLACK MIDDLE-CLASS CHILD

It was important for them to have a sense of identity.

Introduction

This chapter explores the strategies, perspectives and priorities that shape the parenting of the Black middle-class child. We refer to this as a process of 'making up' (borrowing from Vincent and Ball 2007[1]) in an attempt to attend to the complexity of factors, skills and, in many cases, explicit strategising involved. This is a process which is fluid, subject to revision and renegotiation depending on parents' perceptions about their child's personality and specific life experiences or events. Educating the Black child involves, for many, not simply the formal acquisition of schooling and qualifications but also making decisions about the type of child they seek to develop who will be well-placed, resourced, confident and able to succeed professionally and in wider society.

We begin by examining the ways in which parents nurture and endeavour to reinforce Black identity in their child and how they attempt to prepare their children for managing racism. These are matters deemed crucial to surviving and negotiating British society which (all but a small minority of) participants consider racist and saturated by an abundance of negative, stereotypical images of Black people. These are difficult and sometimes painful conversations where the sheer weight and magnitude of the challenges confronting respondents is made starkly apparent. These decisions and the thinking upon which they are based are also inflected, sometimes incisively, by the gender of the child. As we shall see below, parents report differing considerations and concerns that come to bear, depending on the child's gender. We conclude the chapter by examining parents' views and reactions with regard to their child's friendship groups. Our focus is primarily on the relative importance that parents attach to the ethnic and class mix of these groups and the anticipated consequences of this on their child's development.

Preparing the Black child for a racist society

Most participants involved in our study talk about the continuing salience of racism and the need to prepare their children for a racist society. Interestingly, unlike Ochieng's 2010 study into child-rearing practices among Black families, not all of our participants regard being Black – or preparedness to manage racism – as central to the way they raise their children. As with parents' conceptualisations of Black identity and consciousness (discussed in Chapter 1), we note variations in the under-standing of racism and in approaches to dealing with it (Reynolds 2005). Broadly, those parents who we locate towards one end of the identity continuum – those who are consciously or collectively Black – are also those who appear to have thought most deeply about and have a language for making sense of their experi-ences of race and racism. Those (two parents) for whom being Black is merely an incidental aspect of their identity tend to downplay the relative importance of race as a factor influencing how they raise their children. Again, it is not always possible to tease apart concerns about developing a child with a healthy Black identity from those that centre on racism. As already stated, the two closely intersect. The thought and proactive planning around developing a strong Black identity – evident in some of our parents – is, in part, about serving as protection from and readying for White society.

In this regard, Cynthia provides a useful starting point for our analysis. We introduced her in Chapter 1 as embodying a collective Black identity that observes a sense of fit, connection and responsibility to older and younger generations as central to the way that she thinks of herself. Dismayed by the assumption by her children's school (voiced by teachers at a parent-teacher meeting) that Black boys are most likely to underachieve academically, she made the decision to home school them, committed to the belief that a strong sense of 'grounding' – what we might think of as *racial socialisation* – is crucial to their identity:

> ... I need to give my boys a grounding through their primary and junior years. I have to do that for them. (...) They need to know their history. They need to know where they came from. I don't just mean the Caribbean. I mean back to Africa, the journey from Africa to the Caribbean. Their history doesn't start with slavery as is taught. They need to know about the inven-tors, the great kings and queens. They need to know about the influence that Black people have had on this country. They're not aliens in this country. They have every right to be here. They are a part of society. Their parents and grandparents, you know, they fought in the wars. They have family that have fought and died for this country (...) but only *I* can speak that into their lives and I spend a lot of time doing it as well. I just make no apology for it.
>
> *(Cynthia)*

Cynthia regards this cultural and historical foundation as a central and necessary requirement to help ensure that her children (note that these are boys, gender is important here) are able to survive in a 'predominantly White society'. Her passion and commitment to this end is reflected during the interview and in the extract above by the detail of her account (these are clearly matters to which she has given some thought) and by the emphatic repetition of phrases such as 'they need' and 'they have' along with the succinct staccato of her sentences. This is about working to ensure that her sons are 'comfortable in their skin when they're mixing with other cultures'. What is evident is the way in which societal perceptions about Blackness (especially of Black boys) directly inform the manner in which Cynthia strives to raise and protect her sons. Parenting, in this instance, is not an incidental or casual activity – she is home-schooling her children and speaks of the challenges of only relying on her husband's salary as income – there is concerted effort, active planning and strategising involved in the attempt to ensure that her children, her boys, are ready for what lies ahead.

While the parenting work is not as structured or formal, concerns about Black identity also exist for Robert who is someone who speaks quite explicitly about the importance of a Black identity to his experiences and self-perception. Describing how he cultivates this in his children, he explains:

> … I certainly felt it was important for them to have a sense of identity. I don't think that we felt any compelling need to … (…) we have not felt a need to be involved in something structured, which focused on their identity because we have a circle of friends who are all like us in a way. They are professional people. When I say circle of friends I mean a circle of Black friends who are all professional people. They are all highly educated, they are all aware of where they have come from, where they want to go. So they [the children] have got enough, in our view, people who occupy appropriate strata in our society. So (…), it is not obvious to us that they need role models to be consciously provided for them, no, because there are people within our circle who are doctors or dentists, lawyers and so on. I am [an academic], my wife is [a professional] and so on. So the issue of any belief that they (…) couldn't achieve, and that they couldn't see other Black people achieving was not relevant to them.

It should be noted that Robert's children are considerably older than Cynthia's. They are university age (and above) and this is bound to have a significant bearing on attitude towards parenting and parental influence. However, Robert also has a discernible network of 'people like us' who in a very Bourdieusian sense share a similar occupational status, tastes and cultural preferences and form part of the everyday environment of his children's lives. Less concerted effort therefore goes into making up the Black middle-class habitus of his children; there is less of an imperative to be part of something structured. Common to both parents, though transmitted in fundamentally different ways, is a desire to instil in their children the possibility – indeed, the expectation – of Black success. Again, the context of raising Black children in a predominantly White society is pertinent here as is the recognition of the damaging consequences of racism. In fact, everyday racism (that is the more subtle acts of racial subjugation and stereotyping) is regarded as such a given, normal aspect of life that any Black person who questions its existence is regarded with suspicion:

> If another Black person says to me, 'There aren't any issues, we are all equal, racism isn't a problem' depending on who it was I would say, 'Well you've got your head in the clouds because the reality is very different.' I just see that society for me personally is still very negative towards Black people and instead of just being in your face it has just gone underground ...
>
> *(Lorraine)*

Sandrine echoes Lorraine's sentiment describing, in the extract which follows, the perceived shift in cultural thinking and identity that has occurred with her brother who, in her words, has 'married White' and 'all his friends were White':

> He couldn't understand conversations any more. Like we'd be having a conversation about something and he ... you could tell it was just 'whoosh' [sweeps hand over head] he just didn't understand it. We could speak (...) in Patois and he could do that but he didn't understand the essence of what was being said. He lost it because he'd moved out of that realm, out of that circle (...). He almost didn't understand that racism existed. (...) He had this really sort of colour blind approach, it was 'Oh yeah, everyone does that' or 'That happens to everyone' or ... he almost, he seemed ... And he actually said one day 'I've never been discriminated against', and I thought to myself, and I said are you sure or is it because you just didn't notice. And he said 'No, I don't see things like that.'

We highlight similarities in thinking and behaviour between Sandrine's brother and those parents we identify as 'incidentally Black' (see Chapter 1). There is little investment in a collective Black identity and he denies (according to his sister) ever having experienced racism. Sandrine highlights the fact that her brother's wife, friends *and* the area in which he lives are White and this is regarded as a central aspect of or as signalling his racial positioning. Further, while several participants speak of the advantages of using Patois (Chapter 8) when in particular Black spaces or of code-switching when in mainly White spaces (Hewitt 1986) Sandrine's brother is unable to connect with this as a form of cultural adhesive. He misses the 'essence' – the cultural energy – of what is being said. Fanon's thesis that some Black people appropriate unquestioningly the 'language of the civilizing nation' while renouncing Blackness (here Patois) may have pertinence here (Fanon 1967: 9; also hooks 1990). There are similarities in the articulation of his identity with Miles who, it was noted in Chapter 1, also tends not to regard his ethnicity as a key factor in shaping his decisions in relation to his children and their education. He also differs considerably from the majority of respondents involved in the study in the way he talks about and imagines he would handle racism. When asked, for example, about how he would handle a potentially racist situation at his son's school Miles is confident that existing policies and procedures are sufficient and rigorous enough to ensure that the situation will be satisfactorily resolved: 'You would go to the authorities and you say exactly what has happened and thanks very much goodbye, see you later.' Asked to detail how he would manage a situation if his son's *teacher* were found to have behaved in a racially discriminatory manner, he elaborates:

> Well as his parent I would confront that. I would go in and actually say this is the incident. Can you explain it to me? And if I wasn't satisfied with the outcome of that (…) we would then go to the Head, and if we weren't happy with the outcome with the Head we would go to the [Local] Authority. I mean at the end of the day this is what the system is for. It is for everybody to say actually right, if you are not happy with that incident and actually it has not been dealt with to your satisfaction then move on to the next stage up. That is the only obvious thing that I can say.
>
> NR: And would you say that you considered it was racist?
>
> Yes totally, if it were. I think you would be pretty stupid with the policies as they are (…) you would be excluded if you were a teacher and it came out that this (…) smacks of being racist [if you were] then to turn round and say, well think what you like. Well then I would automatically say to myself alright then, let's go to the next stage and actually then pull that person in and [ask] the Head [to come] in and find out what their thoughts are.'

Miles' confidence and reliance on protocol stands out compared with others involved in our study. Indeed, his approach to handling racism is very different from the majority of respondents; he has to imagine a potentially racist situation whereas other parents are able to draw on a repertoire of examples. Interestingly, he also does not speak (like others) of the careful micropolitics or emotional challenges involved when naming racism to White others. He does not expect to encounter resistance along the way. He posits, without hesitation, that he would name the situation as 'racist' if the evidence supported it. Contrast this with Ella, the mother of two primary school children. Whereas Miles has to draw upon a fabricated racist incident to illustrate his argument and struggles with conceptualising racism, Ella has several examples upon which she is readily able to draw – with some pain – throughout the course of the interview. In the situation below, she considers how she would react if her son's teacher behaved in a racist manner:

> If it was something which was a particular teacher in the school who was clearly being consistently racist to him I would have to go in and deal with it. I would have to go in and talk to the teacher, I would have to find out you know what was going on. I have never actually been in a situation where I

have gone out and said, 'You are racist', or 'I think this is an act of racism'. It is something I am very very reluctant to do because you get [slaps hands firmly together] shut down. You get shut down. So although I might acknowledge [to my son] that yes I think this might very much have been racist I am going to go in and deal with it. (...) [my approach would be] 'I am going to try and sort out this situation with you' because I think once you mention to people that you think they have been racist, they clam up but what you can do is you can say that 'this behaviour was a problem'. I am not going to say why it was a problem, in other words 'I think it was a problem because you were racist'. I am going to look at (...) the behaviour that was a problem, how can we tackle it and turn it round?

(Ella)

A willingness to go into the school to explore a means of addressing the problem indicates a desire, on the part of both parents, to protect their child from what is clearly understood to be unacceptable behaviour. However, here the similarity ends. Unlike Miles, Ella makes no mention of formal school policies or guidelines and instead concentrates her focus on nuanced, complex and emotive sensitivities often provoked when the word 'racism' is mentioned. In detailing her *modus operandi* with the school, Ella stresses that it is fundamental to have 'strategies for dealing with professional people'. She is careful, vigilant. She is aware of the power that teachers hold and the ways in which they 'can influence the way things go for your children (...) and make it a very difficult year'. This observation carries considerable salience in the context of the now firmly established body of research charting the differential school experiences of Black pupils (e.g. Gillborn 1999; Ofsted 2001; Wright 1992; Youdell 2003).

Concerns about how to manage racism personally as an adult and how to transmit these strategies to their children are a matter of significant worry for the majority of parents involved in our research. As Ochieng (2010: 65) observes with regard to the families in her study, 'While it is questionable if any amount of preparation can sufficiently dull the pain of racism, families felt that it was important to prepare and teach their children to recognise the existence of racism (...) and how it continues to survive.' There is, on the one hand, a keen imperative to prepare the child for mainstream society and, on the other, a profound worry and reluctance to present the child with the illogical, painful realities of an inequality based on nothing other than the inescapable fact of their Blackness. Richard, for example, worries that his children are too young to discuss racism and his related concerns about their being stereotyped, as Black boys, by teachers at school:

It is difficult because I don't want them to be ... you see I don't want to give them any kind of crutch. You know I don't want to start ... that is the other extreme you see ... and that is why people have that: 'Oh no no, race hasn't been an issue!' Of course it has been an issue. I don't care who you are, race has been an issue, positively or negatively.

(Richard)

This relatively brief comment encapsulates quite evocatively some of the complexities and the psychic violence of racism. Richard recognises how debilitating coming to an awareness of racism can be, especially for young children (his sons were nine and ten years old), and is concerned that this awareness is not subsequently used as an excuse for his children not to achieve. At the same time, he notes 'the other extreme' where their lack of understanding might potentially lead to a naïve, colour-blind approach. He speaks, at one stage in the interview, of his struggle in wanting to both prepare and protect them, laughing at himself saying, 'You can't go around everywhere they go, when they go for a job interview, you can't go, "My son's coming in, please don't stereotype him".' Again, this reveals the extent to which racism is seen as an embedded taken-for-granted part of everyday life. Richard sets out his concerns further:

> I want them to know that it can happen, acknowledge when it is happening, be bright enough to acknowledge when it is happening and deal with it appropriately. But if you start expecting it, you start to deal with people the way they deal with you and then you have lost straight away and that is bad for so many reasons, I can't even be bothered to go into it. (…) it is a complicated issue and unless it is tackled from a number of different ends you can't really do anything about it. In this situation all I can do is deal with my boys and say to them, 'Look' and it has to be done gradually in increments you see. I can't lay all that on them at one point. I can't say to them, [serious voice] 'There is racism, people are going to be racist towards you, so you have to do this'. (…) [If I do] it will become a crutch potentially for them: 'I didn't do so well because I am Black' [or] 'I didn't get this because I'm Black'. I would cry for days if that ever happened to my kids you know (…) So many people have done that to their children (…) saying 'well, you are not going to do anything or you can't do anything because you're Black'. (…) they are not [really] saying that but what they [mean] is 'people aren't going to give you a fair shake because you are Black'…

While Richard deliberates about how to broach the subject of racism to his sons Femi is, by comparison, unequivocal and unapologetic in her stance, insisting that her ten-year-old daughter 'has to see things for what they are'. This is largely informed by the fact that as a young woman Femi was told that her own experiences of unfairness and inequality were *not* the result of racism. This led her to believe that she must have somehow brought the unfairness on herself, that she was 'a bad person' and 'doing it wrong'. Reflecting on this during the interview, Femi insists that growing up with the belief that if you do it right the system will work for you had been deeply damaging to her sense of self and emotional well-being, and she intended to guard her daughter against this:

> This [racism] isn't about you. You know you are arrogant if you think it is. This is a system that you have to function in that is dysfunctional and you can

either (...) become dysfunctional within it and survive or you can choose to stand against it. But if you are going to stand against it there is a high cost. It is high, you know it is not easy to stay sane in this country being Black because all the time you are told things about yourself that are not true and she [her daughter] needs to realise when she is being told these things that aren't true and she has to have some way of measuring for herself what is right, what is wrong. When she is doing enough and when she is not doing enough? You know go back to my schooling. They were so amazed I could speak English. I don't speak any other language but they were so amazed and there was a point when I thought great – all I've got to do is speak – I don't have to do any work because they are so pleased with the fact that I could speak. And you know if I hadn't done that I would be in a very different position today. I don't want her getting waylaid by that kind of nonsense and it is nonsense and there is no point reasoning it out. There is no point being rational about it, it is a waste of time and energy.

(Femi)

Starkly apparent in the above extract is Femi's absolute clarity about the fact that her daughter must be prepared for the inevitable vagaries of racism. There are costs involved in raising a Black child in a White majority society. The choice one is presented with (such as it is) is stark, painful: to either become part of and assimilate into the hegemonic violence and dysfunction that positions Black people as a problem (DuBois 1996) or attempt to counter it. The first approach involves internalising the negative stereotypes and turning a blind eye – becoming colour-blind – to the magnitude of the problem. We might conceptualise this Black colour-blindness as a version of Whiteness; racism is disregarded and the virtues of individual merit and hard work are extolled much like the conservative Black voices in Paul Warmington's *Black British Intellectuals and Education* (Warmington 2014; see also West 1993). This is the very response that Richard hopes to avoid for his children. The second involves remaining aware of and alert to racial inequities – retaining vision – but simultaneously working to forge a healthy existence that is somehow independent of race inequalities. Either way, it is an existence impossibly shaped and bound by the spectre of racism. Black identity and being is inextricably linked with the determining gaze of Whiteness. Fanon's (1967: 82) sobering observation 'for not only must the black man [*sic*] be black; he must be black in relation to the White man' is depressingly poignant here.

However, while conveying our respondents' struggles in terms of racism and their children, it is equally important to reflect the strategic, agentic ways in which they actively work to resist and protect them from the racism that they know is to come. We described earlier how Cynthia home-schools her sons, in part, as an attempt to help forge in them a positive sense of Black identity and protect them from the low expectations of their school. Parents sought to nurture a strong Black identity (and hence guard against racism) in several ways. While most respondents engaged their children in a range of generic classed extra-curricular activities such as performing arts, instrument lessons and tutoring (Vincent *et al.* 2012a) there are attempts, some organic, some concerted, to utilise specific activities as a means of instilling in their children a sense of Black identity and pride. Derick, who lives in a small town outside of London with little ethnic diversity, tells us that learning how to play the steel pans has a deep cultural significance for his (mixed-race) children and a resonance with their heritage. Another parent, Sandrine, signed up her daughter to one of the UK 100 Black Men Chapters[2] with the specific intention that she has 'some strong Black role models' and develops a positive impression of Black men. This explicit 'creating' of Black identity is marked by active doing and planning similar to the ways in which the White middle classes – without concerns around racism – 'make up' the White middle class child (Vincent and Ball 2007). Michael's decision to move his 16-year-old son from a mainly White independent school to a high achieving co-educational sixth form exemplifies this concerted cultivation of a healthy Black identity:

> I think for my eldest child I didn't want him to go to university not having had much contact with Black girls. So he now goes to a college and as I've said before a very very good college where there are lots of Black students. It's really surprising how many Black students there are at this college given its status and given the fact that we normally think of Black students as failing (…) not only did they have a big cohort of Black students, of that a large percentage are girls and I wanted him to be in that environment. I didn't want him to arrive at university not having had any contact with Black girls on a daily basis (…) because I want my children to marry Black girls, absolutely.
>
> *(Michael)*

Choice of establishment for Michael is not only centred on the overall educational success of the college but also is fundamentally located in a desire to ensure that his son mixes with Black girls. There are intergenerational considerations and societal trends to take account of here. Michael unequivocally wants his son (all of his sons) to marry Black girls and, given the number of Black men with a partner outside of their ethnic group (Platt 2009)[3] does not wish to leave this to chance. In this case, it is not just the Black identity of his son that requires cultivation but also the ethnic profile of future generations of his family. While the subject of relationships, identity and race was not the focus for our study, the strength of the sentiment expressed by those parents who did broach the subject indicates that there is clearly scope for further research in this area. Our data suggests concern and considerable reflection about ethnic mix in relationships (we discuss friendship below). Malorie, for example, prioritises her daughter's happiness rather than, she says, the idea of her marrying someone who is also Black:

> … the other thing is she can hardly find a Black partner now (…). The reality is the majority of our Black men do not look at what I call classic Black

women: [their view is] if you are mixed race in some way you are far more attractive than what I call a classic Black woman. So for me (…) wanting her to be happy is more important than worrying about whether another Black person thinks she has sold out …

(Malorie)

Issues of gender and representations of beauty are central here alongside undertones of betrayal and the erosion of cultural respect by 'our Black men' – again this sense of a collective 'us'. These men are perceived to have turned their back on 'classic Black women' in favour of those of mixed heritage. A number of factors are present but remain unspoken in Malorie's observations. We understand the 'classic Black woman' to lack – there is a distinct sense of their missing out, of being overlooked, disregarded – the 'acceptable' lighter skin tone and hair texture of their mixed-race counterparts who seem to be imbued with greater legitimacy in British society. Indeed this harks back to notions of colourism (the favouring by mainstream and minoritised communities of paler skinned minorities) and preoccupations about 'good hair' that remain prevalent today (Hunter 2005; Lorde 2009; Weekes, 1997). In acknowledging this, Malorie concedes that her daughter might marry someone who is not Black, insisting that her daughter's happiness is more important than concerns that she might be judged by other Black people as having 'sold out'. This acceptance may well speak to the shifting and remaking of the (perceived) boundaries of Black identity and community, where to 'sell out' traditionally denotes a losing or forgetting of one's roots (in the way that Sandrine described her brother).

Gender: raising boys, raising girls

Our data indicates that there are discernible variations and worries with regard to raising a Black son compared with raising a Black daughter. Conceptions of beauty predicated on White Western ideals are a central source of apprehension voiced (usually by mothers) by those who have daughters. We might think of Malorie's 'classic Black woman' as a shorthand to help us understand which norms of femininity are being resisted, rejected and recreated. There is resonance with June's observation, when referring to her own daughter, that someone 'who is Black and [who] has got very tight frizzy hair' is not going to be perceived, by mainstream society as attractive. The Black female is not seen to have much legitimacy in White mainstream British society, a point that is reinforced within contemporary forms of social media and popular culture. As we write, for example, we note that a discussion entitled 'why I'm not attracted to Black girls' is trending on twitter centring on themes around Black women's hair (notably weaves) and attitude. Stereotypes about 'acceptable' versions of Black femininity perpetuated through media are seen to make links between hair, skin tone and attractiveness (sexiness) with notions of success, intellect and attitude:

You know Black girls are just getting slated constantly through the media, from all sides, just having … being strong enough to say, no I'm not going to do that, no (…) I think the MTV image, if I think of it like that. And you know even Beyoncé was quite wholesome at one stage, and now I am thinking Beyoncé you don't have to dress like that because you just don't. But she just seems to be … you know Lady Gaga and Rhianna and it is this thing that you have to be sexy to be … a particular type of sexy … to be successful.

NR: What type of sexy?

It is the … Shorts or short skirts, tights, boots, a wig, maybe some colour contact lens and preferably light skin, that sort of image.

(Sandrine)

Sandrine, the mother of a 13 year old daughter, highlights three particularly successful female artists arguing that the ways in which they are positioned reflects notions of female hypersexuality, availability and desire which, in turn, is seen to be inextricably linked to their success. While one of the three artists she mentions is White, we propose that certain versions of femininity intersect with race to leave the 'classic Black woman' firmly on the outside. For example, there was considerable controversy, in 2008, over the alleged 'Whitening' by L'Oréal of Beyoncé's image for a make-up campaign, debates that have continued more recently in 2012 with the release of her new album (Adewunmi 2012; Eriksen 2012). These debates matter because they promote the idea that darker skin tones are socially undesirable[4] (indeed, the general argument is that darker women are not financially lucrative in terms of advertising revenue) and that racism continues to operate at the level of shadism or skin tone. As Hunter (2005: 7) explains: 'Colorism is part and parcel of racism and exists because of it.' So there is an awareness here that not only does being Black-skinned matter within a racist society but the relative shade of it matters too. It is precisely these kinds of issues that concern parents involved in our study. Again, we witness how the raising of the Black child is firmly located within the limiting gaze of Whiteness (Fanon 1967; see also Chapter 7). Both Malorie and Sandrine are highly vigilant of these societal standards and work, where possible, to subvert them. Malorie's earlier comment about 'our Black men' overlooking Black women in the context of intimate relationships implies that even Black men have been seduced by society's (White) norms – rejecting 'conventional' forms of Blackness in favour of a version 'sold' as desirable. In light of this, therefore, there is perhaps a tension with regard to whether we conceptualise Malorie's preparedness for her daughter to partner outside of her ethnic group as genuine choice or the result of circumstance.

Anxieties about femininity, sex, boys and (educational) success come together in uncomfortable, seemingly contradictory ways:

Put together and faced with it constantly what you have is young impressionable Black girls actually feeling that they have to look more European to be considered sexy and therefore you start to get – even within the Black community – this sort of in a sense shadism where beauty then becomes based on hair, skin colour and I suppose body as well, so they become an object.

They are not seen as a person. So boys will see them as an object because again they see them like that on the TV and they see Black men treating them like that on the TV. And so my fear is that there will be a lot of young girls out there who feel that that is what they have to look like, and that actually education isn't sexy. And if we take, alright if we come out of MTV and go into *EastEnders* and have a look at Libby and her sister. Case in point, Libby is the smart one right, look at Libby, look at what they have done to her, she looks frumpy, she is very smart, she has gone to [the University of] Oxford (...) so you have Libby looking like that and then you have Chelsea her sister who a lot of people say is very beautiful you know. She has got the hair and the nails but she's dumb. I'm sorry she's ... some people call it a Black Barbie ... so it is that sort of image whereby, whether it is MTV Base or *EastEnders* you have these images that are basically saying, 'If you want to study, if you want to be educated you are going to be really boring and you are going to look like that.'

(*Sandrine*)

There are various themes pertaining to gender that intersect here. Sandrine is worried that what we might summarise as 'MTV Blackness' (the antithesis of the classic Black woman) becomes the problematic ideal to which both young Black women aspire and which young Black men desire. Her comment about *EastEnders*[5] is interesting and insightful. While Libby is lighter-skinned, she is frequently conveyed as less desirable, as sensible and somewhat dowdy in appearance. She is shorter and larger than her sister. She has natural hair compared with her sister who is darker, tall, slim, wears weaves and has long, artificial nails. Libby is presented in the programme as smart (winning a place at the University of Oxford) whereas Chelsea comes across as more preoccupied with beauty and her appearance (she worked for a period of time in a beauty salon). Sandrine's point is based on whether it is indeed possible for the Black female to exist beyond a stereotype or to represent a 'classic' identity that is uncritically and unproblematically seen as beautiful and intelligent. In attempting to police the boundaries of these versions of Black femininity, she explains that her sister responds, with her own children, by banning MTV in her house. However, Sandrine allows her daughter to watch television on weekends attempting to use it as a tool to facilitate debate – not always wholly welcomed – with her daughter about 'appropriate' forms of fashion, individuality and femininity. The shadism that Sandrine and others mention is not simply contained within skin colour. It is accompanied by a related politics surrounding Black hair, style and texture that continue to act as markers of Black consciousness and beauty and where straighter, more European hair wins over (Weekes 1997). In short, Sadrine is trying to protect her daughter from ingesting a notion of beauty perpetuated by White society, the criteria of which tend to be internalised by the Black community even though they involve disregarding and devaluing Blackness (Weekes 1997; Lorde 2009). This is a powerful example of DuBois' notion of 'double-consciousness', the sense of 'always looking at one's self through the eyes of others, of measuring one's soul by the tape of a world that looks on in amused contempt and pity' (DuBois 1996: 5).

Cynthia, who also has a daughter (not yet of school age) as well as sons, helps demonstrate something of the gender sensitivities that come to bear when working to create the Black middle-class child. She echoes – understandably with less detail given her daughter's age – some of the concerns described above when discussing the potential choice of school for her daughter:

> With my Black boys, with my sons I just felt that I needed more time with them before they hit the system. With her it will be an experiment, I just want her to go out there. Girls just need other girls I think. They need to bicker, you know what I mean, and they need to do their thing.
>
> *(Cynthia)*

Her comment speaks to the differing perceived needs and parenting priorities for boys and girls. She hints at apparent gender differences in socialisation that are felt to require greater vigilance, protection and support for boys as compared to girls. The interaction between Black boys and 'the system' – meaning the education system but it is also possible that she is talking about wider structures within society – is considered to affect boys and girls in varying ways. Prompted to explain the reason for the different choice in schooling her children, Cynthia speaks of the importance for all her children to see Black people in positions of authority but specifically for Black girls to see other Black girls, knowing that 'their hair will be the same as my hair and their mum will have creamed their skin'. Again, as with the parents described earlier, worries about representations of Black femininity are central.

Where explicit concerns are voiced about raising boys, they tend to be centred on attempts to protect them from the perceived dangers of 'the street' and from stereotypes about young Black men that automatically position them as deviant, troublesome and disruptive. We discussed some instances of this earlier when exploring how parents talk to their children about racism. Richard, for example, the father of two primary school-aged boys, expresses reservations about letting them leave the house by themselves, especially if they dressed 'a little bit street'. There is an awareness that certain forms of dress (e.g. hoodies) intersect with prevalent discourse about Black masculinity to further position them as Other (Giroux 2012; Rollock 2007a; Youdell 2003). Simone, the mother of a teenage boy also echoes this saying:

> You know he walks around with his hood up for no reason whatsoever and I said 'I know its fine and you like it but other people find it intimidating basically' and he said 'well I'm not doing anything' and I said (…) 'but it's the perception that comes out in the perception of hoodies in the press …'
>
> *(Simone)*

Possibly the most evocative examples regarding issues around raising Black boys are conveyed by two mothers in our sample: Felicia and Elsa. As we have already mentioned in preceding chapters, Felicia's son originally attended a mainly White independent school but, following a period of racist bullying that the school trivialised and eventually dismissed, she transferred him to a high-performing state sixth form. She concedes that perhaps now, after all that had happened, she was no longer pushing him as hard as she could with regard to his schooling and career ambitions:

> … it is not my personality to [push push push] but that is what I always felt he needed, [I'm not] that sort of a person who is just going to push him because he would then do well. (…) I suppose it is a stereotype (…) I am from Jamaica – and I have often said to him you know, 'You Caribbean boys I think you just need pushing more'. And I have talked to my female Caribbean friends about it and we have got a consensus that perhaps we don't push in the same sort of way and I don't know if it is because when our parents came with … certainly not qualified the way we are qualified now and maybe things were, yes there was racism and all sorts of other problems but still relatively speaking we managed to get through the system fairly well and we haven't to fight and maybe we don't have the same fight in us as other parents did when they came and had to start from scratch and push. And I was saying to him that I think one of the things I know with Caribbean parents is that they want you to do well, yes they want you to have a good education (…) certainly with me I just want to know that he does okay, well not okay but he does well. I would like him to go to university but I wasn't, to me he didn't have to be a lawyer, he didn't have to be a doctor, he didn't have to be the other.
>
> *(Felicia)*

Context is extremely important to extricating the sentiment behind this quote. At the point at which Felicia decided to move her son from the independent school she had quite serious concerns about his emotional health and well-being following the bullying. Recalling this incident during the interview caused her great upset and the conversation was temporarily suspended. She voices concern about data revealing the mental health and suicide rates of young Black men, describing several examples where Black people or boys she knew appeared to be struggling with operating within the education system and within society more broadly: 'By the time I had him (…) I knew of three or four young men, young Black men who had committed suicide and I knew that statistically young men commit suicide and I was concerned about the stresses that they go under and so that is another thing that stopped me from pushing.' It is in the light of this that we need to consider her statement above.

In seeking to make sense of her own views and attitudes to raising her son, she looks towards other Caribbean mothers – friends – who express similar worries about their sons. She considers that a different formation of the racial struggle that confronted her parents might, at least in part, contribute to a lesser drive for academic and career success among her son and his counterparts. She oscillates between questioning her parenting style and critiquing wider societal factors. Of course, both factors may play a role. For example, Ella, in describing an incident with her son (she also has a daughter), argues that certain characteristics considered desirable in White boys are not granted the same legitimacy for Black boys: 'People don't accept the same level of confidence in a little Black boy.' Black girls seem to be on the periphery of such heightened concern and fear (Rollock 2007b).

There is a sense in which the world beyond the confines of the home represents a site of considerable danger, both psychically and physically for Black boys. We highlight similarities here, albeit it differently inflected, with the experience of our respondents as children (Chapter 8). We have already examined Cynthia's strategy to home-school her sons in an attempt to ready them for 'the system', a method not deemed necessary for her young daughter. Ella is worried that 'out on the street' society will merely see her son as 'another Black boy', that is as a threat and a stereotype first, thus influencing how he is dealt with, rather than recognising that he is, in fact, a boy. Elsa expresses similar apprehensions with regard to her teenage son. She describes the struggle she is confronted by, wanting to give him space to develop as a young man and her concerns about the dangers of the street:

> I am just a bit over-protective I suppose, and there are lots of things that we got up to that your mother would have cringed or died or killed you if she had known you what you were up to when you were [son's] age. So give him his space and then I can't choose his friends for him. I can only advise and say, 'Look (...), OK it's one thing going off to a party with someone, but it's another thing when you are in a group of boys even though you are just mates, who are doing nothing, hanging around in the park, because how people perceive that, wrongly or rightly, if there are more than three of you, you are perceived as a gang, and you know you are going to get stopped by the police and you are going to get searched, and you are going to get this', and it's happened to him enough times even when he is in his school uniform ...
>
> *(Elsa)*

Elsa displays a similar parenting style to Felicia that speaks to a deep concern to protect her son while striving not to be overbearing. There is a carefulness as she seeks to moderate apprehensions about societal pressures and surveillance with a desire to allow her son some space to become a young man.

Thus, growing up in the UK is a perilous state for a young Black boy where the attempts to control and protect them remain constant.

Friendships

Considerations of race and class – what we term 'social mix' – saturate our conversations about the friendship groups of our respondents' children (see Chapter 2). The identity characteristics of these groups are seen as an important marker in developing the balanced Black middle-class child. The majority of the children in the sample are reported by their parents as having ethnically mixed friendships, including among their best and close friends, both within and outside of school. Overall, ethnically mixed friendship patterns are seen as highly positive and desirable by our interviewees, both as a form of social learning for the child – preparing them for a global market – and as an indicator of general social progress. Several parents comment on the contrast between their own friendship patterns during childhood and those of their children. In some cases children are constructing their social and racial identities in a markedly different social context and this is almost always viewed as a positive development:

> He has a very mixed group of friends, so that's good.
>
> *(Simone)*

> Their friends are a real mix: Chinese, White girls.
>
> *(Cassandra)*

> He always had friendships across a range of backgrounds. In fact he was saying in his new college he's found it quite strange that the Black children stick together.
>
> *(Felicia)*

> The friends who they mix with, it's very mixed. We have all different type of friends coming back, and I say to them that's very, very important.
>
> *(Candice)*

> I've never grown up with my children to think about Black/White … so they have all different kinds of friends.
>
> *(Gloria)*

> A lot of his friends are African, they're a mixture, but all the friends I've met I like (…) everyone wants to do well, and I think you can see that quality in the kids …
>
> *(Anita)*

Concerns are raised, however, where the child is seen to have friends from just one ethnic group. For example, Samantha reports that her son's friends are 'all White' and that she 'would prefer him to have more of a mix' but 'I can't force him to make friends with people who he doesn't want to'. Friendship mix varies within families also:

> I mean my youngest child, most of her friends are White. The people who come to my house invariably have been White students, she has very rarely brought home any Black friend from school. Primary school was different but at secondary school that's how it panned out. Even now she has gone to university most of her friends are Whites (…) that's the choice that she's made.

Erm, her older sister was different, she had a mixture of friends from Chinese, Indian, whatever, mixed, all the rest of it.

(Anthea)

Samantha and Anthea make observations about their children's friendships but, possibly because of their age (they are teenagers) or due to differing priorities, do not seek to actively shape or alter them. Contrast this to the small number of parents who consciously encourage their children to attend Black social groups or mentoring organisations partly as a way of providing their children with extra skills and experiences and also to ensure that their children mix with other Black children. The earlier comments made by Michael and Malorie about ethnicity and the personal relationships their children pursue are pertinent here.

A very few children in the sample have predominantly Black friendship groups, and a few children and parents deliberately seek out Black friends as a tactic in maintaining an ethnic identity of which they are proud.

They're mixed, predominantly Black. They do have one or two White friends, but they're predominantly Black, Asian ... probably 60:40 Black (...) They choose as they want. They're not marrying them are they?

(Patricia)

My youngest one has gone all out to try to get a hundred per cent Black friendship group, and to be perfectly honest with you I said to her I don't mind. You know when I was at school I wanted to have Black friends but what I want is for your behaviour and standards not to change.

(Brenda)

Once again we see the tensions between different desires and perceived threats, in Brenda's case the feared threat to behaviour posed by an all-Black friendship group. On occasion parents feel the need to intervene and to try to make their children reflect on the implications and consequences of their friendships. These can be fraught discussions and touch on questions about what it means to be Black:

There are some very interesting things for me that are happening. In that my daughter would think 'Oh! She's really Black', because she's got all these Black friends, and I feel that that version is not what I call being Black. I find that *stereotypical* Black, but who knows. So we have some clashes on this but we can discuss it ...

(Brenda)

Different identities, conceptualisations of Black identity infused by a class subtext come into play. For Elsa the threat is not only from 'bad boy friends' but also from a racist society that views Black males as hyper-threatening and acts against them (see also earlier comments by Elsa):

> So I don't think he wants the bad boy friends that much, even though there is a little bit of excitement in there. But I think he knows that it isn't quite the life he wants to be doing when he is thirty or forty, but there is also a lot of – with Black boys, it's about the street cred. So he wants to be seen to be one of them, but at the same time he knows he's not really one of them (…).
>
> *Elsa*

These are tremendously difficult and sensitive issues for parents to navigate with, and on behalf of, their children. Interviewees express particular concerns about how their sons might be perceived (again the significance of gender) and treated negatively on the basis of racist stereotyping, concerns that they explain and try to share with their sons. Black boys must make their way in a social world saturated with racist stereotypes that portray them as dangerous, threatening and volatile. In relation to this, parents are wary of some sorts of friends, as evidenced above. There are 'nice' children and those who are 'not nice' and there are 'bad boys' who may be 'bad' influences. Again we see here the work of 'internalised "embodied" social structures', as Bourdieu (1986: 468) describes them, that is forms of 'class recognition' and 'race recognition' with a distinct subtext of *respectability*, that involves attempts by parents to distance their sons from certain versions of Black boyhood. Indeed, Moore (2008: 497) sees respectability as 'a distinguishing feature of Black habitus', part of which emphasises 'positive self-presentation as a form of social status'. There are distances that need to be kept and a respectability to be maintained.

> I don't want [my daughter] to be friends with her. This girl is constantly telling everybody about her entire life and it is just like well, it is not really appropriate. (…) she has got friends, she is friends with other Black and mixed children as I say. You know, the number of Black children at the school, in her year group, isn't that high but you know, they are there but I wonder …
>
> *(Amanda)*

> [My daughter] made friends with a girl that was younger than her … very sweet, very nice, very polite … it wasn't until quite a bit later that this girl is one of six siblings of a single mother and there was a boyfriend on the scene … had I known I probably would not have agreed to her spending the night because I don't know the family dynamics.
>
> *(Lorraine)*

Social class surfaces in a range of subtle and not so subtle ways. There are complex intersections of language, values, interests and behaviour that shape the Black middle-class habitus and views about their children's friendship groups. There are also questions about identity and *authenticity*, what Matthew (below) refers to as 'having to be a certain way to be Black' (see Chapter 1). In many cases, this (concern about authenticity) involves consideration of the types of issues which are also pertinent when parents reflect on their class identity; not embodying the individualism and privileges of White identity is central. In some families these issues are explicitly addressed and discussed. The nexus of identity, ideology and solidarity is often focused around friendship groups, and commonalities and differences are played out at school and in the neighbourhood. These are complex, painful and sometimes contradictory issues for which there is no simple resolution.

> We've never as a family grouped our kids to have only Black friends or whatever. They're very aware, we've taught them to be very aware of their colour, but also to never let that be an issue in real life … Average Black kids, they say our children are *posh* in the way that they talk, proper Queen's English, all the rest of it. That's a product of their schools and their parenting, but they're very Black, they're very socially conscious, and Black conscious (…) but they have not felt, they don't have that burden of having to be a certain way to be Black, I get it in my job because of the way I speak, am I Black enough? Or you know, 'you have to sell yourself short as a Black man (…) or sell out to get anywhere in life.' So we just taught our children (…) you need these things to be educated, you need to talk properly, at times (…) you have to play by the rules essentially but be proud of who you are.
>
> *(Matthew)*

Matthew, therefore, makes a point of discussing with his children the strategic significance of things like received pronunciation. Language and accent (which are referred to in several other interviews) are markers that construct mundane but significant social exclusions and inclusions. Speech is a marker of class that also has certain intersections with race and is implicated in the management of racisms and the confounding of racist stereotypes. Being consciously or collectively Black and speaking well is not a contradiction although it is in the eyes of mainstream society. In a conscious attempt to rebut the view of such language as 'posh' or a 'sell out', Matthew argues for a position where 'you have to play by the rules essentially but be proud of who you are' (see Chapter 7). Note too his use of 'average Black'. This speaks to a sense that he and his children are different, they do not align in a straightforward way with some average conceptualisation of Black (working-class) identity. They occupy a new, isolated minority (Chapter 1). New identities and versions of Blackness are being brought into being. Anthea discusses a further concern, where the desire for Black peers as friends cannot always be satisfied within middle-class circles:

> My daughters had to make choices in terms of who their friends are, especially the younger one. Are your friends going to be White middle-class

children or Black students who may not be middle class, who might be lower or might be whatever? And that's the dilemma that they both had (...) although you are Black and they would choose, perhaps they have more in common with Black students. (...) But those same Black students, their values, their behaviour, whatever, was slightly different to theirs. So if you are not friends with those groups of girls, who are you going to be friends with?

(Anthea)

The race and class tensions that Moore (2008) discusses are evident again here. Being Black and middle class is not necessarily a straightforward, easy identity; it is to be a minority of a minoritised group. Finding friendship groups which mirror class and ethnic location is not easy. There are complex Bourdieusian distinctions, divisions and relativities involved in the development of racial and class identities: 'Social divisions become principles of division, organizing the image of the social world' (Bourdieu 1986: 417). These families draw upon their practical knowledge of the social (especially racial) world, and schemes of perception and appreciation, to objectify and classify others, most typically through a network of antagonistic oppositions, but these cognitive structures are four-way rather than two-way, that is Black and White middle class, and Black and White working class. These are schema that take shape from and are largely infused by a wider framework of Whiteness (see Chapters 1 and 8). The parents and children are also aware that race and class are written onto the bodily hexis, and that certain forms of this hexis, are in some circumstances positioned as racially unpalatable, to borrow from Carbado and Gulati (2009) or at least racially contradictory. These intersections are sometimes difficult to manage for families and individuals and we might say that the children in the sample inhabit 'intersectional bodies' (see Rollock 2012b).

They don't speak posh, because my younger daughter, what she has with her friends is, what her brother pointed out to her, what you are talking about is a difference in culture. Because quite a few of her friends are relatively well off. I mean when she is quantifying the differences her brother has said these are cultural or class differences you are talking about here. I don't use teapots at home. I have teapots but I don't use them. We have mugs of tea or coffee, but when she is at her friends' they might have tea with teapots for example.

(Anthea)

Parents are attuned to their children's friendships but also aware of the limits of their control. Nonetheless, efforts are made to ensure that children choose the 'right' friends – those who are like them in terms of values, aspirations, demeanour, speech and 'grooming', as Moore calls it. White middle-class parents evince similar concerns but inflected differently in terms of the relations between ethnicity and class (Ball *et al.* 2004.) and the reproduction of privilege. Most significantly, it is difficult to overstate the importance of racism as a complex and changing presence that sets the context for many of these issues and the discussions that parents have with other parents and with their own children.

Conclusion

In this chapter, we have shown that a wide range of variables shape the development and parenting of the Black middle-class child. There are, in many cases, active attempts to nurture a healthy, balanced racial identity which will steep the Black middle-class child in confidence and act as a potential barrier against the racism that is known to be part of wider society. Decisions must be made about when and how to talk with their children about racism while at the same time seeking to guard against the possibility that this awareness will fill their child with a foreboding sense of defeat. Acknowledging racism does not simply mean becoming a victim. It must be acknowledged and the contours of it recognised; there are strategies to be learnt in order to navigate it. We have also shown that individual conceptualisations of Black identity directly inform the types of strategies and approaches deployed to tackle racism and when talking to their child about these issues. Those parents who embody an individualised or incidental Black identity tend to employ less detailed, confident strategies to manage racism.

Gender is an important consideration in raising the healthy Black middle-class child. Having a Black boy means being attendant to stereotypes about the (perceived) Black male threat constant within wider society and the levels of surveillance trained upon them. Parents express concern over whether they are being too stringent and hence pressurising their sons too much or, in contrast, perhaps being too lenient. For girls, there are concerns about notions of femininity, attractiveness and intelligence. Drawing on parents' insights, it is possible to distinguish between 'MTV Blackness' and the 'classic Black woman', the former representing versions of Blackness seen to have credibility in White mainstream society (light skin, long hair, hypersexuality) whereas the latter embodies a version of Black femininity which embraces dark skin and natural hair as beautiful and desirable.

Many of these issues influence the ways in which our respondents view their children's friendship groups. Ethnic and class diversity is welcomed and parents express apprehensions about friendship groups which are solely White or solely Black. In some cases, parents consciously seek out activities run by Black-led organisations to ensure that their children meet 'people like us'. However, race is not the sole concern, for parents seek to encourage their children to make 'nice' friends who embody similar values and principles to them. This is especially the case when befriending other children who are seen to fit an average (that is 'deficient' or disadvantaged) Black stereotype. Parents are concerned that their children will not be misrecognised as being part of this stereotype. Language and accent become markers that set our respondents' children apart from the wider Black group and we are again reminded that to be Black and middle class is a relatively new, emerging identity formation. It is to be a minority of a minority.

We take forward this topic – ways of surviving British society as a raced and classed minority – in the next chapter.

Notes

1   Vincent and Ball (2007) use this term in relation to the White middle classes. While there are some similarities in terms of the work and strategising involved in class reproduction, we wish to stress the considerable differences in privilege, entitlement and experiences of race between the White and Black middle-class groups.
2   100 Black Men is a community-based charity led by Black men providing a range of activities (e.g. mentoring, family days out, educational support) aimed at Black young men and fathers. It is a chapter of the US 100 Black Men of America, which was founded in 1963.
3   Nearly half (48 per cent) of Black Caribbean men in Britain have a partner from a different ethnic group, the highest inter-ethnic relationship rate with the exception of those of mixed heritage backgrounds. The figure for Black Caribbean women is 34 per cent (Platt 2009).
4   The desire for lighter skin is a lucrative business, with cosmetic firms accruing millions of pounds in profit from the trade (see, for example, http://www.bbc.co.uk/programmes/b00nkpmm; http://www.bbc.co.uk/news/world-africa-20444798).
5   Long-running, popular BBC soap opera set in East London, depicting often fraught and controversial themes among the characters.

7

STRATEGIES FOR SURVIVAL

Managing race in public spaces

Sometimes people categorise you.

Introduction

> In public settings, people of color find themselves between the Scylla of
> becoming visible and the Charybdis of remaining silent. If minorities follow
> an analytics of color, they run the risk of incurring white symbolic racism at
> best or literal violence at worst. (…) It becomes a Catch-22 for them. Either
> they must observe the safety of whites and be denied a space that promotes
> people of color's growth and development or insist on a space of integrity
> and put themselves further at risk not only of violence, but also risk being
> conceived of as illogical or irrational.
>
> *(Leonardo and Porter 2010: 140)*

In this chapter, we highlight the complex ways in which race and racism continue
to have resonance in the lives of the Black middle classes despite their successes and
achievements. Barack Obama, elected to his first term of office during the same
period that our research was being carried out, provides a prominent, high-profile
example of precisely the type of arguments that we detail here. For example, at the
start of 2010, just one year after Obama's inauguration, Democratic Senator Harry
Reid was reported to have described the United States as ready to embrace Obama
as president because he was a 'light-skinned' African American with 'no Negro dialect unless he wanted to have one' (MacAskill 2010; Preston 2010). Historic forms
of race categorisation – here calling upon colourism and assessments of skin tone
hierarchy and intellect – inform and shape what we might crudely conceptualise as
'the Black experience' despite (or as we will argue in what follows *because of*) their

achievements (Hill 2002; Hunter 2005). Simply put, race matters irrespective of success or class status (see Chapter 1). In this chapter, we are particularly interested in the ways in which the Black middle classes conceptualise and respond to racism. As we shall see, they often deploy (sometimes subconsciously) careful, highly strategic forms of agency and resistance as they work to navigate and secure a legitimate place within British society.

The continuing significance of race

Barack Obama's 2008 presidential win triggered wide-ranging commentary in both the US and the UK about the role of race and success in contemporary Western societies. His win instilled in many (notably White) commentators, the sense of a new era of understanding in racial politics:

> Years from now, I hope we can view his presidency as the one that turned around our economy, ended two wars and created thousands of jobs, but *at the very least, we will always view him as the president who changed the face of race relations in America.*
>
> *(Richert 2008: emphasis added)*

In the same year that Obama was sworn in, the Department for Work and Pensions in the UK published a study reporting the findings of statistical research into the probability of White and minoritised applicants securing a job interview. They found that minoritised candidates with a 'foreign sounding' name had to send 74 per cent more applications compared with their White counterparts in order to be called for an interview *despite holding the same qualifications and experience.* Commenting on these findings, the authors conclude:

> It is hard to avoid the conclusion that racial discrimination accounts for a proportion of the 'ethnic penalty' in labour market outcomes.
>
> *(Wood et al. 2009: 47)*

Within politics more broadly, there has been a discernible shift away from engagement with race and racism. Despite well-established equalities legislation and policy-makers' explicit public rejection of inequity, racism continues to shape the thinking and actions of mainstream British society.

Leading Black academics such as Stuart Hall and bell hooks offer a series of powerful, critical analyses of the ways in which stereotypical representations of the Black body – that is those marked as Other by the colour of their skin – persist in popular culture and the mass media. Black bodies are characterised as vehicles of mystical strength, hypercriminality and hypersexuality (Hall 1997; hooks 1992), representations which have persisted since the Transatlantic Slave Trade, albeit in more subtle form. These contemporary cultural depictions both resist and restrict the possibility of fluid, diverse Black identities and in so doing set the criteria by which a narrow and unsophisticated version of 'Blackness' is defined (see also Chapter 1). Iris Young's theorisation of identity formation is useful here:

> The rational subject does not merely observe, passing from one sight to another like a tourist. In accordance with the logic of identity the scientific subject measures objects according to scales that reduce the plurality of attributes to unity. Forced to line up on calibrations that measure degrees of some general attribute, some of the particulars are devalued, defined as deviant in relation to the norm.
>
> *(Young 1990: 125)*

We have already shown that there are certain norms associated with the Black body, which retain subtle permanence in British society and with which our Black middle-class participants have to contend. Borrowing from Young and Fanon (1967) we demonstrate how 'objects', or in this case identities, that are seen to deviate from these norms automatically trigger curiosity, fuel confusion, warrant inspection. Demands are made of our respondents to account for their 'deviation' from the Black stereotypical norm. It is through this conceptual lens that we can better understand Senator Reid's alleged remarks about Barack Obama. Simply put, Obama stimulates curiosity and intrigue not just because he is the first Black President of the United States but because he also is seen as an aberration, an oddity in light of normative popularisations of Black identity. While his difference from the norm is odd, it also allows him a certain degree of acceptance (though this is perilous, fragile and always subject to interrogation) by white mainstream society.

In this chapter, we examine how the Black British middle classes navigate the public terrain, marked as it is by class and race discrimination. We are especially concerned with how, given the restrictive norms and stereotypes imposed upon them, they are able to construct strategies for survival. Bourdieu is especially useful to our analysis and to theorising our respondents' strategies as tactical forms of what we might think of as a unique Black capital which helps them negotiate their way through white society. In carrying out this analysis, we also draw closely on the work of Karyn Lacy (2007) whose examination of the identity construction processes of middle-class African Americans in three different communities in Washington, DC, is particularly pertinent. Lacy skilfully demonstrates how middle-class Blacks have at their disposal a range of resources – a 'cultural toolkit' (Moore 2008: 498) – including language, mannerisms, clothing and credentials that allows them to create what she terms 'public identities' to minimise or mediate against discriminatory treatment:

> Public identities are (…) purposeful, instrumental strategies that either reduce the probability of discrimination or curtail the extent of discrimination middle-class Blacks face in their public interactions with white strangers (…) [Middle-class Blacks] assert public identities in order to convince others that they are legitimate members of the middle class.
>
> *(Lacy 2007: 73)*

These public identities provide a useful framework through which to examine how our Black middle-class respondents are able to elicit some degree of agency in light of the discriminations they face in their interactions with white others generally and with education establishments in particular. Our focus in this chapter is primarily on their experiences within wider White society. The themes discussed lend crucial context to understanding parents' views and experiences of the education system and the ways in which they work to navigate their children successfully through it.

We begin by examining how the public identities of the Black middle classes were formed. More specifically, we are interested in moments when they became race aware and how they made sense of and responded to early incidents of racism. Our analytical journey starts at school, a place which epitomised for the vast majority of our respondents a sense of isolation and memories of racial discrimination. We contend that the school (and other places in which they were a racial minority) served as a potential learning ground, forcing them to acquire the public identities upon which they later draw as adults.

Coming to race awareness: the childhood experiences of the Black middle classes

We asked respondents to describe their experiences of secondary school. Few accounts were entirely positive. Most highlighted the challenges, isolation and pain of being the only or one of few Black children in the pupil population, a phenomenon which was exaggerated for those living in rural or less urban areas. School represented, for our participants, a site where they came to learn exactly how they were viewed by White peers and school staff. Vanessa describes memories of when, aged 13, she started at a state secondary school not long after her arrival in the UK from Jamaica:

> I remember children coming up to me to find out if my bottom was White or Black because they just had no idea at all (…) I couldn't believe that anyone could be so ignorant as to not know (…) they were shocked about my hair not being the same as theirs. (…) they were just intrigued about me as a person and in turn I was intrigued that they didn't know … because I don't think I (…) was that conscious of this difference between White and Black children [pauses] even though I know that I missed (…) my family surroundings of Jamaica. I was shocked at how little they knew (…) and had to ask (…). I just couldn't understand (…) because I don't think I had that sort of consciousness and it wasn't until later on that I developed the realisation of [pauses] of the fact that this difference was actually maintained in (…) society.
> *(Vanessa)*

The first point to note from Vanessa's recollection of her school experience is that clearly in relation to the proportion of White children to Black within the school she is in a minority (she mentions this later in the interview). This alone, however, does not automatically point to racial subjugation. It is the inquisitional role assumed by the White children coupled with their racial intrigue vis-à-vis Vanessa's relatively powerless role of the inspected that is pertinent here. Vanessa is an object of curiosity. She is fixed as subject. That her White peers proceed to exhibit curiosity about her bottom, as opposed to any other less sexualised parts of her anatomy, speaks to a gendered and racialised preoccupation with the Black female form that is steeped in historical classification (Cooper 2005; Young 1990). The children's fascination has uncomfortable historical undertones which hark back to White fascination with Saartjie Bartman,[1] otherwise known as the Hottentot Venus, in the nineteenth-century (Hobson 2003). This 'negating activity' (Fanon 1967. 83) to which Vanessa is subjected contributes to the development of a relational identity formation. That is, she begins to make sense of and examine her raced and gendered identity *in relation to* those aspects of her otherness that are picked out and met with intrigue by White peers. She becomes intrigued at their intrigue, shocked at their questions and confused by their lack of understanding. While she lacks, as a child, the race awareness she later develops as an adult, it is likely that this negative experience will have a different impact on her compared to her Black counterparts who were born and spent their formative years in the UK. It may be that growing up around a majority Black community in Jamaica is likely to have served as some form of protection for Vanessa. We make conceptual links here with the protective benefits of Black collectivity, as discussed in Chapter 1.

This almost zoological examination by White people of the Black body also extended to a fascination with Black hair. Brenda recalls 'everyone [White children] wanting to feel your hair' and that this constant singling out treatment as being somehow different, as being spectacle (Hall, 1997), impacted negatively on her ability to learn. Monica, like Vanessa, initially spent some of her early childhood overseas. She echoes Brenda's sentiment when recalling her schooling there:

They were fascinated with your hair. They were fascinated with your skin. (…) they'd literally come up and touch you [laughs]. It was funny and the teachers didn't quite know what you were about. It was that surreal. They really and truly did not know that you were the same (…) [that] it was just the colour of your skin that was different and maybe your hair. (…) then [in] upper school where I was the only Black [pupil] I remember getting into an argument with a teacher. It was a geography class and they wanted us to go away and do research on where we'd come from and of course, I come from England so I went away and did my research, presented it to the class and he said, 'Oh that's all very well and good Monica, but (…) we all know that Black people don't live in England' (…). I said, 'Well somebody needs to go back over there and tell all the Black people that I left there to get out because that's where I was born.' He didn't believe me. My mum had to send my birth certificate in; he really and truly did not believe me.

(Monica, teacher)

Monica's experience, even though not within the English education system, mirrors the experiences of respondents discussed above. This extract reveals how the regime of Othering, of postcolonial curiosity, is not exercised simply by her peers. The adamant refusal on the part of the teacher to accept Monica's account of her origins as valid not only reinforces a notion of Whiteness as privileged and 'expert' but simultaneously trivialises and invalidates her knowledge, and specifically her knowledge about her own identity, as legitimate. It speaks both of the *invisibility* of Blackness through the teacher's lack of awareness that Black people can and do reside in England – all the more troubling because of his role as educator – and, without contradiction, draws attention to Monica's simultaneous *visibility*; she is only allowed to exist in an identity that *he* judges appropriate for Black-skinned persons. This is a disturbing Fanonian example of not just the ways in which limitations are imposed on the Black body, on the Black psyche, but also of how these limitations are defined, imposed and assessed by White people. Returning to Monica's account we note that the incident was drawn out over several weeks with the teacher threatening to issue her with a fail if she did not subscribe to his understanding of Black migration and living patterns. It is only the production by her mother of Monica's birth certificate that sees the teacher appeased and the situation finally resolved. This is a powerful, painful account. It is dehumanising. It demonstrates that not only is there a denial of her identity and experience in the playground as White peers touch and poke at her but that she is not safe even within the teaching and learning confines of the classroom.

Similarly, in Chapter 3, we describe Gabriel's experience of repeatedly trying to gain membership of the school chess club and the disparaging retort made by his teacher: 'I didn't think *you people* played chess.' Not only does this account reveal the endemic nature of racism at the time, but it also highlights the determination and unflinching resolve – conscious or otherwise – with which Gabriel managed it. It is precisely Gabriel's refusal to take no for an answer that sees him achieve his goal (admission to the club) and as a secondary, and arguably unforeseen, consequence challenge the teacher's racist stereotyping. As we shall see, such 'persistence' is just one of the forms of strategies developed by our respondents, as passed down from their parents, as ways of surviving racism.

School represents a site of a battle for survival in terms of persistent low teacher expectations about their academic potential (see Chapter 3) and with regard to their cultural identity and heritage. In terms of context, it is important to remember that our respondents were attending school in the 1970s and early 1980s. This was a period in British popular culture marked by infrequent yet stereotypical depictions of Black people. A popular television sit-com of the time, *Mind Your Language*,[2] to which one interviewee refers, reflects much of the type of racist stereotyping that was prevalent and with which many of our respondents had to contend. Being called 'nigger' or 'wog' was commonplace along with denigrating references to monkeys. Interviewees speak of the hurt that such experiences caused, making them feel despondent and think of leaving the education system altogether. Those who did recount such events to their parents were introduced, via their advice and responses, to what we recognise as the foundations of a skill set or set of resources for managing racism:

> Both parents (…) would just say, you've got to be strong (…) and answer back and tell them [White pupils] what for. And that is what I did but you couldn't do that all the time but that is what I did actually and I had to become quite aggressive – not aggressive but really assertive, otherwise you would be trampled on … So it [school] was really not a pleasant experience.
>
> (Paulette)

PATRICIA: And I said [to my mum] 'This girl jumped me and beat me up.' My mum said [Jamaican accent] 'Beat you up? Beat up wha'? When I know … you must can fight anybody ten years more than you. Beat up? Anytime anybody hit you again, you tek a brick, you tek a stick, you tek a stone and you lick dem becaa' if you come in 'ere again wid dat … backsiding fuh you' [i.e. I will beat or severely reprimand you!].

So from that day [smacks of hands together for emphasis] dust didn't touch my fist. I'm telling you. Any any *any*body [repeats for emphasis], no matter how big. No matter how big and anybody who come with that 'Black bastard' 'cause that was like [accent] 'Ay up … Black bastard.'

NR: That was the way they'd greet you?

PATRICIA: It was normal.

NR: Was this at school? Outside of school?

PATRICIA: Both. Walking to school, you'd have people shout out in their cars and there weren't that many on the road so you'd see the car coming and you'd see it drifting away. 'Ay, you Black bastard!' Honestly [and they'd say] 'Nigger lover' to your friend walking to school. Simple as that.

Both accounts convey the challenges of growing up Black in 1970s Britain. These are not inequities of class but clearly and unequivocally discrimination based on the colour of their skin. We also witness how their parents respond to and teach their children how to react when confronted by racism. Learning how to defend yourself, be it verbally or physically, is seen and stringently reinforced as an essential require-ment for the young Black child. To fight back is to retain some degree of agency, to present strength in the face of adversity. These examples not only speak to differences in the socialisation of the Black child compared with their White counterparts but also draw attention to their relative isolation when outside the home.

Respondents' parents also reminded them that in order to succeed at school, in employment and elsewhere in British society they have to work twice as hard, if not harder, than their White counterparts. To be Black within a racist context demands constant vigilance. Note Patricia's comment 'it was normal'. To be Black, in this context, is to recognise from early on that there is no level playing field and opportunities are not equal. Our respondents must be alert. They must be ready to respond to and protect themselves from the constant threat of racism.

It is worth remembering that, as children, our Black middle-class respondents are developing an identity which is minoritised and which is wholly distinct from their parents, whose racialised identities were mainly formed under a geographical, temporal and postcolonial context very different from theirs. These retrospective glimpses into interviewees' childhoods not only tell us about the challenges they endured, but also provide insight into moments or experiences that reinforced a positive sense of identity and self-worth. We start to comprehend the ways in which they begin to develop additional strategies to negotiate a less fraught and more humanising existence. The television series *Roots*,[3] aired during 1977, illustrates this point well:

> (…) we are talking about my secondary education when *Roots* came out and how people then responded to that film and the injustice that you saw in that film. And how I responded was to say that I can have it. That Black people have gone before me and have died before me so that I can have what I have today. And I don't want to throw it away. I refuse to throw that away what has gone before me. So that is my defining moment. (…) Others I remember (…) responded by saying that I am not going to work for no White man (…) but I chose to respond in a different way. I said I was going to go out and get what is mine and I know what I am capable of earning and what I am capable of doing.
>
> *(Joan)*

Several interviewees make reference to *Roots* and its significance to their childhood identity. Several of our respondents described how *Roots* facilitated in them a sense of racial awareness which extended beyond their immediate situation and locale. That is to say, what was previously regarded as a set of individual experiences became resituated within a wider, historical context which spoke to a collective reality as Black people subjugated at the hands of White people. Commenting on her school experience, Eleanor reflects 'there was no understanding (…) of who you are, of promoting who you are, and I think the first sort of any sort of understanding we had of us as Black people in society was when *Roots* the film came on.' Note the way Joan (above) speaks of conceptualising her injustice as an extension of those Black people who have died and 'gone before'; they have paid the ultimate sacrifice for being Black upon which she now feels compelled to build. The racist acts of the classroom, the playground and the street are relocated, magnified within a broader envisaging of identity and belonging. This is the foundation of the collective Black identity that we described in Chapter 1. Joan gains strength in knowing that she is not alone and Patricia, who we met earlier, reveals a similar sense of agency, of determination:

> [I was] ten [years old] (…) when *Roots* came out. And so [that was] what my mum was saying to me [about working hard]. I've seen this here *Roots* and we're doing history and I'm learning about Elephantiasis and African people

in mud huts and things like that in school. So I'm panicking 'cos I'm thinking 'I can't miss [lessons]' and I just could not talk. I could not play with these [White] people and I'd bring my book and at playtime you'd see me sitting there with the book. (…) because I'm thinking 'There's no way. I can't miss a beat, because if I miss they're gonna put me to the bottom'.

Despite the fact that her mother has reminded her constantly about 'studying her books', it is the fear generated by watching *Roots* – a stark representation of race inequality – that galvanises Patricia into what we can think of as a form of 'racial resistance' (Moore 2008: 49). She now recognises that the name-calling and fights to which she has been subjected are not about her as an individual. There is a bigger fight to be faced that is not about the individual – and Roots exposes this for her – namely racism.

We now have some insight into our respondents' childhood experiences of racism. Some recoil at the starkness of the oppression facing them, while others work to face it head on with steeliness and determination. We observe how their parents inculcate in them strategies and means by which to survive racism. However, our analysis does not simply end here. Following Moore (2008: 495), we seek to better understand the boundaries and content of these racial identities and how race and class come together and 'vary according to the context, particularly the social, economic and cultural resources that groups have available to them'.

Playing the game: deployment of cultural capital to survive Whiteworld

We have seen that for our respondents school acted as a formative space of learning in terms of developing a racial identity imbued with minoritised status. While in some cases their parents advised about how to navigate and survive these enduring moments of tension, such guidance tended to be perfunctory, lacking in sufficient tactical detail to enable respondents to successfully manoeuvre through the raced complexities of daily British life. It is only through the gradual process of assessing and testing out a range of responses themselves that respondents have been able to begin to forge a path for surviving Whiteworld. In this section, we demonstrate how the experience of being a racialised minority along with acquiring middle-class status (albeit resisted as a self-definition by the majority) has enabled our interviewees to use their class position to signal status and hence a degree of legitimacy (though fragile and subject to interrogation) to their White counterparts. In making this argument, we continue to borrow from Bourdieu to set out the weight given to the social value of 'secondary characteristics' which, though they often remain unnamed, 'function as tacit requirements' to access social spaces or membership or inclusion in elite groups (Bourdieu 1986: 102). In this case, the groups and spaces mainly refer to educational establishments, that is schools and further and higher education institutions, but also include and draw on references to wider fields, the rules of entry to which are closely policed by a dominant White middle-class majority. The following comment from Miles provides a useful starting point from which it is possible to start to set out a distinction between primary/explicit characteristics (qualifications, hard work) and those which are secondary in nature:

> My mum, her line to me always was (…) 'If you work hard enough you can get anything you want to, all you need to do is work hard enough'. (…) There [was] only one thing that [was] said. There is a style of walking if you want to be a bad man walking down the street, you kind of hop and draw your leg along, and I do remember mum saying, 'If you ever walk like that I really will break your leg!' (…) I'm talking about my grandparents as well, they always want the best for you. They always want you to speak properly, to act properly and to have good values.
>
> *(Miles)*

The adults around Miles when he was growing up clearly articulate that merely working harder than your White counterparts, while important, is not sufficient to succeed. Adopting particular forms of embodied capital, in this case not walking like he is from the street, accent and values, are seen to further distinguish desirable from unwanted forms of being. Asked to expand on this statement, Miles refers to different 'cultural styles' or personas that are seen as appropriate to given contexts. Indeed comments about speech, accent and being 'articulate' feature frequently in discussions with interviewees, especially in relation to questions about class identification. Of importance here are not simply the values attributed to these various capitals but the simultaneous (mis)recognition of judgments assigned to alternative forms of the same property (Bourdieu 1986). For example, Miles, in extolling the importance of speaking 'properly', does so relationally, denouncing the value of Patois, a Jamaican colloquial form of verbal exchange: 'Yeah [speaking properly means] not speaking in Patois. Speaking clearly, and being able to be understood really (…), no street talk or anything along those lines, just as I'm speaking now.' We use this particular example as a means of introducing the thesis being 'racially salient' (Carbado and Gulati 2004: 1658), that is 'performing' and embodying aspects of cultural capital seen to be racially defined are not only undesirable within Whiteworld but also, as a result, become repositioned and uncritically accepted as undesirable by some Black middle classes themselves. We return to this subject later.

Language and accent are regarded as central tools that enable Black middle-class respondents to signal their class status to White others. In these sophisticated ways they are able to facilitate the creation of an invisible demarcation between themselves as middle class and other Black people from working-class backgrounds. Cassandra reveals some of the benefits of deploying her accent and the ways in which others respond:

> I get that reaction [of surprise] (…) a lot when people meet me (…) You can see (…) the wheels are going 'Ah she is a Black woman' because I don't

necessarily unless I want to sound like a Black person, I don't necessarily sound like a Black person (…) I'm very proud of being a Black woman but I think well, what is important is that people begin to listen to you and hear the way that you speak. Hear that you might have a level of education. So [for] example, I go into a shop and I am not happy with the way that I have been treated and I perhaps will tell the person that (…), they might try to fob me off and I insist to speak to the manager and you can very quickly see the realisation that I am actually not perhaps just dealing with somebody that does not know how to handle themselves. (…) And so I find that when the manager will come out and I am speaking and (…) not raising my voice but (…) just (…) putting my point across that usually I will get what I want. (…) I think that sometimes people categorise you, they expect you to be whatever stereotypical kind of screeching not able to be articulate (…) Black female …

This is a particularly interesting comment that exemplifies some of the nuanced complexities of raced and classed identity politics and stereotypes. 'Sounding Black', to borrow Cassandra's terminology, operates to denote a certain lack of education – there may be similarities here with Miles' reading of Patois – but also conveys more than this. Accent is conflated with comportment, in this case composure and politeness as an embodied form of capital, along with persistence and knowledge that enables her to take her complaint to the highest channels and obtain the outcome she seeks. This is the first point to note about Cassandra's statement. Second, her comment exposes how gender intersects with race and class, resulting in a reading of the Black female working-class body as uneducated and lacking in verbal and physical restraint. By making use of accent as a signifier of her middle-class status, Cassandra works to position herself as distinct from her Black female working-class counterparts. She is engaging in what Lacy (2007: 75) terms *exclusionary boundary work* in order to make known her class status and hence decrease the likelihood that she will be treated in a discriminatory way on account of her race. In order to do this successfully the Black middle classes must have awareness of the politics of both Black and White identities so they are able to access and deploy their capital appropriately. This is certainly evident with Cassandra. That she recognises her actions as part of the requirement to assert a public identity in a dominant White society is evidenced when she explains that when with her Black colleagues, she code-switches[4], with her speech marked instead by the use of Patois.

There is, however, a third point to be made. While she correctly identifies her actions as part of the unspoken[5] *rules of racial engagement* (Rollock 2012a) she also becomes complicit in *mis*recognising this form of capital (accent) as legitimate when, on meeting Dr Rollock for her interview, she expresses surprise at *her* race. The arbitrary criteria of Whiteworld that she recognises and deploys to her advantage, therefore, become the very basis by which she assesses raced and classed identity. In other words, in a perverse reformulation of DuBois' notion of double consciousness, Cassandra is not merely looking at herself through the eyes of

(White) others (necessary to allow her the insight to use her middle-class accent in appropriate settings) but she has 'forgotten' that she is doing so.

In addition to exclusionary work, the Black middle classes also carry out *inclusionary boundary work*, that is emphasising similarities (perhaps in values or pastimes) and shared experience with the White middle classes, in an attempt to minimise the distinction between the two groups. In the following extract, for example, Jean (a college lecturer) reveals how she enacts this:

> 'Cos I don't know if they [teachers] forget when they're (…) in the school (…) that there's actually two parents sitting [t]here [at the governors' meeting]. So we're all sort of speaking the language, *I call it the language of Whiteness. It's like you've got to be part of that in order to communicate in certain situations.* So the governing body communicates in a very White middle-class language. So they forget themselves and start making these derogatory remarks about parents and (…) [I] sort of [sit] there thinking 'Oh, so this is it'. [You] see very much what their core beliefs are … the parents … that they serve (…) [are from] a deprived community; [the] majority of parents are English as an additional language. [Emphasis added]

Here we observe that it is not merely accent and comportment that facilitates inclusion into White middle-class spaces – here conversations at governors' meetings – but the acquisition of a particular style of communication. This dual role (she is a minority playing at the language of a majority group) enables her to gain a 'perspective advantage' that those excluded from the centre or the 'norm' can experience as their analysis becomes multi-layered, becomes 'both' 'and', 'beyond the normative boundary of the conception of Self/Other' (King 1995, cited in Ladson-Billings and Donnor 2008: 373).

There is a further complexity to this analysis. Middle-class Black people also carry out what we think of as *authenticity signalling work* to let other Black people know that, even though they are sending one set of messages to Whiteworld (to gain acceptance and inclusion and to indicate their difference from working-class Blacks), they recognise many of these performances as a set of quite deliberate strategies.[6] They have not been entirely subsumed by this dominant ideology (and their enactments of it) and hence forgotten their Black roots and identity. Therefore we contend that the Black middle classes are living through not a double consciousness (as DuBois has famously theorised) but instead through a set of *multiple* consciousnesses as they move back and forth between the class and race divides within different social spheres populated by audiences and actors of varying race and class backgrounds. Richard's experience neatly exemplifies this multi-perspective:

> And then I've got the Black professional me almost [so] that when I'm around other Black professionals there is almost signals you have to send out to other Black professionals to let them know that you are for real, that you are here to work, you are not a joker. You are not someone who is just in there to

make up the quota as another Black guy (...). You didn't get on [simply] because you are Black (...) you have to let them know that because other Black professionals are sometimes a bit wary of you because they've worked really hard to get where they've got and they think well who are you? *What are you about? Where are you coming from? Are you one of those or one of us? And so you have to negotiate that a lot of the time which is strange.* You have to do that and sometimes you have to do that with White professionals as well. You have to say, hey look you know I'm not just here, I didn't just get here, I know what I'm talking about, *so you are constantly having to prove yourself all the time on a number of levels* ... [Emphasis added]

(Richard)

Of course, as Jean's earlier remarks indicate, the performance of these public identities includes the site of the school where, although as parents they engage in similar acts of monitoring and surveillance as White middle-class parents, specific concerns about their raced identities and racism modulate the nature of their interactions differently. In this chapter, we have sought to attend to the processes through which the Black middle classes develop public identities that are beyond the context of the school. There is a final point to be made. Constantly assessing and navigating these various public terrains can be exhausting and while we have detailed the resilience and agency exercised by many of our interviewees, there were some who spoke of the fatigue and challenge of manoeuvring through this relentless inequity and between these endless spaces marked by the demands of race and class:

I started doing it [putting on a mask of performance] consciously so in the mornings I would get in my car and I would have very loud reggae music, probably the windows down, people would always look and think, seeing a woman in a suit and think it is inappropriate music isn't it? And I would get on the tube and I would be playing (...) music but that is me, that is me without a mask. When I get off the tube and I walk up to the doors [of my work building] and I come through the revolving doors and I say, 'Good morning' the mask is on. It is my good morning [that the switch happens], 'Good Morning' [brightly] because my language has changed. I wouldn't speak like that at home, like 'Good Morning, how are you?' [bright and breezy] So I have become in a sense much more formal, quite closed, but it is almost like Superman going ...is it Superman? (...) then I sit down and start my work, the mask is on. If I have a phone call, if I get a call on my mobile and it is one of my friends, my sister or something, I will always just go out and say [*normal voice*], 'I can't speak, what is it?' [whispering] And then I come back in.

(Sandrine)

We witness the extent to which Sandrine's engagement in her workspace demands energy and concerted effort. Her account does not suggest a seamless, fluid and empowering transition in the management of public identities; rather it speaks to the suppression of her true self, a self that she argues has no legitimacy in her place of work and which we see exemplified via the careful way in which she handles personal telephone calls. We might think of reggae as a metaphor reflecting a sense of freedom and her cultural heritage. This music is awkwardly juxtaposed against the stiff, quiet formality of her workplace. There is a forlornness to this, a sense of not fitting in, of not belonging. Her account has resonance with Lorraine's powerful desire (Chapter 1) for a room of her own, a space in which she does not feel bound by the race and class limitations of wider society.

Conclusion

In this chapter, we have demonstrated the complex ways in which Black middle-class respondents come to an understanding of their status as racially minoritised and how their middle-classness enables them to access a set of capitals to perform a unique, classed form of racial resistance. The Black middle classes strategically make use of a range of resources including accent, language and comportment to signal their class status to White others to ultimately minimise the effects of racial discrimination. In reaching this conclusion, our aim has not been to lay claim to the primacy of race over class or vice versa but to understand how these particular forms of constructed identities operate in relation to one another. As evident throughout this book, racism persists as part of British society, albeit often in subtle, everyday forms, and even middle-class Black people remain judged based on the colour of their skin. However, they have at their disposal relative power and privilege to help them mediate racial injustice in a way that, on account of differences in access to and deployment of cultural capital, is not available to their Black working-class counterparts (hooks 2000). While this can help provide some insight into the nuances of racisms and the various forms in which it manifests, it should not obfuscate the pain and damaging consequences that racism causes. We also ought not to underplay the amount of energy and effort that is sometimes required of the Black middle classes as they work to successfully navigate White spaces. As with their childhood selves, there is an extra aspect to their socialisation and fit in mainstream society which is directly shaped by racism and the varying characteristics of Whiteness. This chapter helps us to understand the micropolitics of being Black and middle class and hence puts into greater context the ambivalence and hesitations they express about their class location (see Chapter 1).

There is a broader point to be made. The very need for these classed public identities – this Black middle-class cultural capital – provokes questions about the extent to which British society is socially just. It raises fundamental questions about race equity if *even* middle-class Black people – who have achieved many of the traditional benchmarks of social achievement and success – are obliged to carry out extra work in order to gain some level of legitimacy and acceptance within White society. Second, we are interested in whether the notion of 'inclusion' for Black people really means becoming 'racially palatable' and hence 'peripherally or unstereotypically nonwhite' (Carbado and Gulati 2005: 1658). The public identities that they deploy in mainly White spaces are those which mirror White middle-class behaviour or, at least, will minimise their racial difference when with them. If so, this represents not an advancement of race equality but the maintenance of an imbalanced status quo, the rules of which are determined by White society. That this society remains oblivious to (or uninterested in) the demands it places on the Black middle classes speaks to the unexamined power and privileges embedded in Whiteness.

Notes

1   The public exhibition of Baartman in London, 1810, caused a 'public scandal' not just due to the law abolishing slavery three years earlier but due to the semi-naked manner in which she was 'displayed' (Gilman 1992). Hobson (2003: 90) notes that 'by virtue of skin color [*sic*], femaleness and body shape – Baartman became a "freak" in Europe [enabling] Westerners [to further] prescribe racial and cultural differences and, hence, their "superiority" as Europeans in comparison with African people and cultures.'
2   Running from 1977 to the mid-1980s, the television sit-com *Mind Your Language* focused on adult students of an English as a Foreign Language evening class. The programme and its humour centred on the misunderstandings of the foreign students' engagement with the English language and drew heavily on cultural stereotypes of their individual countries of origin.
3   Based on the novel of the same name by Alex Haley, *Roots* charts the life of African born Kunta Kinte who was captured in his teens and taken to the 'New World' where he was sold into slavery. The story reveals the pain and challenges of slavery and proceeds to follow subsequent generations of Kinte's family through the abolition of slavery and into modern times.
4   'Code-switching' denotes the ability to switch from one dialect or vernacular to another (Hewitt 1986). Here we suggest that this is informed by signifiers of class and cultural background.
5   Unspoken, that is, within wider society. In 'safe' company many Black middle classes often switch between forms of parlance and colloquialisms not to delineate class position but to lend nuance and dramatic effect to storytelling or, in some conditions, to signal 'authenticity' to Black strangers.
6   Of course, we are not suggesting that these 'class acts' are always conscious or deliberate. In many instances our respondents embody and perform 'middle-classness' as a fundamental element of their habitus.

8

CONTINUITY AND DIFFERENCE ACROSS THREE GENERATIONS

We can't give you wealth but we can give you education.

Introduction

This final chapter is an account of mobilities – social and spatial – across three generations. As well as asking respondents about their childhood experiences of education, we also sought to elicit an understanding of their parents' degree of interaction with their school and/or their learning and how they considered issues of race and class to be viewed and experienced by their children. We focus on the different ways in which race and class intersect in shaping notions of Black identity as well as attitudes towards education and subsequent educational practices. We note that the broad nature of racism has changed across this generational span, although it persists in more subtle, insidious forms. Further – and quite fundamentally – we contend that race cannot be simply 'added on' to class analyses. This chapter illustrates how the two intersect, in complex ways, in different historical 'moments'.

Defining generations

As well as analysing the ways in which race and class shape the priorities, actions, values and beliefs of our cohort of middle-class, middle-aged Black adults, we also look before and after them, to their parents and their children, to see what these specific spatial and temporal trajectories reveal about changes in race and racial inequality in England.

In our data, the first generation is the respondents' parents, migrants from the Caribbean to the UK in the 1950s and 1960s. The respondents themselves are mostly second-generation Black British citizens who have achieved educational and labour market successes, often in challenging circumstances. They have been socially mobile, from the predominantly working-class occupations held by their parents to their current professional employment. They now seek to embed and reproduce their class assets and advantages through their children – the third generation – and education plays a key role in their thinking and planning for the future. Their strategies with regard to education are directed towards further social mobility for their children into what they perceive to be more secure positions than their own within the middle classes, or at least the social reproduction of their achieved position: 'a thrust inscribed in the slope of the past trajectory' as Bourdieu (1986: 333) puts it. Over and against this, however, they are acutely aware of the racism that still exists in education, employment and wider society and seek ways of inculcating their children against this. Even as they are engaged in such acts, their own class position remains 'ill-defined, open, risky and uncertain' (Bourdieu 1986: 345).

We find Mannheim's (1952) paper on *The Problem of Generations*, which considers the impact of generational experience across class and geographical lines, useful in facilitating our analyses of the three different age groups/time periods. Mannheim argued that a generation could be defined in terms of collective response to a traumatic event or catastrophe that unites a particular cohort of individuals into a self-conscious age stratum; thus generations may exhibit a distinctive consciousness and different situational responses. Racism can be considered a trauma in this way. That is to say, for each generation in our study the forms of racism experienced at school and elsewhere differ significantly, as do responses to racism and the politics of race relations:

> Racism does not stay still; it changes shape, size, contours, purpose, function – with changes in the economy, the social structure, the system and, above all, the challenges, the resistances to that system.
>
> *(Sivanandan 2002: 2)*

Mannheim draws attention to what Pilcher (1994: 489) calls the 'dialectic of history and biography', meaning that each social generation has a distinctive historical consciousness:

> … each social generation, although contemporaneous with other social generations, has a distinctive historical consciousness which leads them to experience and approach the same social and cultural phenomena differently.
>
> *(pp. 488–9)*

Neither Mannheim's original paper nor Pilcher's later commentary consider that racism might be a factor distinguishing which cultural and social phenomena are particularly affecting for a generation. We must put this in context. To speak of racism in this way also requires acknowledgment of the generational shifts among White people in their acts of racism and in the performance of Whiteness. Each generation of the Black family is operating within and in response to this wider relational and contextual frame (Fanon 1967). We note also that Mannheim's focus on the traumatic event, while an appropriate way of describing the potential effects of single incidents of racism on individuals, might also seem to suggest that racism is a unitary entity, with clearly defined, fixed boundaries which sit outside of everyday normality. Instead, through our use of Critical Race Theory, we recognise racism to be pervasive, a result of racist attitudes, preconceptions and expectations being deeply embedded in routines, 'common sense' and long-established ways of operating among White people. Racism today is differently encoded and performed than when respondents' parents came to the UK but it remains, nonetheless, a persistent norm in their lives.

Socio-political context across the generations

We set out key aspects of the socio-political context in the Introduction. However, it is worth restating here for the purposes of this chapter that a significant dimension of generational consciousness is the intersection of opportunity and oppression in relation to education policy. The policy context has changed over time from the assimilationist approaches of the 1960s – when most of our respondents' parents arrived – through colour-blind, multicultural and antiracist approaches to education, to the 'aggressive majoritarianism' (Gillborn 2008: 81; Tomlinson 2008) of the present day. Education policy rhetoric and practices have differently framed awareness of racial inequality, as well as offering and denying educational opportunities in different ways. In 1965, for example, policies sought assimilation, and the dispersal (bussing) of Black and other minority ethnic children was officially sanctioned as a way of ensuring that Black and minority ethnic children did not become concentrated in particular schools. Through the 1960s and 1970s, there was increasing concern from Caribbean-origin parents regarding the underachievement of their children – leading to their establishment of the supplementary school movement – which was reflected and further galvanised by the publication of Bernard Coard's book *How the West Indian Child Is Made Educationally Subnormal in the British School System* (Coard 1971).

During the 1970s, when most of the study's respondents were at school, education policy moved away from an official emphasis on assimilation to one of integration. The first official enquiry into race and education was published as the Rampton Report in 1981, and acknowledged that racism affected Black children's achievements, yet the findings were diluted in the later Swann Report (1985) and little meaningful action was taken. Those of the respondents who were educated at urban schools during the late 1970s and 1980s were sometimes on the receiving end of multicultural education.[1] This was criticised for its superficiality by those arguing for a more robust anti-racist approach (Troyna and Carrington 1990). The latter was taken up in several urban local education authorities in the 1980s. However, the protests against police brutality and economic deprivation in Brixton and Toxteth in 1981 showed how little real progress had been made towards race equality. In more general terms, like their White working-class counterparts, the respondents, as children, were caught up in the messy transition in the 1970s from grammar and secondary-modern schooling to comprehensive education. Many of those who did make it to grammar school experienced the alienating and damaging 'dividing practices' – the sense of marginalisation, of feeling and being positioned as Other – described by Jackson and Marsden (1962).

The third generation in our research was born in the shadow of Stephen Lawrence's murder and the subsequent inquiry into his death (Macpherson 1999) which highlighted the prevalence of institutional racism in public sector organisations, and which saw education as the primary means of seeking to address racism within future generations (Macpherson 1999; Rollock 2009). Schools had a short-lived duty under the Race Relations (Amendment) Act 2000 to record all instances of racial abuse, a responsibility abolished by the Coalition government elected in 2010. An emphasis on generic equalities and social exclusions has replaced specific concern with racism and sexism, as demonstrated by the abolition of the Commission for Racial Equality and its replacement by a joint Equalities and Human Rights Commission (EHRC) which itself has seen its powers diminished (Ramesh 2012).

In 2009, the year of Obama's election, an EHRC/MORI survey based on 1,498 interviews with people from different ethnic groups found an increasingly relaxed approach to cultural diversity and ethnic difference. The findings indicate that 49 per cent of participants were at ease with the multicultural nature of the UK and optimistic about it being 'tolerant' in relation to race. This optimism was particularly noted in the under 25s, which led the report to define them as the 'Obama generation' (EHRC/MORI 2009). However, this trend should not be overstated – there are many counter-indicators. The same report noted, for example, relatively little trust among Black and minority ethnic communities where the police are concerned. Elsewhere, head teachers reported a rise in the number of racist incidents in schools between 2007 and 2010 (Talwar 2012) and, crucially, the EHRC/MORI findings sit (as we have already mentioned) within a wider socio-political context in which policy-makers and leading public figures advocate the wholesale rejection of institutional racism as relevant within contemporary British society. Yet in 2007 – just two years prior to the EHRC/MORI report – Richardson reprinted Coard's arguments from 1971 to emphasise the slow pace of change and the entrenched nature of racial discrimination in education (Richardson 2007). Despite rhetorical changes over the intervening period, Black children continue to face challenges in compulsory and higher education, including lower average attainment, increased likelihood of permanent exclusion, under-representation at elite universities and less likelihood of being awarded first-class degrees (EHRC 2010a).

Educational strategies of the first generation

The majority of respondents explain that their own parents, the first generation in our data set, had little direct engagement with schools in the UK. In part this is because of a different, more distant climate of home–school relations generally in the 1960s and 1970s. However, there were also several other factors that influenced this relationship. Parents brought with them to the UK a (short-lived) faith in the

British education system which had been informed by their experience of it in the Caribbean. There was a ready expectation that not only would hard work and dedication on the part of the pupil be recognised and rewarded by the school, but that teachers would have the same investment in raising and educating their child as was the case back home:

> My father wasn't necessarily familiar with the [education] system and neither was he necessarily challenging of [it] because he came from a cultural perspective where people believed in teachers' attitudes and teachers' interests in the education of children was actually demonstrated. So to an extent the system that existed, he felt was fair. (…) he believed in inherent fairness of the British (…) system.
>
> *(Robert)*

> … like I said my mother came here (…) believed that the White system was absolutely fair and they [that generation] believed you know, you will get the right to go through, you know if you go to school you learn your lessons, you just go on (…) but they didn't know in my opinion, what to expect. They just wanted the best for us. My mum wanted the best for me.
>
> *(Anthony)*

It is important to recognise the generational habitus that respondents' parents brought with them in their migration from the Caribbean where, in fact, the cultural landscape and mores were very different. Ensuring the child received a good education and future was not seen as merely the parents' responsibility but the teacher shared in this commitment; Robert speaks of a head teacher making it part of his 'daily duties' to enquire after any child who was not in school. In this sense, a 'community' was involved in raising the child. Britain presented a profoundly different cultural landscape:

> Disappointment and disillusionment of many kinds were the everyday experience of the 1950s settlers. It cannot be denied that the West Indians, in particular, had totally unrealistic expectations. The anti-imperialist tradition notwithstanding, their ideas about Britain were largely derived from a colonial education system in which Britain was revered as the 'mother country'. (…) What they found here dismayed and shocked them.
>
> *(Fryer 1984: 374)*

Barbara recalls that her parents did not particularly understand the system but – in line with Fryer's observations – were of the opinion that it was the role of the school to give her an education: 'They shouldn't openly be discriminating against me because I'm Black', a viewpoint espoused by Cynthia's parents also. Racism was a new, shocking, painful reality with which these new immigrants had to contend. Robert reflects that he does not believe his father ever really 'came to grips with racism operating in the institutionalised sense', revealing both the emotional challenge of racism as well as its sheer endemic magnitude. Thus we begin to evidence the marking out of invisible boundaries and consciousness between generations. Gabriel's father, for example, experiences racism, as an adult, in the workplace while his son learns of it during his formative years within the context of the school:

> ... my parents' aspirations were very firmly within traditional middle-class aspirations, I would say, despite our actual living standards and all the other features of our [life] but race was in and out of our house and in school every day. My parents experienced at work horrendous things, you know, my parents in tears – sometimes my father with tears running down his face and then my school experience ...
>
> (Gabriel)

Gabriel's account vividly conveys the sobering, powerful image of a young child – a boy – witnessing his father, a grown man, reduced to tears through events that both mirror his own school experiences and which are preparing him for the adult world. Others, recognising the racism and barriers, instilled in their children the need to work harder than, 'to be 10 times better, or a 100 times better than a White person' (Lorraine) in order to succeed, a strategy that simply would not have been necessary in their own early years. These differing positionalities reveal not just broader generational distinctions in the conceptualisation of and responses to racism but, in some cases, signal potential *within*-family differences about the nature of political resistance and survival:

> ... the support came from peers rather than from my parents' generation (...) we were supporters of the notion of Black power [and] they couldn't understand why we would want to support any notions of Black power. So that created a political divide. And it was a sort of chilling experience at 17, 18 to be confronted with my father's generation to say that Black power is of no use to the world and I said well actually we have a White power regime in the world! Power is not colourless, it's not neutral.
>
> (Robert)

The extent to which respondents' parents engaged with school was informed also by the pressures they faced in their new jobs in Britain, in many cases having not just to 'settle for a lower job status than they had enjoyed at home' (Fryer 1984: 374) but (as the above comment from Gabriel indicates) also having to cope with racist abuse and stereotyping. Therefore, practically (often parents were holding down more than one job or working long hours) and emotionally, intervention into their children's school experience was not always feasible. Grace describes her parents as 'placid' and 'accepting'; Richard describes his as 'wanting a quiet life', 'fitting in', a response that needs to be contextualised with reference to the crude and overt racism of the 1960s and 1970s. A few had no contact at all with the school although most went to parents' evenings and almost all conveyed to their children a strong sense of the importance of education and the expectation that they do well at school:

> Mum was a nurse, father was a lorry driver and the only thing throughout all of our upbringing, you know, 'we can't give you wealth but we can give you education' and they paid and they sent us to a private (…) school.
>
> *(Cynthia)*

> I did very well at school and […] my parents …. coined 'Education, education, education' long before Mr Blair … they both had this vision of what education could do for their children and they, I wouldn't hesitate from using the word inculcate, they indoctrinated us about the value of education and what we needed to do at school.
>
> *(Gabriel)*

A small number were more heavily involved in their children's education. These were usually (though not always) those from more middle-class backgrounds in the Caribbean, whose own education allowed them to be active as well as aspirational around their children's education. Lucy describes her parents:

> My mum was very academic, she was a teacher in Dominica and when she came over here she pursued a career in nursing […] Dad was a civil servant […] My parents were fully involved [with school]. You know in terms of primary school where you had activities, my mum and dad would participate [in those] my dad used to teach cricket at school … through to secondary school where there were parents' evenings. My parents always attended all those things, you know [curriculum] option meetings … they were fully involved in my and my brother's education.
>
> *(Lucy)*

Given provocation, however, some generally non-interventionist parents would act (e.g. Isabelle's parents challenged her placing within the lower status CSE rather than O-level groupings) but for most there was an expectation that the teachers were the experts and knew best. Josephine's father, for instance, accepted that his daughter needed a remedial speech class while she was at primary school because she spoke with a strong Barbadian accent (having spent her early years in Barbados). Most respondents were told by their parents that if they went to school, and paid attention, they would learn, pass exams and then would have access to a better job and a better life than their parents.

The majority of the respondents' characterised their own orientation towards their children's education as very different from their parents who had not been 'proactive', 'hands on' (Isabelle), did not 'intervene' or have a long-term 'strategy' (Michael). Joan characterised her mother as having the will for her daughter to succeed but not the knowledge of the education system. Joan herself who works for a local education authority, feels she has both. In this sense, they learned *from* and learned to be different *to* their parents. However, it would be misleading to characterise the respondents' parents as simply passive. Their approach was largely one of survival and protecting their families from the racist economic and social conditions they encountered. Another strategy often mentioned was the development of an active and collective aspect to thinking about education and this was evidenced through the collective movements and activists for economic and race equality at the time (Sivanandan 1983). In our study, while some respondents said their parents unreflexively chose local schools, other parents used social networks of neighbours or friends to glean information and help create a climate of expectation. For example, Felicia had a successful educational career as the first Black child at a Jewish primary school, chosen on the advice of a White neighbour, and Isabelle describes the encouragement of fellow immigrants from St Vincent in her town to study hard and to reach university.

Second-generation: class mobility, schooling and race

Respondents, by and large, grew up and attended school in the 1970s and 1980s. They have experienced social mobility, often occupying spaces – university, the workplace – that are predominantly White. They are a classed and raced minority. They have also experienced some degree of change in the nature of how race and racism are enacted. They have developed middle-class identities (see Chapter 1) under the historical trajectory of equalities legislation and policy guidance, and changing public opinion about the existence of racism:

> Excluded groups are therefore not the victims of more traditional and overt racism but more subtle incarnations of even more insidious practices. (…) A constant aspect of this new racism is its ability not to be recognized as the explicit or overt racism of the past as it transforms itself into debates about citizenship, immigration, nationhood. A 'safe' distance emerges for these discourses from the more identifiable biological or phenotype explanations of racial hierarchies and inferiority or superiority, and results in amorphous types of racism that are difficult to detect and much easier to deny.
>
> (Hylton 2009: 14)

Respondents also identify subtle (and not so subtle) forms of racism such as being perceived as the one who does not quite 'fit in', who is positioned as 'other', the continued stereotypes of Black people as being prone to aggression, of being uninterested in education, as being from inadequate families. Such persistent racism threatened families' ambitions for their children.

Memories of school

Like many respondents Gabriel has good memories of some teachers, but also like many others, he was also routinely confronted by racism. We described in Chapter 3 his being called names (golliwog, jungle bunny) and being subjected to other denigratory remarks. The chances of White teachers and peers behaving in a racist manner was to some extent arbitrary or at least unpredictable, but some tendencies are discernible from the data. For example, Ruby had mixed experiences, related largely to the degree to which individual educational settings were ethnically mixed. She was 'dispersed' (bussed to a school outside her immediate locality, a policy designed to hasten the assimilation of Black and ethnic minority children and placate the fears of White parents) to what became a relatively ethnically mixed primary school in a White working-class area and 'has no recollection of racism at all. At all.' Following this, she went to a grammar school where she was part of a very small Black minority: '"Wog" was a common phrase at that time wasn't it [the 1970s]? "Oh, no offence" I got fed up of "no offence", five years of "no offence".' Her sixth form experience at a different, more ethnically mixed school was much better. She then went to a London university and 'for the first time [as a young adult] met White people I didn't think were racist.' Similarly Rachel, a student at another London university with a multi-racial intake, found there for the first time 'teachers that care'.

The respondents' stories suggested that the chances of meeting racism increased in certain circumstances, one of these being a Black minority in a grammar school: 16 out of 62 respondents (26 per cent) attended a grammar school. Much has been written about the experience of White working-class children in grammar schools, their marginalisation and their sense of being 'other' (Lacey 1970; Jackson and Marsden 1962). For the respondents, the focus of the discrimination they received was based on the colour of their skin.

Some, like Gabriel, met physically violent and abusive racism, others experienced acts of racial Othering, for example in the form of repeated questions about skin and hair (Chapter 7; see also Rollock 2012b). Paulette refused to give much detail about her school experiences, firmly stating, 'I don't want to go over that thank you. It was not pleasant.' As children, these parents experienced a sense of isolation. Elizabeth responded to her largely White middle-class grammar school by 'hiding'. Rachel noted, 'I didn't get involved in a lot of stuff at school, a lot of extra curricular stuff because I didn't really feel part of what was going on ... I wasn't properly integrated and I was getting a lot of racial abuse on a daily basis from children.' Isabelle talks about the long-term effect on her of being 'not seen as equal'.

> The message I got about being Black [was] I knew there was prejudice and I knew that people would not like me because of the colour of my skin and I don't know how any child recovers from that ... I think to attach a judgment to the colour of my skin, I never got over that, I couldn't get over that.

She describes the embodiment of White privilege in middle-class girls at her grammar school with 'beautiful hair, very healthy looking skin, slender, the way they talked was very refined', girls who 'didn't talk to you with the same ease with which they spoke to other people, people they related to better'. For Isabelle, such girls grew up to be the mothers outside her daughter's independent school. 'In the playground … there were lots of parents around with their huge umbrellas when it was raining. I don't know why people in that kind of space have these huge umbrellas …' Umbrellas here act as a domestic signifier of exclusion and distinction. Isabelle reflects that the success she enjoyed speaking to a school meeting using her professional expertise shows how far she has come from her previously marginalised identity, but that has not made the journey less painful, and she is concerned not to pass on feelings of inferiority to her daughter (also in a minority at her school).

> I talk to her about Blackness to her regularly, but I talk across the spectrum, not just us as victims … She takes pride in who she is. Her colour doesn't dominate her life. It's who she is but it's not everything to her, she sees herself as [daughter's name] first. I am just amazed.

A sense of being 'other' was also instilled through more subtle signals, which highlighted difference and non-belonging, even through the polite veneer of seemingly innocuous actions. As a working-class Black girl at a largely White middle-class grammar school Lorraine found 'in many ways I became a teacher's pet because I was the only Black girl in my year, and in some ways people went *over the top* to be nice to me' (emphasis added). The difference in the race and class capitals she brought from home and that of the other children and the school was palpable and emphasised her difference.

> In primary school you got taunts about race, but not so much in secondary school … I think class became more of an issue … In English lessons we'd been asked to bring in newspapers from home to talk about … when everyone else brought in *The Times*, I was bringing in, you know, the *Daily Mirror* … There was quite stunned silences, I really do think my English teacher didn't actually know what to say. […] No one said anything horrible but you sensed that this was just not the done thing […] So much revolved around having read *Alice in Wonderland*, *Wind in the Willows*, there were all these references to classic children's literature … No one knew about the Anansi[2] tales or anything like that. It was always this sense of being the odd one out, trying hard not to stand out […] Not letting the race down. I couldn't ever relax while at school.
>
> *(Lorraine)*

It is perhaps unsurprising given the weight and tenor of these experiences, coupled with the low expectations of many teachers and often poor careers advice, that most respondents did not achieve great educational success at school. Indeed nearly half of the respondents who have a degree achieved that qualification as adult returners (not an unusual path for Black Caribbean graduates (Mirza 2009b)).

Racism, class and isolation

The second generation in this study, the respondents, have succeeded despite racism. They have fulfilled their parents' hopes and (often) their expectations of social mobility:

> … around the age of about 21 something came up again where I said, there is no way I would live in [poor North London borough], no way, my parents live in [London borough], there is no way I would live in [that borough]. My friends were like 'Why? We grew up here [in that area]'. And this is where they wanted to live. And I said 'absolutely not, my parents did not travel five thousand miles from [the Caribbean] arriving in this country with nothing in their hands, nothing in their pockets, to buy a house in [area], for me to buy a house in [that same area]. That's not what they want!'
>
> *(Michael)*

And yet they have not escaped racism. The apparently smooth surface of the professional workplace also reveals flaws. Rachel maintains that it is seen as normal and natural for White people to have other professional White colleagues while Black professional colleagues are somehow misplaced and seen as unusual; Black people in her workplace do not feel accepted and are rarely sponsored or mentored by senior White colleagues. Claudette also speaks of similar issues, a sense that her cultural identity and experience are not quite understood:

> I've worked with White people who are really interested [in race] but there's a certain amount of explaining sometimes that you have to do [with] White people and I have to do that everyday of my life and sometimes I want to just talk to someone who (…) understand some of the things I'm talking about.

As we discussed in Chapter 7, the strain of living in a society where Whiteness is the norm extracts psychological costs – described by Jean like wearing a 'tight pair of shoes' – which, in some cases, is compounded by their mobility into the middle classes and away from their family origins. From a generational perspective, Jean is clear that she does not want her children to feel they have to show 'one face out there and a different face at home because I have seen [the costs] so much'. Sandrine develops this theme, noting that with her White middle-class colleagues she is sometimes unwittingly excluded by the conversation; she gives the example of books and plays with which she is unfamiliar (although she notes later that she regularly goes to the theatre, but not necessarily to watch White mainstream productions) and being asked what she did during her gap year when in fact she did a part-time degree as an adult returner while working. Here intersectional tensions, and the damage that they can do, come into view. In addition, different forms of *disidentification* are enacted in the tensions between where you are now and where you come from. Both Jean and Sandrine describe the pressure derived from not being able to be yourself in predominantly White workplaces, but Sandrine does not feel entirely at ease with her family either, not all of whom have been socially mobile into the middle classes. She feels compelled to leave out areas of her experience, namely her professional working environment (as a manager in central government), when with her family. It is with her Black work colleagues that she feels the least need for a 'mask'. They share the same class *and* race positions and therefore she feels she can relate with them as a 'whole' person 'as opposed to half a person or three quarters'. As Bourdieu (1986: 337) notes: '"Taking off" always presupposes a break, and the discovery of former companions in misfortune is [...] one aspect of this.' Again, we note this underlying sense of isolation among the Black middle classes (see Chapter 1).

There are raced and classed calculations to be made in mainly white spaces and in the spaces of family and (certain) friends. Lorraine speaks of the possibility that her parents might be offended by her views of their television habits and exercises care in her comments about this. Sensibilities of taste and preference, imbued with markers of class, serve to impose a further generational distance between Lorraine and her family – a distance acquired through the class mobility that Lorraine has experienced and which her family have sought for her. Sandrine expresses similar concerns, explaining that while generic acts or conversations 'about the TV, having dinner, eating rice and peas and chicken, washing up, telling off the kids' are safe territory with her family, she has to redact or simplify conversations that relate to her work. Her family do not understand the detailed micropolitics of her workplace nor are they able to offer strategies about how to handle conflict or problems that she experiences there. Thus there are costs to achieving class mobility, to being among the first Black middle classes; the family home too becomes a place of possible isolation.

Race and class within the Obama generation

Parents are aware that their children's identities and experiences are being differently shaped by race and class. The more affluent respondents, especially, having come from economically disadvantaged working-class backgrounds, were very aware that their children were growing up in more secure and comfortable surroundings. The younger generation in some cases also articulate Blackness in ways that differ from their parents, and this can sometimes lead to family perturbations. It should be noted here that our accounts stem from the children's parents and not the young people themselves; children may articulate their experiences differently. Parents were proud and pleased that their children were confident, but their comments about their children's sense of entitlement – which they themselves have worked to develop – were in some cases tinged with ambivalence. This is for two reasons. One is their awareness of the difference between their position – the fragility of being socially mobile and being first-generation middle class, and the sense of 'boundary crossing' which that position elicits – and the more established social position they hope their children will hold. They inhabit a space where class and race intersect differently from their children. Richard captures these intersectional, generational nuances:

> I never went out to a restaurant when I was young … My son who is 11 … We were having a discussion about how, about the fact that he didn't feel that his scallops had been browned off enough … I didn't even know what a scallop was when I was his age! I had never eaten one. I was highly unlikely to be in a place where I would be getting things like that. And I thought he has been all over the world, he has travelled, and at that age I hadn't done any of that stuff … He will just grab a menu and go to me 'is that a kind of roux sauce dad?' And I am thinking 'you are 11. You should be eating fishfingers and beans like I was!'
>
> *(Richard)*

The second reason for ambivalence is anxiety, the anxiety that their children's security, confidence and promise might be undermined or even destroyed by racism and, furthermore, that this is a danger *some* of the children, at the present time, do not see. Both Malorie and Robert noted that their children had called them racist because of their emphasis on race.

> It is difficult to convey … it is outside of your experience [said to White interviewer] … but it's really happening, and that's why I am driven to say to [my daughter] and my niece and nephew … 'you need to be aware, you need to be aware that things happen because of the colour of your skin, yes?' And sometimes – it depends how receptive they are to it – but sometimes they just say 'oh, you're racist'.
>
> *(Malorie)*

Robert comments that his children have been 'shielded and protected' by their relatively affluent lifestyle. Dawn also notes that her daughter and younger relations 'seem to have bought into [the] whole multiculturalism idea', and Jean further comments that the younger generation is one 'that is sleepwalking into thinking that everything [racism] has gone, done, dusted. Whereas I think a lot of the racist stuff that goes on is actually very subtle.' These differences in conceiving of racism appear to be, in some cases, shaped by the simple fact of their youth – these children and young people have yet to encounter the racially formative and predominantly White spaces of university, the workplace or other adult social spaces. It is also informed by differing conceptualisations of Blackness among this third generation. Femi, for example, despite the explicit debates had within the home about identity, racism and inequality, notes 'with some disgust' that her daughter has a 'very limited concept of herself as Black'. A similar sentiment is expressed by Robert who concludes that his children seem not to have a need to think about themselves as Black in quite the same way as he did as a young man and Janet observes that her children are growing up having being raised by Black British parents as opposed to parents who have a firm Caribbean grounding. Identity is shifting; notions of Blackness are changing across generations:

> ... there was a young Black woman [at a public talk] who said that she was young, she was female, she was Black and she was gay but she felt that none of those things defined her. Now there is a little bit of me that was offended actually because I thought, well actually I am very proud to define myself as a Black woman and I would never want to do anything other, and a bit of me felt that you know people didn't go through the struggles so that you could dismiss the fact that you are Black or gay or whatever. But then the other side of the coin is that she has the confidence and maybe she hasn't gone through the kinds of difficulties that I might have, and maybe that is a really positive thing that she doesn't have to question anything about being Black or being a woman or being gay.
>
> *(Lorraine)*

We should not be surprised by this. The race struggles and class transition that respondents went through today look different. The notion of identities shaped by 'collective action and consciousness' (Gilroy 1981: 212) that marked the race and class struggles of the 1960s, 1970s and 1980s is being reconstituted as the socio-political landscape changes (Warmington 2014). It is marked by the fuzzy boundaries of a new generational dynamic, namely the beguiling lure of post-racialism:

> Today, we have to recognise the complex internal cultural segmentation, the internal frontlines which cut through so-called Black British identity. And perhaps where these internal divisions are most acutely registered, where these lineaments of change are explored most vigorously concerns young people and their cultures. (...) Blackness in this context may be a site of positive affirmation but is not necessarily any longer a counter identity, a source of resistance.
>
> *(Hall 2000: 127)*

However, it would be a mistake and oversimplification to state that the third generation live free of racsim. In an overt example, Malorie describes how her niece, a student, was greeted by monkey noises as she travelled to her university lodging just outside London. In other cases racism manifests less overtly but nonetheless continues to draw on stereotypes of Black people as 'other'. Derick's teenage daughter, for example, is expected by her White peers to know everything about Black music. Some mothers also speak about the pressure on their teenage daughters to adopt a European light-skinned notion of beauty by, for example, straightening their hair (see Chapter 6). This may not be a modern phenomenon, but arguably the increased availability of different forms of media serve to bombard children with images of largely White or light-skinned celebrities. Mothers also reference the behaviour and self-presentation of the few Black characters in TV programmes. As Robert pointedly notes, 'The UK isn't a different place [than in the past] although the same things might be done differently.'

Respondents acknowledge that while they were the first in their family to go to university, their children are traversing a path already trodden about which they, as parents, can provide insights. The third generation can draw upon the strategies of their parents and are less likely to experience similar levels of class or race isolation:

> (…) I am not 100 per cent confident that things have changed that critically for the younger generation but I think that they perceive things differently and that might be a good thing. I think [my daughter] will probably be better off starting out having the confidence to not worry about whether she is the only Black person or not, whether the reality has changed or not. Just her attitude will probably make life easier for her than it was for me.
>
> *(Lorraine)*

Concluding thoughts

The first generation in this study came to the UK with high hopes for their children and found an education system pervaded by crude racisms. While the resources and opportunities to confront these directly were not always available to them, they were able to instil their children with a sense of drive and the possibility of advancement. Now, for the parent respondents, their class resources and accumulated educational assets are key 'to reducing the probability that racial discrimination will determine important outcomes in their lives' (Lacy 2007: 112), and are helping them prepare their children for success in the education and labour markets.

In this chapter, we have emphasised the particularity of Black experiences of upward social mobility. While they share some of the same insecurities and ambivalences (Reay 2001), the respondents' experiences are different to those of White 'border crossers'. They are members of a visible minority and, despite their mobility, they express reservations about being 'middle class', seeing that designation as owned and protected by a privileged and more affluent White majority. Membership of a Black middle class is a relatively new and emergent identity. It is characterised by isolation, by searching for a space in which to be comfortably Black and middle class. Our intersectional analysis demonstrates that race cannot be simply 'added on' to class. Race and racism change how class works, how it is experienced, and the subjectivites available to individuals. As the data illustrates, the two intersect, in complex ways, at different historical 'moments'. As we have suggested above, the intersection for members of the third generation – the Obama generation – is likely to be different to that lived by their parents and grandparents. These young people are portrayed by their parents as self-confident Black children and young adults, sure of their identity, accumulating academic qualifications and a range of other skills and capabilities which offer future opportunities. Even those educated in mainly White settings are growing up in a country with a diverse, multi-racial population and a growing Black middle class. Their experiences of disadvantage and privilege are configured differently and are played out in a different cultural-political context. To be Black in this context is also differently shaped, differently informed. In this sense they inhabit a different 'generational location', as Mannheim calls it, to their parents. There is evidence here of an original and distinctive consciousness and a different dialectic of history and biography. However, it is important to think about what has stayed the same, as well as what has changed, across these three generations. Racism and race inequality has changed but it has not disappeared. For the third generation, racism may be less likely to assail them as explicit vicious abuse, but still retains the potential to undermine, to marginalise and to threaten. They may potentially present new forms of resistance to this racism, informed by the specific 'lineaments' (Hall 2000: 127) of their raced identities and the (classed) cultural capitals they bring to bear. There are plenty of examples in our data of moments when racisms of various kinds threaten to negate class resources and block or curtail educational opportunity (see Chapters 3 and 4). Racism in the labour market persists and there may also be consequences of the current economic crisis which disproportionately threaten this group, particularly the decline in public sector employment (Devabhai 2012; Gillborn 2012; Unison 2012). While most of the third-generation children appear for the most part, with the support of their parents, to be surviving and thriving in a White-dominated society, 'the ever present possibility of [racial] stigmatization' (Lacy 2007: 73) remains.

Notes

1 Multicultural education meant 'adding on' references to other cultures in the curriculum (the 'Three Ss' of saris, samosas and steel bands (Troyna and Carrington 1990). Antiracist approaches emphasised the explicit promotion of racial equality.
2 Anansi, featuring in Caribbean and West African fables, is a clever spider, outwitting those around him.

CONCLUSION

A colour-blind future?

Introduction

> All black people know that no matter your class you will suffer wounds inflicted by racism.
>
> *(hooks 2000: 98)*

> ... the low attainment and poor progress of Black Caribbean students cannot be accounted for by social class or, indeed, by a wide range of student, family, school and contextual variables. The results mitigate against common explanations of Black Caribbean-White British gap related to socioeconomic deprivation, parental involvement or student attitudes to school.
>
> *(Strand 2011: 217)*

In this final chapter, we concentrate on three principal areas. First, we draw together the discussions and analyses of the preceding chapters to summarise the impact of social class in the experiences and perspectives of our Black middle-class respondents. Drawing closely on Bourdieu, we then refine our arguments to demonstrate how the deployment of class capitals is shaped by, and intersects with, race and racism to ultimately limit the educational chances of Black middle-class families in different ways. This finding is highly significant. It explains why quantitative research consistently fails to account for the lower academic attainment of Black Caribbean pupils, even after taking account of social class and other key factors. Perhaps most importantly, our research fundamentally challenges the political insouciance that surrounds race inequalities in education and across society, where the primary concern has become social class. In concluding the chapter, we reflect on both the challenges and reality of racism and how the political focus on social mobility alone to address educational disadvantage will leave untouched the issues presented in this book.

Class capitals and race

To be Black and middle class is to exist in an amorphous space between the White middle classes and the Black working class. As we have seen, the majority of the Black middle-class respondents experience a sense of dislocation and discomfort in aligning with the label 'middle class' (Chapter 1). While some of these uncertainties reflect broader misgivings evidenced when people are asked about class identification generally (Savage *et al.* 2001), others relate specifically to the ongoing presence of race and racism in their lives. In fact, we cannot understand the experiences of the Black middle classes without attending to the role of race and racism. As Ball (2003b: 168) argues, class identities are 'relational, made by distinctions and classifications of self and others' and it is important to remember that these identities do not exist in a reified, contained state. Dominant notions of class within the British context are racialised; they are shaped and informed by Whiteness even when Whiteness is not explicitly named. Some of the discomfort voiced by participants about aligning with a middle-class identification stems precisely from a reluctance to be associated with a term ('middle class') which for many is always and already inflected with Whiteness which in turn they characterise as individualistic and hyperprivileged. Instead, some Black middle-class people speak of valuing what we term 'moral capital' – that is an awareness and concern about the circumstances of others alongside a recognition of the value of goods and people around them. Moral capital, in this context, stems from a memory of a working-class past, of an understanding of what it is to have nothing. In becoming middle class, there is a desire to hold onto this capital as a way of remaining grounded and not becoming aligned with Whiteness. It is the continued presence of racism along with an understanding of the characteristics of Whiteness which imposes and reinforces boundaries and distinctions between the Black middle classes and their White peers. The class identities of the Black middle classes are shaped and distinguished, therefore, in relation to classifications of not just social class but also race; as their parents' generation were a distinct fraction of the working class (Ramdin 1987), the Black middle classes are now a distinct classed and raced fraction of the middle class.

It is important to note that the racism with which the Black middle classes have to contend is nuanced, subtle, often covert. It is rarely the explicit, crude racism of far-right extremist groups. This quiet racism presents via 'coded signifiers' (Hylton 2009: 14) and racial micro-aggressions (Rollock 2012a; Solorzano *et al.* 2000; Sue *et al.* 2008). It is characterised within our research by White people's polite dismissal of the possibility that Black families can be intelligent, knowledgeable or achieve at the highest levels, by a refusal to treat Black families as equal or to regard their concerns as legitimate. Race is seldom explicitly named but the assumptions, beliefs and stereotypes upon which such interactions are based betray an underlying belief in racial difference. Black middle-class families are alert to the probability of such practices by Whites and work in careful and often highly strategic ways to avoid or minimise their engagement with these acts and to seek successful educational returns for their children. Our examination of the class strategies of the Black middle classes has enabled us to uncover and shed light upon the moments at which these boundaries are made and such distinctions reinforced. However, it would be a mistake to conceptualise the identities and experiences of the Black middle classes *only* through the lens of racism. Cultural identity, heritage and values transmitted through pastimes, foods, music and key points of cultural reference also act as what we describe as a 'cultural adhesive', sometimes facilitating connections with other Black people:

> I didn't know who John Lennon was until he was assassinated, I didn't know who he was. If someone said 'John Lennon', I couldn't tell you, and that was a product of my upbringing where in my home it was John Holt, it was Bob Marley, it was Mohammed Ali, in our home even without it being a statement.
>
> *(Nigel)*

Our findings on school choice (Chapter 2) exemplify some of the assessment and careful monitoring deployed by parents as they pursue their priorities for their children. Those who focus on academic excellence in the selection of schools (academic choosers) understand that this will often mean sacrificing the likelihood of their child mixing with pupils from a range of ethnic backgrounds and, moreover, also increase the probability of their child experiencing racism. Independent schools and state schools which are predominantly White are viewed as likely arenas for such incidents. The decision to send their child to these schools requires not just economic resources but also time and vigilance to maintain watch over their children once there, to ensure their continued educational attainment *and* to guard against racism. This type of raced emotional labour and risk-taking fundamentally differs from that needed by White middle-class families.

We also identify from our school choice data those whom we term 'social choosers', that is they regard the ethnic and social class mix of the pupil population as key priorities. These parents often seek, among other factors, to distance themselves from particular kinds of Black pupils and their parents, whom they regard as uninvolved and uninterested in education. Our findings, therefore, speak not just to the factors involved in school selection but also enable us to tease out the parameters of distinction that some Black middle-class parents perceive set them apart from certain other Black parents.

Parents' concerns do not end at the point of school selection (and indeed 'choice' in this area is limited for most). We heard many accounts of low teacher expectations about the academic capabilities of their children *even when* previous school-based evidence clearly documented the same students' capacity for excellence (Chapter 3). Respondents report instances of their child being lauded for good behaviour when, in fact, their academic work required attention and improvement, of their child being moved down to lower ability groups despite performing at the same level as pupils in the top group, of being overlooked for a leading role in the school play despite excellence in drama, of being pacified by teachers to accept low grades as sufficient success despite keenness and questions from both pupil and parents about how to do better. Such practices (lack of support and low expectations) are more pronounced in situations where the child has been or might be labelled as having special educational needs (SEN) or a disability (Chapter 4). The field of disability and inclusive education is fraught with contradictions and complexities (Slee 2011) but our data suggests that Black parents and their children face an extra challenge because of inequalities of race. Black middle-class respondents who mention special educational needs report numerous instances where schools have failed to provide adequate support and guidance following diagnoses. In other situations, students who had highlighted their experience of racism in school found themselves viewed as candidates for SEN referrals. In this way, the system shifted blame and attention away from institutional practices back onto the alleged deficit of the individual child. Facing such challenges, parents mobilise their considerable class capitals in order to (fight to) secure guidance and support for their children. This includes seeking out independent assessments, carrying out online research, consulting literature and even soliciting the help of psychologists to broker and expedite assistance from the school. It is difficult to do justice to quite how much effort and work parents expend in asking for help from teachers and school support staff yet find that their efforts are frequently rebuffed or ignored altogether. This aspect to the education of Black children is rarely mentioned in headlines about attainment and school experience.

Parents in our study vary in the ways in which they engage with the school and in their response to what we might define as schools' intransigence. In Chapter 5, we set out these responses along a continuum with those who are *determined to get the best* at one end and those who are *hoping for the best* at the other. Those in the former category closely plan and carefully monitor their children's educational trajectory, employing tutors and signing their children up for a range of extra-curricular activities in a bid to complement their academic career and prepare them for employment within a global marketplace. These parents are proactive in their engagement with the school and are prepared to move the child if dissatisfied with any aspect of their education. At the other end of the continuum are parents who value education but not at any cost or above all other considerations. They are hopeful that their child will achieve academically and are proactive in their engagement with school yet they also recognise the challenges and competitiveness of the education system and are sensitive to the impact that this environment might have on their child. Their focus, therefore, centres mainly on the child's immediate wellbeing and happiness. These findings rebut the stereotype that uncritically positions Black parents as uninterested and uninvolved in their children's education.

There are many instances where the accounts of racism are difficult or painful to recount (one participant refused to share details of her school experiences because she did not wish to recall the trauma of the racist incidents she suffered) but perhaps none more so than in Chapter 6 where parents share their concerns about how best to raise a balanced and culturally aware Black middle-class child. If they have sons, parents worry about prevalent stereotypes that situate Black males as an object of fear and threat. Anxieties centre on the dangers of what might happen to them outside of the home via the possible lure or violence of gangs and the dangerous and unpredictable surveillance and treatment by the police via stop and search procedures. Indeed, racial disproportionality in stop and search is an issue on which campaigners have been active for many years (Bowling and Phillips 2007; EHRC 2010b).

Parents' concerns about raising their daughters vary from those cited in relation to raising boys. While age is an important variable in shaping the articulation of parental anxiety, principal worry centres on protecting daughters from normative conceptions of beauty that position White women (and hence light skin and long hair) as desirable, to the direct denigration of what one mother calls 'the classic Black woman' (i.e. having natural hair and being Black/dark-skinned). Negative images of Blackness are displayed via television, music videos and other form of media and evidenced in daily encounters as parents go about their usual business of shopping or taking children to/from activities. These incidents can serve as teachable moments, a means of initiating discussion and teaching their children about race and identity. In some cases, parents explicitly teach about Black history and highlight successful Black figures in order to compensate for the shortcomings of the education system and to give their children a proud grounding in their identity.

For many of the parents we interviewed, the topic of racism is seen as a painful, awkward but necessary conversation for parents to have with their children. Age is again important here: when is the most appropriate age to broach such a difficult issue? Some parents work to gently introduce the idea that racism exists in order to ready their child for the real world and to ultimately help provide them with the tools for dealing with it. Yet, at the same time, they express heartfelt apprehension and hesitation about the possibility of poisoning their (primary school aged) child's reality with such damning news. Either way, they are aware through the stories that their children bring home from school and from their interactions with peers that race already has presence in their lives.

Our data also highlight the complex and changing nature of racism and, in relation to this, there are important generational differences in the engagement and comprehension of racism to be noted. Participants told us how they felt their (older) children viewed racism and their parents' response to it. In Chapter 8, we note that children seem far more optimistic in their outlook, sometimes even judging their parents' concerns and warnings to be a sign of racism.

There are two overarching conclusions we draw from these findings. First, racism is not static. It changes in formation and the ways in which it is enacted in relation to local and broader historic context. The overt forms of racism (name-calling, crude exclusion and denigration by teachers and peers) participants experienced as children are less evident today but, as mentioned above, have been replaced by more subtle forms of racial subjugation. We should not be surprised if racism in the twenty-first-century context is differently inflected, given shifts in thinking and equalities legislation. We also should not be seduced by the beguiling idea that racism is no longer a problem in British society (Mirza 2010). In embracing an intersectional approach, we pay heed to the need to contextualise racism across generation and context, as evolving and responding to different times, spaces and narratives. While racism morphs across space and time, inequalities of race persist. A second point here is that we are hearing the views of the children second hand via their parents and, given their ages (eight to 18 years), it may be that their views and engagement with the dynamics of race and racism will become more honed as they enter public and work spaces in which they are a racial minority. As Frazier (1997: 214) insightfully reminds us, 'The children of the black bourgeoisie can not escape the mark of oppression.'

Bourdieu, Critical Race Theory and the continuing significance of racism

We reflect, in this section, on the contribution our findings make to our engagement with Bourdieu and Critical Race Theory. Our principal aim, in carrying out the research, has been to examine and identify the complexities of advantage and disadvantage that are played out as Black middle-class families support their children through the education system. Specifically, we have been concerned to explore how parents mobilise their class resources in their pursuit of educational goals and how race and racism mediate these processes.

In revisiting our theoretical influences, it is worth reminding ourselves of the way in which Bourdieu conceptualises 'capital'. He states that we need to understand it as a 'social relation' (p.113):

> ... an energy which only exists and only produces its effects in the field in which it is produced and reproduced [and that] each of the properties attached to class is given its value and efficacy by the specific laws of each field.
>
> *(Bourdieu 1979: 113)*

In other words, each field or site of operation – we have focused on the education system – is governed by specific rules or ways of operating and conducting the business of that social encounter. These rules dictate the normative ways of operating yet they are often unspoken and arbitrary in nature. Thinking about this in practice, this is why Jean (Chapter 7) talks of employing the 'language of Whiteness' – which she later explains as a formal, impersonal language employed by White middle-class members of the governing body – in order to be heard, for her views to be read as having some degree of legitimacy, during those meetings. She says, 'You've got to be part of that in order to communicate in certain situations.' The (unwritten) procedure of the governors' meeting dictates that this is the most effective way of being heard. This is why, in part, other Black middle-class parents describe the need for a proficiency at code-switching, that is speaking with a particular accent and vernacular in mainly White spaces compared with when with Black colleagues or at home. It is not simply the resources at one's disposal but how they are used. They are, in Bourdieu's terms, deploying their cultural capital in accordance with the norms of the field in which they are operating. As we have shown, at some length, there are many instances in which Black middle-class families do deploy or work to deploy their class capitals to their advantage.

However, we have also documented moments where despite their best efforts, their complaints or proactive requests for support from the school have come to nothing and they have had to seek alternative solutions. Here we witness class capitals intersect with the barriers of race and are reminded, through Critical Race Theory, of the normality of racism as an ordinary 'ingrained feature of our landscape' (Delgado and Stefancic 2000: xvi). Racism manifests in the form of low expectations about the level of excellence Black pupils are able to achieve and in the unfulfilled promises that children's needs will be met with appropriate adjustments and support. Parents often work to subvert and challenge such barriers. For example, faced by repeated refusal by a head teacher to nurture his son's excellent drama skills and give him a speaking part in the school play, Michael moves him to another school while noting that had his son been 'blond and blue-eyed' such concerted attempts at recognition would not have been necessary. Class capitals are operating here through Michael's confidence and ability to approach the head teacher and make such a request and, when met with refusal, through his preparedness and actions of moving him to another school. Michael is also cultivating a particular habitus in his son in which high educational expectations are the norm alongside a confidence to engage with those in senior positions and demand the best.

Similarly, following advice from his son's tutor about his son's writing difficulties and concerned that his son might not be working to his fullest potential, Nigel and his wife approached the Head Teacher of his primary school to explore how using a laptop might support his son's learning. This incident is described at greater length in Chapter 4; however, we note here how despite deploying their cultural capital to establish (through research and conversation with others) the basis for their son's difficulties and despite the relationship (social capital) they enjoy with the Head Teacher 'who we were very friendly with', their efforts were unsuccessful. The idea of the laptop is rejected on the grounds that it might set a poor precedent with other pupils. Nigel and his wife leave the meeting feeling 'disappointed' and 'surprised' by this response but nonetheless redirected and mobilised their class capitals to support their son to win entry to a fee-paying school. Again, we witness the ways in which various forms of capital are brought to bear upon a situation to garner educational support and advantage for their children. In each case, and in many examples throughout this book, we have demonstrated how Black middle-class families' efforts have been thwarted by unsupportive school staff. In other words, despite attempting to deploy their capitals successfully, the value or worth attached to them is often rejected or not read as legitimate. That is to say that while the possession and deployment of 'appropriate' classed capitals is central to being able to successfully navigate the education field, of equal importance are the attributes assigned to individual actors within that field.

> In practice, that is, in a particular field, the properties, internalized in dispositions or objectified in economic or cultural goods, which are attached to

agents are not all simultaneously operative; *the specific logic of the field determines those which are valid in this market, which are pertinent and active in the game in question, and which, in the relationship with this field, function as specific capital –* and, consequently, as a factor explaining practices. This means, concretely, that *the social rank and specific power which agents are assigned in a particular field depend firstly on the specific capital they can mobilize, whatever their additional wealth in other types of capital ...*

[Emphasis added] (Bourdieu 1979: 113)

In extending Bourdieu to incorporate an analysis of race and racism, we contend that the power and social rank of individual agents depends not simply on the capital that they can mobilise but, crucially, on their perceived fit within that field, what Bourdieu describes as the 'homogeneity of dispositions' (p. 110). Therefore, while the Black middle classes *possess* legitimate forms of capital *and* deploy it within the applicable context, the actual worth and power assigned to their capital is dependent on White power-holders or agents in that field. Put another way, there are two stages to the successful mobilisation of capital: it needs to be appropriately deployed by agents *and* also *be recognised and accepted as legitimate by other agents* within the field. Both stages need to be operational for the capital to have any ultimate worth or effect. It is our contention that while the Black middle classes deploy their capital, the fact of their Blackness and the ongoing fact and permanence of racism means that it is not recognised as having worth or much value by Whites:

> While Bourdieu does not make explicit mention or acknowledgement of the way in which race intersects with class in the formation and reproduction of class capitals, in conceptualising Black skin as a form of embodied capital and by drawing upon analyses of the way in which social capital is restricted to those with the most 'harmonious' fit, it is my thesis that race – in the form of White identity and Whiteness – is, in fact, quietly present in his work. The dispositions that are seen to comprise 'fit' are exactly those which keep the Black middle classes on the fringes of middle classness.
>
> *(Rollock 2014: 449)*

The intersection of their middle-class status with their raced identity is positioned, we argue, by Whites as representing an inharmonious fit, as being against the natural order of things and it is this that accounts for the amount of extra work in which the Black middle classes have to invest in order to secure the best educational opportunities for their children. The dialectic which is established 'between dispositions and positions, aspirations and achievements' (Bourdieu 1979: 110) is not one that readily or seamlessly embraces Black Caribbean families as part of this 'objective destiny' (ibid.).

In the introduction to this book we quoted an extract from Bourdieu about the role of the family and school in shaping academic capital:

> Academic capital is in fact the guaranteed product of the combined effects of cultural transmission by the family and cultural transmission by the school (the efficacy of which depends on the amount of cultural capital directly inherited from the family).
>
> *(Bourdieu 1979: 23)*

We have seen the ways in which, despite the best hopes and efforts of Black middle-class families, and despite their sharing similar forms of cultural capital to their White middle-class counterparts, the effects of cultural transmission by the school work to limit, through racial stereotypes and low expectations, the potential for academic excellence of Black pupils.

The pessimism of racism: hope for the future

> Is Critical Race Theory pessimistic? Consider that it holds that racism is ordinary, normal, and embedded in society ... Is medicine pessimistic because it focuses on diseases and traumas?
>
> *(Delgado and Stefancic 2001: 15)*

In drawing together our analysis of the educational strategies of the Black middle classes, we have been able to point to the role of both race and social class in shaping their experiences. Race and racism are a constant presence in their lives and during their engagement with the education system. One of the most common criticisms of Critical Race Theory is that it views racism as so powerful and deeply entrenched that the perspective effectively breeds hopelessness: *if racism is as fundamental to society as you say it is*, so the criticism goes, *then any attempt to fight it must be condemned to failure, so what's the point?* This argument has been answered numerous times by critical race scholars who highlight the countless victories that have been won (at national, local and individual levels) and who emphasise the constant need for active strategising and resistance if past victories are to be maintained and new ones realised in the future (cf. Bell 1992; Delgado 1995; Gillborn and Ladson-Billings 2010). The Black middle-class parents' experiences, hopes and fears – that we have documented in this book – signal a further dimension to this issue. The majority of our respondents view racism as a powerful (often complex and subtle) presence in their lives and one that, although uncomfortable, they *must* find ways to address as they steer their children through schooling and into adulthood. We have considered their strategies at length and their successes (in their own right as professionals in high-status positions and as parents) offer further hope for the future. In addition, we have been struck by some parents' testimony about the transformative impact that even a single positively oriented teacher can have:

> I had this teacher called [Mr Edmonds], who was actually Welsh (...) and he made a very big impression on me because for whatever reason he saw that

I was capable of doing something (…) he seemed to think I was capable, he talked to me and never had a bad word to say. Which was quite incredible because [the] next year I had another teacher who was very, very different, in fact the very opposite. And even when I left his class, this [Mr Edmonds] continued to, yeah to be encouraging, to talk to me, to be encouraging to me (…) even now, fifty years later, I remember this guy, and my sister and I constantly talked about him, because the impact that he had on me was so marked.

(Robert)

We have noted that chronically low teacher expectations are a factor that our respondents encountered when they were children *and* when they interacted with schools as adults. Interestingly, Karyn Lacy's research with Black middle-class adults in the US revealed a strikingly similar situation, with respondents able to recall the names of specific teachers who left an especially strong impression (positive or negative). Here Brad describes his high school guidance counsellor:

[She] 'told me that I should not go to Michigan because I probably wouldn't make it, and should go to a trade school. [That way] I would have a job, [and] I could support my family.' He pauses, visibly upset. Then with sarcasm, he adds, 'She was great' (…) 'she was a White woman. Miss Blupper. I remember her name.'

(Lacy 2007: 84–5)

More happily, Gloria remembers the name of a teacher she first encountered when she was eight years old:

'I was always the first one he would ask about a question and if I couldn't answer, tut tut tut, because he expected it of me, never forgot, I even remember his name, [Mr Cole] and we're talking about 40 odd years ago. Because again, you think of the impact a teacher makes on one's life and he made me feel special because remember I'd just come into the country more or less, so that was a positive experience.

(Gloria)

Several of our respondents pointed to individual teachers who had made a real difference to their schooling, for example:

We had a really good teacher (…) she was lovely and she took a real interest in a handful of us girls and helped us to kind of research what we wanted and needed …

(Paulette)

We had one teacher who had travelled quite a lot and, on times when I would be quite tearful and really wanted to go back to Jamaica, he'd sit me down and say, you know, I've been to Barbados and, you know, I understand the difference, so he was quite well spoken and seemed to understand the problems I was feeling whether they were real or imagined and that I think supported me through school ...'

(Vanessa)

In these extracts we witness the enormous impact that good teachers can have upon children and, in addition, glimpse one of the most hopeful findings to emerge from our study. The presence of just one positive, supportive teacher who pays attention, has high expectations and nurtures a child can have a remarkable impact, even amid the routine racism of low expectations and heightened surveillance faced by Black children in contemporary schools and society. These simple, but hugely important, insights point to one of the key strengths of qualitative research that offers rich insights and nuance about people's lives in comparison with the findings of statistical research alone.

Qualitative research in education is extremely popular but also frequently criticised. On the one hand, the approach can provide detailed, powerful insights into the everyday processes that lie behind wider patterns of educational achievement and underachievement. On the other hand, the technique is generally slow and labour-intensive; interviews have to be designed, piloted, conducted, transcribed, analysed and re-analysed over time. It would be easy to dismiss the challenges experienced by participants described in this book as the mere anecdotal ramblings of a handful of disgruntled Black parents but to do so would be naïve for several reasons. First, it overlooks the wider historical context in which the study is situated (see Introduction): the issue of low Black academic attainment and differential treatment at school has long been a feature and concern, if not among policy-makers, among parents, community activists and stakeholders for several decades. Second, in drawing upon an analysis that centres the experiences of Black middle-class families, we have been able to document the challenges with which even they have to contend despite their varied and complex range of class capitals: *being middle class does not mean having transcended racism.* Further – and this third point is worth emphasising – these parents are not passive or apathetic upon encountering racism. Racism is a reality in their lives and they invest a considerable amount of time and energy working out how best to manage and circumnavigate it. There is evidence of this throughout the many examples offered in this book but it is perhaps most salient in Chapter 7 where we explore how Black middle-class respondents strategically, but not always consciously, deploy key markers of their class position such as accent and language to negotiate and secure (possible) inclusion by White people. The narrative which many Black middle classes learnt as children of having to work harder than White peers in order to succeed at school is reconstructed in the workplace and as they struggle to get their children through school successfully. Many of these actions and strategies go unnoticed by the White majority, in part because it benefits them not to acknowledge or see them.

Whites are born into a world that is racially harmonious with their sense of self. (…) it does not take long for white children to recognise that the world belongs to them, in the sense that whites feel a sense of entitlement or ownership of the material and discursive processes of race. From the means of production to the meanings in everyday life, whites enjoy a virtual monopoly of institutions that make up the racial landscape.

(Leonardo 2009: 112)

Our data, therefore, presents a direct challenge to discourses which indicate that to name or acknowledge racism as a lived experience is to be a victim or, as commonly presented in popular media, is to 'have a chip on your shoulder' or to 'play the race card'. Parents we spoke with, across England, recognise racism as a reality but work to succeed and encourage their children to succeed within school despite it.

Finally, we return to the extract from Strand (2011) with which we opened this chapter. Even when controlling for social class, Black Caribbean pupils do not make the expected gains in academic attainment. The findings of our study, which has examined the educational strategies of Black Caribbean heritage families, go some way to explaining this continued inequity. In this light, government and policy fixation on improving educational outcomes through a colour-blind focus on poverty and social mobility alone can have only a limited effect on Black Caribbean families. Targeted engagement and intervention is required to tackle racism and to finally dismantle the culture of low teacher expectations that respondents experienced as children and which they continue to confront as parents.

REFERENCES

Acker, J. (2006) *Class Questions: Feminist Answers*. Lanham, MD: Rowman & Littlefield.

Adewunmi, B. (2012) 'So what if Beyoncé's skin colour is looking lighter', *Guardian*, Shortcut Blogs, 17 January. Online at: http://www.guardian.co.uk/music/shortcuts/2012/jan/17/beyonce-skin-colour-lighter (accessed 20 September 2012).

Agyeman, G. (2008) 'White researcher – Black subjects: exploring the challenges of researching the marginalised and "invisible"', *Electronic Journal of Business Research Methods*, 6 (1): 77–84. Online at: http:www.ejbrm.com (accessed 15 August 2014).

Annamma, S. A., Connor, D. J. and Ferri, B. A. (2013) 'Dis/ability Critical Race Studies (DisCrit): theorizing at the intersections of race and dis/ability', *Race Ethnicity and Education*, 16 (1): 1–31.

Araujo, M. (2007) '"Modernising the comprehensive principle": selection, setting and the institutionalisation of educational failure', *British Journal of Sociology of Education*, 28 (2): 241–57.

Archer, L. (2010) '"We raised it with the head": the educational practices of minority ethnic, middle-class families', *British Journal of Sociology of Education*, 31 (4): 449–69.

Artiles, A. (2011) 'Toward an interdisciplinary understanding of educational equity and difference: the case of the racialization of ability', 2011 Wallace Foundation Distinguished Lecture, *Educational Researcher*, 40 (9): 431–45.

Artiles, A. and Trent, S. C. (1994) 'Overrepresentation of minority students in special education: a continuing debate', *Journal of Special Education*, 27 (4): 410–37.

Artiles, A., Trent, S. C. and Palmer, J. D. (2004) 'Culturally diverse students in special education: legacies and prospects', in J. A. Banks and C. A. McGee Banks (eds), *Handbook of Research on Multicultural Education*. San Francisco: Jossey-Bass, pp. 716–35.

Atkinson, W. (2011) 'From sociological fictions to social fictions: some Bourdieusian reflections on the concept of "institutional habitus" and "family habitus"', *British Journal of Sociology of Education*, 32 (3): 331–47.

Ball, S. J. (1981) *Beachside Comprehensive: A Case Study of Secondary Schooling*. Cambridge: Cambridge University Press.

Ball, S. J. (2003a) *Class Strategies and the Education Market*. London: Routledge.

Ball, S. J. (2003b) 'The risks of social reproduction: the middle class and education markets', *London Review of Education*, 1 (3): 163–75.

Ball, S. J., Rollock, N., Vincent, C. and Gillborn, D. (2011) 'Social mix, schooling and inter-sectionality: identity and risk for Black middle class families', *Research Papers in Education*, 28 (3): 265–88.

Ball, S. J., Vincent, C., Kemp, S. and Pietikainen, S. (2004) 'Middle class fractions, childcare and the "relational" and "normative" aspects of class practices', *Sociological Review*, 52: 478–502.

Barker, M. (1981) *The New Racism*. London: Junction Books.

Barnes, C., Mercer, G. and Shakespeare, T. (1999) *Exploring Disability: A Sociological Introduction*. Oxford: Polity.

BBC News (2010) 'English rules tightened for immigrant partners', http://www.bbc.co.uk/news/10270797 (accessed 7 July 2011).

Bell, D. (1992) *Faces at the Bottom of the Well: The Permanence of Racism*. New York: Basic Books.

Beratan, G. D. (2012) 'Institutional Ableism and the Politics of Inclusive Education: an Ethnographic Study of an Inclusive High School'. Unpublished PhD thesis, Institute of Education, University of London.

Blair, M. (2001) *Why Pick on Me? School Exclusions and Black Youth*. Stoke-on-Trent: Trentham.

Blanchett, W. J. (2010) '"Telling it like it is": the role of race, class and culture in the perpetuation of Learning Disability as a privileged category for the white middle class', *Disability Studies Quarterly*, 30 (2). Online at: http://dsq-sds.org/article/view/1233/0 (accessed 28 November 2013).

Bodovski, K. (2010) 'Parental practices and educational achievement: social class, race and habitus', *British Journal of Sociology of Education*, 31 (2): 139–56.

Bourdieu, P. (1979) *Distinction: A Social Critique of the Judgment of Taste*. Cambridge, MA: Harvard University Press.

Bourdieu, P. (1987) 'What makes a social class? On the theoretical and practical existence of groups', *Berkeley Journal of Sociology*, 23 (1): 1–17.

Bourdieu, P. (1990) *In Other Words: Essays Towards a Reflexive Sociology*. Cambridge: Polity Press.

Bourdieu, P. (1993) *Distinction: A Social Critique of the Judgement of Taste*. London: Routledge.

Bourdieu, P. (1997) 'The forms of capital', in A. Halsey, H. Lauder, P. Brown and A. Stuart-Wells (eds), *Education, Culture, Economy, Society*. Oxford: Oxford University Press, pp. 46–58.

Bourdieu, P. and Passeron, J. (1977) *Reproduction in Education, Society and Culture*. London: Sage.

Bourdieu, P. and Wacquant, L. (1992) *An Invitation to Reflexive Sociology*. Cambridge: Polity Press.

Bowling, B. and Phillips, C. (2007) 'Disproportionate and discriminatory: reviewing the evidence on police stop and search', *Modern Law Review*, 70 (6): 298–322.

Bozalek, V., Carolissen, R., Leibowitz, B. and Boler, M. (eds) (forthcoming) *Discerning Critical Hope in Educational Practices*. London: Routledge.

Bradbury, A. (2013) *Understanding Early Years Inequality: Policy, Assessment and Young Children's Identities*. London: Routledge.

Brah, A. and Phoenix, A. (2004) 'Ain't I a woman? Revisiting intersectionality', *Journal of International Women's Studies*, 5 (3): 75–86.

Brooker, L. (2002) *Starting School: Young Children Learning Cultures*. Buckingham: Open University Press.

Brown, A. L. and Donnor, J. K. (2011) 'Toward a new narrative on Black males, education, and public policy', *Race Ethnicity and Education*, 14 (1): 17–32.

Byrne, B. (2006) *White Lives: The Interplay of 'Race', Class and Gender in Everyday Lives*. London: Routledge.

Cabinet Office (2003) *Ethnic Minorities and the Labour Market*, Final Report, March. London: TSO.

Cameron, D. (2011) PM's speech at Munich Security Conference, Munich. Online at: http://www.gov.uk/government/speeches/pms-speech-at-munich-security-conference (accessed 28 November 2013).

Cameron, D. (2012) Speech to the Confederation of Business Industries (CBI), 19 November.

Carbado, D. and Gulati, M. (2004) 'Race to the top of the corporate ladder: what minorities do when they get there', *Washington and Lee Law Review*, 61: 1645–93.

Cassen, R. and Kingdon, G. (2007) *Tackling Low Educational Achievement*. York: Joseph Rowntree Foundation.

Clark, K. and Drinkwater, S. (2007) *Ethnic Minorities in the Labour Market: Dynamics and Diversity*. Bristol: Policy Press.

Coard, B. (1971) *How the West Indian Child Is Made Educationally Subnormal in the British School System*. London: New Beacon Books, reprinted in B. Richardson (ed.) (2005) *Tell It Like It Is: How Our Schools Fail Black Children*. London: Bookmarks, pp. 27–59.

Colley, H., James, D., Tedder, M. and Diment, K. (2003) 'Learning as becoming in vocational education and training: class, gender and the role of vocational habitus', *Journal of Vocational Education and Training*, 55 (4): 471–98.

Collins, P. H. (1991). *Black feminist thought: Knowledge, consciousness and the politics of empowerment*. New York: Routledge, in Horvat, E.M. (2003), The interactive effects of race and class in educational research: Theoretical insights from the work of Pierre Bourdieu, Penn GSE Perspectives on Urban Education, volume 2 issue 1. Online at https://www.urbanedjournal.org/archive/volume-2-issue-1-spring-2003/interactive-effects-race-and-class-educational-research-theoret

Commission for Racial Equality (CRE) (1992) *Set to Fail? Setting and Banding in Secondary Schools*. London: Commission for Racial Equality.

Communities Empowerment Network (2005) *Zero Tolerance and School Exclusions*. Special Issue of the *CEN Newsletter*, vol. 5, issue 6.

Connolly, P. (1998) *Racism, Gender Identities and Young Children: Social Relations in a Multi-Ethnic, Inner-City Primary School*. London: Routledge.

Cooper, C. (2007) 'School choice as "motherwork": valuing African-American women's educational advocacy and resistance', *International Journal of Qualitative Studies in Education*, 20 (5): 491–512.

Cooper, F. R. (2005) 'Against bipolar Black masculinity: intersectionality, assimilation, identity performance, and hierarchy', *University of California Davis Law Review*, 39: 853–906.

Crenshaw, K. (1995) 'Mapping the margins: intersectionality, identity politics, and violence against women of color', in K. Crenshaw, N. Gotanda, G. Peller and K. Thomas (eds), *Critical Race Theory: The Key Writings that Formed the Movement*. New York: New Press.

Crossley, N. (2008) 'Social class', in M. Grenfell (ed.), *Pierre Bourdieu: Key Concepts*. Stocksfield: Acumen Press.

Crozier, G. (1998) 'Parents and schools: partnership or surveillance?', *Journal of Education Policy*, 13 (1): 125–36.

Crozier, G. (2005) '"There's a war against our children": black educational underachievement revisited', *British Journal of Sociology of Education*, 26 (5): 585–98.

Crozier, G., Reay, D., James, D., Jamieson, F., Hollingworth, S., Williams, K. and Beedell, P. (2008) 'White middle class parents, identities, educational choice and the urban comprehensive school: dilemmas, ambivalence and moral ambiguity', *British Journal of Sociology of Education*, 29 (3): 261–72.

Davis, K. (2008) 'Intersectionality as buzzword: a sociology of science perspective on what makes a feminist theory successful', *Feminist Theory*, 9 (1): 67–85.

Daye, S. (1994) *Middle Class Blacks in Britain: A Racial Fraction of a Class Group or a Class Fraction of a Racial Group?* Basingstoke: Macmillan Press.

Delgado, R. (1995) *The Rodrigo Chronicles: Conversations about America and Race.* New York: New York University Press.

Delgado, R. (2011) 'Rodrigo's reconsideration: intersectionality and the future of critical race theory', *Iowa Law Review*, 96: 1276.

Delgado, R. and Stefancic, J. (eds) (2000) *Critical Race Theory: The Cutting Edge*, 2nd edn. Philidelphia: Temple University Press.

Delgado, R. and Stefancic, J. (2001) *Critical Race Theory: An Introduction.* New York and London: New York University Press.

Department for Children, Schools and Families (2008) *Youth Cohort Study and Longitudinal Study of Young People in England: The Activities and Experiences of 16 Year Olds: England 2007.* London: DCSF.

Department for Children, Schools and Families (2009) *Special Educational Needs (SEN) – A Guide for Parents and Carers. A Commitment from the Children's Plan.* Nottingham: DCSF.

Department for Education (DfE) (2013a) *GCSE and Equivalent Attainment By Pupil Characteristics in England, 2011/12*, SFR 04/2013. London: DfE.

Department for Education (DfE) (2013b) *Permanent and Fixed Period Exclusions from Schools and Exclusion Appeals in England, 2011/12*, SFR 29/2013. London: DfE.

Devabhai, N. (2012) 'Social care cuts are hitting black and minority ethnic communities hardest', *Guardian*, 5 March. Online at: http://www.theguardian.com/social-carenetwork/2012/mar/05/cuts-black-ethnic-minority-carers-hardest (accessed 28 November 2013).

Developmental Adult Neuro-Diversity Association (DANDA) (2011) 'What Is Neuro-Diversity?', http://www.danda.org.uk/pages/neuro-diversity.php (accessed 28 September 2012).

Developmental Adult Neuro-Diversity Association (DANDA) (n.d.) Online at: http://www.patient.co.uk/support/DANDA.htm (accessed 15 July 2014).

Dixson, A. (2006) 'The fire this time: jazz, research and critical race theory', in A. D. Dixson and C. K. Rousseau (eds), *Critical Race Theory in Education: All God's Children Got a Song.* New York: Routledge, pp. 213–30.

DuBois, W. E. B. (1996) *The Souls of Black Folk.* London: Penguin.

Eagleton, T. (1992) 'Doxa and common life: in conversation with Pierre Bourdieu', *New Left Review*, 191: 111–21.

Edwards, R. (1990) 'Connecting method and epistemology: a White woman interviewing Black women', *Women's Studies International Forum*, 13 (5): 477–90.

Equality and Human Rights Commission (EHRC) (2010a) *How Fair Is Britain? Equality, Human Rights and Good relations in 2010: The First Triennial Review.* London: EHRC.

Equality and Human Rights Commission (EHRC) (2010b) *Stop and Think: A Critical Review of the use of Stop and Search Powers in England and Wales.* London: EHRC.

Equality and Human Rights Commission/Ipsos MORI (2009) 'New Commission poll shows British institutions need to "keep up with Obama generation"'. Online at: http://www.equalityhumanrights.com/news/2009/jan-may/new-commission-poll-shows-british-institutions-need-to-keep-up-with-obama-generation/.

Equality Challenge Unit (2012) *Equality in Higher Education: Statistical Report 2012 Part 2: Students.* London: Equality Challenge Unit.

Eriksen, A. (2012) 'White out of order! Beyoncé is looking several shades lighter in promo shoot for her new album', *Daily Mail*, Tuesday, 17 January. Online at: http://www.

dailymail.co.uk/tvshowbiz/article-2087388/Beyonc-white-skin-row-Controversial-photo-shows-singer-looking-shades-lighter-usual-tone.html (accessed 20 September 2012).

Everett, J. (2002) 'Organizational research and the praxeology of Pierre Bourdieu', *Organizational Research Methods*, 5: 56–80.

Fanon, F. (1967) *Black Skin, White Masks*. London: Pluto Press.

Francis, E. (1993) 'Psychiatric racism and social police: Black people and the psychiatric services', in W. James and C. Harris (eds), *Inside Babylon: The Caribbean Diaspora in Britain*. London: Verso, pp. 179–205.

Frazier, E. F. (1997) *Black Bourgeoisie*. New York: Simon & Schuster.

Fryer, P. (1984) *Staying Power: The History of Black People in Britain*. London: Pluto Press.

Gentleman, A. (2013) 'Equality Commission loses its office, but is it losing its purpose?', *Guardian*, 25 January. Online at: http://www.theguardian.com/society/2013/jan/25/equality-commission-office (accessed 12 October 2013).

Gerrard, J. (2013) 'Self-help and protest: the emergence of Black supplementary schooling in England', *Race Ethnicity and Education*, 16 (1): 32–58.

Gillborn, D. (1990a) *'Race', Ethnicity and Education: Teaching and Learning in Multi-Ethnic Schools*. London: Unwin Hyman/Routledge.

Gillborn, D. (1990b) 'Sexism and curricular "choice"', *Cambridge Journal of Education*, 20 (2): 161–74.

Gillborn, D. (1999) 'Fifty years of failure: "race" and education policy in Britain', in A. Hayton (ed.), *Tackling Disaffection and Social Exclusion: Education Perspectives and Policies*. London: Kogan Page.

Gillborn, D. (2006) 'Rethinking white supremacy: who counts in "whiteworld"', *Ethnicities*, 6 (3): 318–40.

Gillborn, D. (2008) *Racism and Education: Coincidence or Conspiracy?* London: Routledge.

Gillborn, D. (2010) 'The colour of numbers: surveys, statistics and deficit-thinking about race and class', *Journal of Education Policy*, 25 (2): 253–76.

Gillborn, D. (2012) 'Intersectionality and the primacy of racism: race, class, gender and disability in education'. Keynote presented at the Annual Conference of the Critical Race Studies in Education Association (CRSEA), Teacher's College, Columbia University, June.

Gillborn, D. and Demack, S. (2012) 'The still moving right show – talking justice while widening gaps', *Race Equality Teaching*, 31 (1): 4–10.

Gillborn, D. and Ladson-Billings, G. (2010) 'Education and critical race theory', in M. Apple, S. Ball and L. Armando Gandin (eds), *The Routledge International Handbook of the Sociology of Education*. London: Routledge, pp. 37–47.

Gillborn, D. and Mirza, H. S. (2000) *Educational Inequality: Mapping Race, Class and Gender*. London: Ofsted.

Gillborn, D. and Youdell, D. (2000) *Rationing Education: Policy, Practice, Reform and Equity*. Buckingham: Open University Press.

Gillborn, D., Rollock, N., Vincent, C. and Ball, S. J. (2012) '"You got a pass, so what more do you want?": race, class and gender intersections in the educational experiences of the Black middle class', *Race Ethnicity and Education*, 15 (1): 121–39.

Gillies, V. and Robinson, Y. (2012) '"Including" while excluding: race, class and behaviour support units', *Race Ethnicity and Education*, 15 (2): 157–74.

Gilman, S. (1992) 'Black bodies, white bodies: towards an iconography of female sexuality in late nineteenth century art, medicine and literature', in J. Donald and A. Rattansi (eds). *'Race', Culture and Difference*. London: Sage and Open University Press.

Gilroy, P. (1981) 'You can't fool the youths ... race and class formation in the 1980s', *Race and Class*, 23: 207–22.

Giroux, H. A. (2012) 'Hoodie politics: Trayvon Martin and racist violence in postracial America', *Truthdig*. Online at: http://www.truthdig.com/report/item/hoodie_politics_trayvon_martin_and_racist_violence_in_post-racial_america_2 (accessed 10 October 2012).

Hall, S. (1993) 'Cultural identity and diaspora'. Online at: http://www.unipa.it/~michele.cometa/hall_cultural_identity.pdf (accessed 21 September 2012).

Hall, S. (1996) 'Cultural identity and cinematic representation', in H. A. Baker Jr, M. Diawara and R. H. Lindeborg (eds), *Black British Cultural Studies: A Reader*. London and Chicago: Chicago University Press.

Hall, S. (1997) *Representation: Cultural Representations and Signifying Practices*. London: Sage.

Hall, S. (2000) 'Frontlines and backyards: the terms of change', in K. Owusu (ed.), *Black British Culture: A Text Reader*. London: Routledge.

Hallam, S. (2002) *Ability Grouping in Schools: A Literature Review*. London: Institute of Education, University of London.

Hallam, S. and Toutounji, I. (1996) *What Do We Know About the Grouping of Pupils by Ability? A Research Review*. London: Institute of Education, University of London.

Hanlon, G. (1998) 'Professionalism as enterprise: service class politics and the redefinition of professionalism', *Sociology*, 32 (1): 43–63.

Harris, A. P. (1990) 'Race and essentialism in feminist legal theory', *Stanford Law Review*, 42: 581–5.

Harris, J. (2013) 'Britain's diversity was lauded during the Olympics. But no longer', *Guardian Online*, 21 July. Online at: http://www.guardian.co.uk/commentisfree/2013/jul/21/uk-diversity-olympics-no-longer (accessed 15 August 2014).

Harry, B. and Klingner, J. K. (2006) *Why Are So Many Minority Students in Special Education? Understanding Race and Disability in Schools*. New York: Teachers College Press.

Heath, A. and Cheung, S. Y. (2006) *Ethnic Penalties in the Labour Market: Employers and Discrimination*, Project Report. Leeds, Crown Copyright. Online at: http://webarchive.nationalarchives.gov.uk/20130128102031/http://statistics.dwp.gov.uk/asd/asd5/rports2005-2006/rrep341.pdf.

Hendrix, K. (2002) '"Did being Black introduce bias into your study?": Attempting to mute the race-related research of Black scholars', *Howard Journal of Communication*, 13 (2): 153–71.

Hewitt, R. (1986) *White Talk Black Talk: Inter-racial Friendship and Communication Amongst Adolescents*. Cambridge: Cambridge University Press.

Hill, M. (2002) 'Skin color and the perception of attractiveness among African Americans: does gender make a difference?', *Social Psychology Quarterly*, 65 (1): 77–91.

Hill-Collins, P. (2006) *Black Sexual Politics: African Americans, Gender, and the New Racism*. New York: Routledge

Hobbs, T. (2013) 'Why I needed to fight those "pushy parents"', *Daily Telegraph*, 3 August. Online at: http://www.telegraph.co.uk/education/10220416/Why-I-needed-to-fight-those-pushy-parents.html (accessed 20 August 2013).

Hobson, J. (2003) 'The "batty" politic: toward an aesthetics of the Black female body', *Hypatia*, 18 (4): 87–105.

Holloway, L. (2012) 'Equality watchdog ditches race experts', Cllr Lester Holloway blog, 2 November. Online at: http://cllrlesterholloway.wordpress.com/2012/11/02/equality-watchdog-ditched-race-experts/ (accessed 13 December 2013).

hooks, b (1990) *Yearning: Race, Gender and Cultural Politics*. Toronto: Between the Lines.

hooks, b (1992) *Black Looks: Race and Representation*. Cambridge, MA: South End Press.

hooks, b (2000) *Where We Stand: Class Matters*. New York: Routledge.

Horvat, E. M. (2003) 'The interactive effects of race and class in educational research: theoretical insights from the work of Pierre Bourdieu', *Penn GSE Perspectives on Urban Education*, 2 (1). Online at: http://www.urbanedjournal.org (accessed 15 August 2014).

Horvat, E., Weininger E., and Lareau, A. (2003) From social ties to social capital; class differences in the relations between school and parent networks, *American Education Research Journal*, 40, 2: 319–51.

Hunter, M. L. (2005) *Race, Gender and the Politics of Skin Tone*. New York: Routledge.

Hylton, K. (2009) *'Race' and Sport: Critical Race Theory*. London: Routledge.

Ignatiev, N. (1997) 'How to Be a race traitor: six ways to fight being white', in R. Delgado and J. Stefancic (eds), *Critical White Studies: Looking Behind the Mirror*. Philadelphia: Temple University Press.

Irwin, S. and Elley, S. (2011) 'Concerted cultivation? Parenting values, education and class diversity', *Sociology*, 45 (3): 480–95.

Jackson, B. and Marsden, D. (1962) *Education and the Working Class*. London: Routledge & Kegan Paul

James, D., Reay, D., Crozier, G., Beedell, P., Hollingworth, S., Jamieson, F. and Williams, K. (2010) 'Neoliberal policy and the meaning of counterintuitive middle class school choices', *Current Sociology*, 58 (4): 623–41.

Jordan, B., Redley, M. and James, S. (1994) *Putting the Family First*. London: UCL Press.

King, J. E. (1995) 'Culture centered knowledge: Black studies, curriculum transformation and social action', in J. E. Banks and C. M. Banks (eds), *Handbook of Research on Multicultural Education*. New York: Macmillan.

Kingston, P. (2001) 'The unfilled promise of cultural capital', *Sociology of Education*, 74: 88–99.

Korhonen, A. (2005) 'Washing the Ethiopian white: conceptualising Black skin in renaissance England', in T. F. Earle and K. J. P. Lowe (eds), *Black Africans in Renaissance Europe*. Cambridge: Cambridge University Press.

Lacey, C. (1970) *Hightown Grammar*. Manchester: Manchester University Press.

Lacy, K. (2007) *Blue-Chip Black: Race, Class and Status in the New Black Middle Class*. Berkeley, CA: University of California Press.

Ladson-Billings, G. (2011) 'Boyz to men? Teaching to restore Black boys' childhood', *Race Ethnicity and Education*, 14 (1): 7–15.

Ladson-Billings, G. and Donnor, J. (2008) 'The moral activist role of critical race theory scholarship', in N. K. Denzin and Y. S. Lincoln (eds), *The Landscape of Qualitative Research*. Thousand Oaks, CA: Sage.

Ladson-Billings, G. and Tate, W. (1995) 'Toward a critical race theory of education', *Teachers College Record*, 97 (1): 47–68.

Lareau, A. (1989) *Home Advantage*. London: Falmer Press.

Lareau, A. (2001) 'Linking Bourdieu's concept of capital to the broader field', in B. Biddle (ed.), *Social Class, Poverty and Education*. New York: RoutledgeFalmer, pp. 77–100.

Lareau, A. (2003) *Unequal Childhoods*. Berkeley, CA: University of California Press.

Lareau, A. and Horvat, E. M. (1999) 'Moments of social inclusion and exclusion: race, class and cultural capital in family-school relationships', *Sociology of Education*, 72 (1): 37–53.

Lash, S. (1993) *Pierre Bourdieu: Cultural Economy and Social Change*. Cambridge: Polity Press.

LeCompte, M. D. and Preissle, J. with Tesch, R. (1993) *Ethnography and Qualitative Design in Educational Research*. San Diego, CA: Academic Press.

Leonardo, Z. (ed.) (2005) *Critical Pedagogy and Race*. Malden, MA: Blackwell.

Leonardo, Z. (2009) *Race, Whiteness and Education*. New York: Routledge

Leonardo, Z. and Broderick, A. A. (2011) 'Smartness as property: a critical exploration of intersections between whiteness and disability studies', *Teachers College Record*, 113 (1).

Leonardo, Z. and Porter, R. (2010) 'Pedagogy of fear: toward a Fanonian theory of "safety" in race dialogue', *Race Ethnicity and Education*, 13 (2): 139–57.

Lindsay, G., Pather, S. and Strand, S. (2006) *Special Educational Needs and Ethnicity: Issues of Over- and Under-representation*, Research Report RR757. London: Department for Education and Skills.

Lorde, A. (2009) 'Is your hair still political?', in R. P. Byrd, J. B. Cole and B. Guy-Sheftall (eds), *I Am Your Sister. Collected and Unpublished Writings of Audre Lorde*. New York: Oxford University Press.

MacAskill, E. (2010) 'Democrat resists calls to quit over Obama race comments', *Observer*, 10 January. Online at: http://www.guardian.co.uk/world/2010/jan/10/harry-reid-obama-race (last accessed 28 February 2010).

McCall, L. (2005) 'The complexity of intersectionality', *Signs: Journal of Women in Culture and Society*, 30 (3): 1771–800

McDermott, N. (2013) 'Pushy parents "are chasing lost dreams" trying to make their children succeed', *Mail Online*, 20 June. Online at: http://www.dailymail.co.uk/news/article-2344790/Pushy-parents-chasing-lost-dreams-trying-make-children-succeed.html (accessed 20 August 2013).

McKenley, J. (2005) *Seven Black Men: An Ecological Study of Education and Parenting*. Bristol: Aduma Books.

McKenzie, K. (2011) 'Being Black is bad for your mental health', *Guardian*, Comment is Free. Online at: http://www.guardian.co.uk/commentisfree/2007/apr/02/comment.health (accessed 15 February 2011).

Macpherson, W. (1999) *The Stephen Lawrence Inquiry*. London: Stationary Office.

Mannheim, K. (1952) 'The Problem of Generations', in *Essays on the Sociology of Knowledge*. London: Routledge & Kegan Paul.

Manton, K. (2008) 'Habitus', in M. Grenfell (ed.), *Pierre Bourdieu: Key Concepts*. Stocksfield: Acumen Press.

May, T. (2013) Speech to the Tory Party Conference, Manchester. Online at: http://www.theguardian.com/politics/video/2013/sep/30/tory-conference-theresa-may-police-stop-and-search-concerns-video (accessed 17 October 2013).

Maylor, U. and Williams, K. (2011) 'Challenges in theorising "Black middle-class" women: education, experience and authenticity', *Gender and Education*, 23 (3): 345–56.

Measor, L. (1983) 'Gender and the sciences: pupils' gender-based conceptions of school subjects', in M. Hammersley and A. Hargreaves (eds), *Curriculum Practice: Some Sociological Case Studies*. Lewes: Falmer.

Medhurst, A. (2000) 'If anywhere: class identifications and cultural studies academics', in S. Munt (ed.), *Cultural Studies and the Working Class*. New York and London: Cassell.

Mills, C. W. (1959) *The Sociological Imagination*. London: Penguin.

MIND (2009) *Psychiatry, Race and Culture*. London: MIND.

Mirza, H. S. (2009a) 'Plotting a history: Black and postcolonial feminisms in "new times"', *Race Ethnicity and Education*, Special Issue 'Black Feminisms and Postcolonial Paradigms: Researching Educational Inequalities', 12 (1): 1–10.

Mirza, H. S. (2009b) *Race, Gender and Educational Desire: Why Black Women Succeed and Fail*. Abingdon: Routledge.

Mirza, H. S. and Joseph, C. (eds) (2010) *Black and Postcolonial Feminisms in New Times: Researching Educational Inequalities*. London: Routledge.

Mirza, H. S. and Reay, D. (2000) 'Spaces and places of Black educational desire: rethinking Black supplementary schools as a new social movement', *Sociology*, 34 (3): 32–58.

Mirza, M. (2010) 'Rethinking race', *Prospect*, Issue 175, October. London: Prospect Publishing.

Montgomery, A. (2006) '"Living in each other's pockets": the navigation of social distances by middle class Blacks in Los Angeles', *City and Community*, 5 (4): 425–50.

Moore, A. (2011) 'Is it payback time for pushy parents?', *Daily Mail*, 6 May. Online at: http://www.dailymail.co.uk/home/you/article-1381201/Is-payback-time-pushy-parents.html (accessed 20 August 2013).

Moore, K. (2008) 'Class formations: competing forms of Black middle-class identity', *Ethnicities*, 8 (4): 492–517.

Morgan, D. (1989) 'Strategies and sociologists: a comment on Crow', *Sociology*, 23 (1): 25–9.

Muir, H. (2012) 'Black and Muslim members lose Equalities Commission roles', *Guardian*, 1 November. Online at: http://www.theguardian.com/society/2012/nov/01/black-muslim-members-equalities-commission-roles (accessed 12 December 2013).

Mullard, C. (1973) *Black Britain*. London: George Allen & Unwin.

Nash, J. (2008) 'Rethinking intersectionality', *Feminist Review*, 89: 1–15.

Nind, M. (2008) 'Learning difficulties and social class: exploring the intersection through family narratives', *International Studies in Sociology of Education*, 18 (2): 87–98.

O'Grady, S. (2009) 'Children left shattered by their pushy parents', *Daily Express*, 30 September. Online at: http://www.express.co.uk/news/uk/130900/Children-left-shattered-by-their-pushy-parents (accessed 20 August 2013).

Obama, B. (2013) 'President Obama Speaks on Trayvon Martin'. Online at: http://www.youtube.com/watch?v=MHBdZWbncXI (last accessed 22 July 2013).

Ochieng, B. (2010) '"You know what I mean": the ethical and methodological dilemmas and challenges for Black researchers interviewing Black families', *Qualitative Health Research*, 20 (12): 1725–35.

Ochieng, B. and Hylton, C. (2010) *Black Families in Britain as the Site of Struggle*. Manchester: Manchester University Press.

Ofsted (2001) *Improving Attendance and Behaviour in Secondary School*. London: Ofsted.

Oliver, M. (1996) *Understanding Disability: From Theory to Practice*. Basingstoke: Macmillan Press.

Oliver, M. L. and Shapiro, T. (2006) *Black Wealth, White Wealth: A New Perspective on Racial Inequality*. Oxford and New York: Routledge.

Pahl, R. E. and Wallace, C. D. (1985) 'Forms of work and privatisation on the Isle of Sheppey', in B. Roberts, R. Finnegan and D. Gallie (eds), *New Approaches to Economic Life*. Manchester: Manchester University Press.

Pajaczkowska, C. and Young, L. (1992) 'Racism, representation, psychoanalysis', in J. Donald and A. Rattansi (eds), *'Race', Culture and Difference*. London: Sage, pp. 198–219.

Pattillo-McCoy, M. (1999) *Black Picket Fences: Privilege and Peril Among the Black Middle Class*. Chicago: University of Chicago Press.

Phillips, D. and Sarre, P. (1995) 'Black middle-class formation in contemporary Britain', in T. Butler and M. Savage (eds), *Social Change and the Middle Classes*. London: UCL Press.

Phillips, T. (2009) *Stephen Lawrence Speech: Institutions Must Catch Up with Public on Race Issues*. Speech to mark the tenth anniversary of the Stephen Lawrence Inquiry, London. Online at: http://www.equalityhumanrights.com/about-us/our-work/key-projects/race-in-britain/event-ten-years-on-from-the-macpherson-inquiry/stephen-lawrence-speech-institutions-must-catch-up-with-public-on-race-issues (accessed October 2013).

Pilcher, J. (1994) 'Mannheim's sociology of generations: an undervalued legacy', *British Journal of Sociology*, 45 (3): 481–95.

Platt, L. (2009) *Ethnicity and Family. Relationships Within and Between Ethnic Groups: An Analysis using the Labour Force Survey*. London: EHRC and Institute for Social and Economic Research, University of Essex.

Power, S., Edwards, T. and Whitty, G. (2003) *Education and the Middle Class*. Buckingham: Open University Press.

Preston, J. and Bhopal, K. (2012) 'Conclusion: intersectional theories and "race": from toolkit to "mash up"', in K. Bhopal and J. Preston (eds), *Intersectionality and Race in Education*. London: Routledge.

Preston, M. (2010) 'Reid apologizes for racial remarks about Obama during campaign', *CNN News*, 9 January. Online at: http://www.cnn.com/2010/POLITICS/01/09/obama.reid/index.html (accessed 28 February 2010).

Ramdin, R. (1987) *The Making of the Black Working Class*. London: Gower.

Ramesh, R. (2012) 'Equality and Human Rights Commission has workforce halved', *Guardian*, 15 May. Online at: http://www.theguardian.com/society/2012/may/15/equality-human-rights-commission-cuts (accessed 15 August 2014).

Rausch, C. (2012) '"Fixing" Children: Producing a Hierarchy of Learners in Primary School Processes'. Unpublished PhD thesis, Institute of Education, University of London.

Reay, D. (1997) 'The double-bind of the "working class" feminist academic: the success of failure or the failure of success?', in P. Mahony and C. Zmroczek (eds), *Class Matters: 'Working Class' Women's Perspectives on Social Class*. London: Taylor & Francis.

Reay, D. (1998) *Class Work : Mothers' Involvement in Children's Schooling*. London. University College Press.

Reay, D. (2001) 'Finding or losing yourself? Working-class relationships to education', *Journal of Education Policy*, 16 (4): 333–46.

Reay, D. (2004) 'It's all becoming a habitus' – beyond the habitual use of habitus in educational research', *British Journal of Sociology of Education*, 25 (4): 431–44.

Reay, D., Crozier, G. and James, D. (2011) *White Middle Class Identities and Urban Schooling*. London: Palgrave Macmillan.

Reay, D., Davies, J., David, M. and Ball, S. (2001) 'Choices of degree or degrees of choice? Class, "race" and the higher education choice process', *Sociology*, 35 (4): 855–74.

Reynolds, T. (2005) *Caribbean Mothers: Identity and Experience*. London: Tufnell Press.

Reynolds, T. (2009) 'Exploring the absent/present dilemma: Black fathers, family relationships and social capital in Britain', *Annals of the American Academy of Political and Social Science*, 624 (12): 12–28.

Rhamie, J. (2007) *Eagles Who Soar: How Black Learners Find the Path to Success*. Stoke-on-Trent: Trentham.

Richardson, B. (2007) *Tell It Like It Is: How Our Schools Fail Black Children*. London: Bookmark Publications

Richert, M. (2008) 'Four words for 2008', *Guardian*, 30 December. Online at: http://www.theguardian.com/commentisfree/cifamerica/2008/dec/30/word-of-the-year-2008?INTCMP=SRCH (accessed 10 March 2014).

Riddell, S. (2009) 'Social justice, equality and inclusion in Scottish education', *Discourse: Studies in the Cultural Politics of Education*, 30 (3): 283–96.

Rollock, N. (2006) *Black School Governors in London*. London: London Metropolitan University.

Rollock, N. (2007a) 'Legitimising Black academic failure: deconstructing staff discourses on academic success, appearance and behaviour', *International Studies in the Sociology of Education*, 17 (3): 275–87.

Rollock, N. (2007b) 'Why Black girls don't matter: exploring how race and gender shape academic success in an inner city school', *Support for Learning*, 22 (4): 197–202.

Rollock, N. (2007c) *Failure by Any Other Name? Educational Policy and the Continuing Struggle for Black Academic Success*. London: Runnymede Trust.

Rollock, N. (2009) 'Educational policy and the impact of the Lawrence Inquiry: the view from another sector', in N. Hall, J. Grieve and S. P. Savage (eds), *Policing and the Legacy of Lawrence*. Cullompton: Willan.

Rollock, N. (2012a) 'Unspoken rules of engagement: navigating racial microaggressions in the academic terrain', *International Journal of Qualitative Studies in Education*, 24 (5): 517–32.

Rollock, N. (2012b) 'The invisibility of race: intersectional reflections on the liminal space of alterity', *Race Ethnicity and Education*, Special Issue 'Critical Race Theory in England', 1: 65–84.

Rollock, N. (2013a) 'A political investment: revisiting race and racism in the research process', *Discourse: Studies in the Cultural Politics of Education*, 34 (4): 492–509.

Rollock, N. (2013b) 'Race and racism in a post-racial age: twenty years since the murder of Stephen Lawrence', National Union of Journalists' Claudia Jones Annual Lecture. London: Thomas Reuters.

Rollock, N. (2014) 'Race, class and the "harmony of dispositions"', *Sociology*, 48(3), 445–51.

Rollock, N., Gillborn, D., Vincent, C. and Ball, S. (2011) 'The public identities of the Black middle classes: managing race in public spaces', *Sociology*, 45 (6): 1078–93.

Rollock, N., Vincent, C., Gillborn, D. and Ball, S. (2013) '"Middle class by profession": class status and identification amongst the Black middle classes', *Ethnicities*, 13 (3): 253–75.

Savage, M. (2000) *Class Analysis and Social Transformation*. Berkshire: Open University Press.

Savage, M., Bagnall, G. and Longhurst, B. (2001) 'Ordinary, ambivalent and defensive: class identities in the North West of England', *Sociology*, 35 (4): 875–92.

Savage, M., Bagnall, G. and Longhurst, B. (2005) *Globalisation and Belonging*. London: Sage.

Sayer, A. (2002) 'What are you worth? Why class is an embarrassing subject', *Sociological Research Online*, 7 (3). Online at: http://www.socresonline.org.uk/7/3/sayer.html (accessed 15 August 2014).

Sayer, A. (2005) 'The moral significance of class', *Sociology*, 39 (5): 947–63.

Sewell, T. (2010) 'Master class in victimhood', *Prospect*, October, pp. 33–4.

Shiner, M. and Modood, T. (2002) 'Help or hindrance? HE and the route to ethnic equality', *British Journal of Sociology of Education*, 23 (2): 209–32.

Sivanandan, A. (1976) 'Race, class and the state: the black experience in Britain,' *Race and Class*, 17: 347–68.

Sivanandan, A. (1983) 'Challenging racism: strategies for the '80s', *Race and Class*, 25 (1), 1-11.

Sivanandan, A. (1993) 'The Black Politics of Health', *Race and Class*, 34 (4): 63-9.

Sivanandan, A. (2002) The contours of global racism. Speech delivered to the conference 'Crossing Borders: the legacy of the Commonwealth Immigrants Act 1962', London Metropolitan University. Available at http://www.irr.org.uk/news/the-contours-of-global-racism/ (accessed July 2014).

Skeggs, B. (2004) *Class, Self, Culture*. London: Routledge.

Slee, R. (2011) *The Irregular School: Exclusion, Schooling and Inclusive Education*. London: Routledge.

Sleeter, C. (1987) 'Why is there Learning Disabilities? A critical analysis of the birth of the field in its social context', in T. S. Popkewitz (ed.), *The Formation of the School Subjects: The Struggle for Creating an American Institution*. Philadelphia: Falmer Press, pp. 210–37.

Small, S. (1994) *Racialised Barriers: The Black Experience in the United States and in England in the 1980s*. London and New York: Routledge.

Smith, D. J. and Tomlinson, S. (1989) *The School Effect: A Study of Multi-Racial Comprehensives*. London: Policy Studies Institute.

Solomon, R.P., Portelli, J., Daniel, B.-J. and Campbell, A. (2005) 'The discourse of denial: how white teacher candidates construct race, racism and "white privilege"', *Race Ethnicity and Education*, 8 (2): 147–69.

Solorzano, D., Ceja, M. and Yosso, T. (2000) 'Critical race theory, racial microaggressions and campus racial climate: the experiences of African American college students', *Journal of Negro Education*, 69 (1&2): 60–73.

Soto, R. (2008) 'Race and class: taking action at the intersections', *Diversity and Democracy*, 11 (3): 12–13.

Strand, S. (2007) *Minority Ethnic Pupils in the Longitudinal Study of Young People in England (LSYPE)*. London: DCFS.

Strand, S. (2008) *Minority Ethnic Pupils in the Longitudinal Study of Young People in England Extension Report on Performance in Public Examinations at Age 16*, Research Report DCSF RR-029. London: DCSF.

Strand, S. (2011) 'The limits of social class in explaining ethnic gaps in educational attainment', *British Educational Research Journal*, 37 (2): 197–229.

Strand, S. (2012) 'The White British–Black Caribbean achievement gap: tests, tiers and teacher expectations', *British Educational Research Journal*, 38 (1): 75–101.

Sue, D. W., Capodilupo, C. M. and Holder, A. M. B. (2008) 'Racial microaggressions in the life experience of black Americans', *Professional Psychology: Research and Practice*, 39 (3): 329–36.

Sukhnandan, L. and Lee, B. (1998) *Streaming, Setting and Grouping by Ability*. Slough: NFER.

Swartz, D. (1997) *Culture and Power: The Sociology of Pierre Bourdieu*. Chicago: University of Chicago Press.

Talwar, D. (2012) 'More than 87,000 racist incidents recorded in schools', *BBC News*. Online at: http://www.bbc.co.uk/news/education-18155255 (accessed October 2013).

Tikly, L., Haynes, J., Caballero, C., Hill, J. and Gillborn, D. (2006) *Evaluation of Aiming High: African Caribbean Achievement Project*, Research Report RR801. London: Department for Education and Skills.

Todd, L. (2003) 'Disability and the restructuring of welfare: the problem of partnership with parents', *International Journal of Inclusive Education*, 7 (3): 281–96.

Tomlinson, S. (1981) *Educational Subnormality: A Study in Decision-making*. London: Routledge & Kegan Paul.

Tomlinson, S. (1987) 'Curriculum option choices in multi-ethnic schools', in B. Troyna (ed.), *Racial Inequality in Education*. London: Tavistock.

Tomlinson, S. (2005) 'Race ethnicity and education under New Labour', *Oxford Review of Education*, 59 (1): 10–21.

Tomlinson, S. (2008) *Race and Education: Policy and Politics in Britain*. Berkshire: Open University Press/McGraw-Hill.

Touré (2011) *Who's Afraid of Post Blackness? What It Means to Be Black Now*. New York: Free Press.

Troyna, B. and Carrington, B. (1990) *Education, Racism and Reform*. London, Routledge.

Unison (2012) Online at: http://www.unison.org.uk/asppresspack.

Valentine, G. (2007) 'Theorizing and researching intersectionality: a challenge for feminist geography', *Professional Geographer*, 59 (1): 10–21.

Vasagar, J. (2010) 'Twenty-one Oxbridge colleges took no black students last year', *Guardian*, 6 December. Online at: http://www.guardian.co.uk/education/2010/dec/06/oxford-colleges-no-black-students (accessed 15 August 2014).

Vincent, C. (1996) *Parents and Teachers: Power and Participation*. London: Falmer Press.

Vincent, C. and Ball, S. (2006) *Childcare, Choice and Class Practices*. London: Routledge.

Vincent, C. and Ball, S. (2007) '"Making up" the middle class child: families, activities and class dispositions', *Sociology*, 41 (6): 1061–77.

Vincent, C. and Martin, J. (2002) 'Class, culture and agency: researching parental voice', *Discourse*, 23 (1): 108–27.

Vincent, C., Rollock, N., Ball, S. and Gillborn, D. (2012a) 'Being strategic, being watchful, being determined: Black middle-class parents and schooling', *British Journal of Sociology of Education*, 33 (3): 337–54.

Vincent, C., Rollock, N., Ball, S. and Gillborn, D. (2012b) 'Intersectional work and precarious positionings: Black middle class parents and their encounters with schools in England', *International Studies in Sociology of Education*, 22 (3): 259–76.

Vincent, C., Ball, S., Rollock, N. and Gillborn, D. (2013a) 'Three generations of racism: Black middle class children and schooling', *British Journal of Sociology of Education*, 34 (5–6): 929–46.

Vincent, C., Rollock, N., Ball, S. and Gillborn, D. (2013b) 'Raising middle class Black children: parenting priorities, actions and strategies', *Sociology*, 47 (3): 427–42.

Walters, S. (2012) *Ethnicity, Race and Education*. London: Continuum.

Warmington, P. (2014) *Black British Intellectuals and Education*. London: Routledge.

Watt, N. (2014) 'Theresa May's stop and search plan delayed by government wrangling', *Guardian*, 22 January. Online at: http://www.theguardian.com/law/2014/jan/22/theresa-may-stop-search-plan (accessed 15 August 2014).

Weekes, D. (1997) 'Shades of Blackness: young female constructions of beauty', in H. S. Mirza (ed.), *Black British Feminism. A Reader*. London: Routledge.

Weis, L. (2004) *The Remaking of the American White Working Class*. London and New York: Routledge.

West, C. (1994) *Race Matters*. New York: Vintage Books.

West, E. (2010) 'Black pupils and bad behaviour – only a black academic can state the obvious', *Daily Telegraph*, 23 September. Online at: http://blogs.telegraph.co.uk/news/edwest/100055001/black-pupils-and-bad-behaviour-only-a-black-academic-can-state-the-obvious/ (accessed 15 August 2014).

Wiliam, D. and Bartholomew, H. (2004) 'It's not which school but which set you're in that matters: the influence of ability grouping practices on student progress in mathematics', *British Educational Research Journal*, 30 (2): 279–93.

Wood, M., Hales, J., Purdon, S., Sejersen, T. and Hayllar, O. (2009) *A Test for Racial Discrimination in Recruitment Practice in British Cities*, Research Report No. 607. Norwich: Department for Work and Pensions.

Woods, P. (1976) The myth of subject choice, *British Journal of Sociology*, 27 (2): 130–49.

Woods, P. (1977) How teachers decide pupils' subject choices, *Cambridge Journal of Education*, 7 (1): 21–32.

Woods, P. (1979) *The Divided School*. London: Routledge & Kegan Paul.

Wright, C. (1986) 'School processes – an ethnographic study', in J. Eggleston, D. Dunn and M. Anjali (eds), *Education for Some: The Educational and Vocational Experiences of 15–18 year old Members of Minority Ethnic Groups*. Stoke-on-Trent: Trentham, pp. 127–79.

Wright, C. (1992) *Race Relations in the Primary School*. London: David Fulton.

Wright, C., Weekes, D. and McGlaughlin, A. (2000) *'Race', Class and Gender in Exclusion from School*. London: Routledge.

Wright, O. (2012) 'Fewer jobs and lower pay: Black graduates pay price in jobs crisis as majority fail to find work', *Independent*, 23 April. Online at: http://www.independent.co.uk/news/uk/politics/fewer-jobs-and-lower-pay-black-graduates-pay-price-in-jobs-crisis-as-majority-fail-to-find-work-7669134.html?origin=internalSearch (accessed 17 September 2012).

Yosso, T. (2005) 'Whose culture has capital: a critical race theory discussion of community cultural wealth', *Race Ethnicity and Education*, 8 (1): 69–91.

Youdell, D. (2003) 'Identity traps or how Black students fail: the interactions between biographical, sub-cultural and learner identities', *British Journal of Sociology of Education*, 24 (1): 3–20.

Youdell, D. (2006) *Impossible Bodies, Impossible Selves: Exclusions and Student Subjectivities*. Dordrecht: Springer.

Young, I. M. (1990) *Justice and the Politics of Difference*. Princeton, NJ: Princeton University Press.

AUTHOR INDEX

SUBJECT INDEX